MW01492388

# MOMENTS OF
# TRUTH

365 DEVOTIONALS TO HELP YOU LIVE
MOMENT BY MOMENT CLOSE TO THE SAVIOR

## ADRIAN ROGERS

**Moments of Truth**

Adrian Rogers

Published by Love Worth Finding Ministries, Inc.
          Memphis TN 38183-0300

Copyright © 2024 Love Worth Finding Ministries, Inc. All rights
reserved. No part of this publication may be reproduced, stored in a
retrieval system, or transmitted in any form by any means, electronic,
mechanical, photocopy, recording or otherwise, without the prior
permission of the publisher, except as provided by USA copyright law.

Words in brackets within scripture quotations added for clarity. Unless
otherwise marked, all scripture taken from the New King James
Version. Copyright © 1982 by Thomas Nelson, Inc. Used by permission.
All rights reserved.

# God Created Human Beings,
# Not Human Doings

Do you wake to an alarm and run a hundred miles an hour until you collapse into bed at the end of the day? Say no to *doing* first thing every morning and start with simply *being*.

*Being* the child of the living God is the most important thing about you—being at peace in His presence, being receptive to His direction, and being faithful to His mission.

That's what Jesus showed us in His time on Earth. He didn't run a hundred miles an hour. Theologians have speculated Jesus walked about three miles an hour. He stopped to see, to hear, and to help people. Most importantly, He pulled away from the crowd for moments of truth with His Father.

He knew how to be at peace: "I and My Father are one" (John 10:30). He knew how to be receptive: "...Father, if it is Your will, take this cup away from Me; nevertheless not My will, but Yours, be done" (Luke 22:42). He knew how to be on mission: "My food is to do the will of Him who sent Me and to finish His work" (John 4:34).

You can too. For the next 365 days, in addition to your regular study of God's Word, start each day with a devotional reading, then look up the associated Scripture and meditate on who God is—for you, in you, and through you.

Thank Him moment by moment throughout each day as He brings the truth of Christ into focus in your life.

And *be* blessed!

So it was when the people set out from their camp to cross over the Jordan, with the priests bearing the ark of the covenant before the people, and as those who bore the ark came to the Jordan, and the feet of the priests who bore the ark dipped in the edge of the water...Then the priests who bore the ark of the covenant of the LORD stood firm on dry ground in the midst of the Jordan, and all Israel crossed over on dry ground, until all the people had crossed completely over the Jordan.

**JOSHUA 3:14-15A, 17**

**PONDER THIS** Why is it that some of us don't follow God? Why don't we get into the Jordan? We don't believe God. I'll give you an illustration. The reason some people don't tithe is that they don't really believe God. Malachi 3:10 says, "'Bring all the tithes into the storehouse, that there may be food in My house, and try Me now in this,' says the LORD of hosts, 'If I will not open for you the windows of heaven and pour out for you such blessing that there will not be room enough to receive it.'" Now, if a person believed that verse, would he tithe? Sure, who wouldn't want God to open the windows of Heaven and pour out a blessing so great he couldn't even receive it? Do you know why we never get into Jordan or whatever it may be that God commands us to do? It's because we really don't trust God. And you know why we don't trust God? Because we don't know God. You can't trust someone you don't know.

- What is difficult for you when it comes to trusting God?
- In what ways would you say you know God well? In what ways would you say you don't know God well?

**PRACTICE THIS** Write out some areas where you need to place your trust in God this year.

Why are you cast down, O my soul? And why are you
disquieted within me? Hope in God, for I shall yet
praise Him for the help of His countenance.

**PSALM 42:5**

**PONDER THIS** Did you know there's someone who's always talking to you? There's that old flesh, and it is constantly talking to you, and that's where negative thinking comes from. That mindset is the one we inherited from Adam. That soul is saying, "You deserve this. You can never be better. You'd be better off dead." In those moments, do you know what you need to do? You need to talk back. That's what David did. He took his soul by the scrap of the neck, looked it in the face, and said, "Why are you this way, O my soul?"

Do you ever talk to yourself? You should. David was talking to himself. He was taking a firm inward look and doing some spiritual analysis. He asked himself this question, "Why am I depressed?" You need to ask yourself that question and be honest. You can answer it perhaps better than anybody else because nobody knows you like you. There are so many reasons we find ourselves in this state, whether it is from a hurting heart or the loss of something or someone we love. I challenge you in those times when life looks grey to ask yourself that question: Why am I so depressed? "Why are you cast down, O my soul?" If you are struggling with clinical depression, go get a checkup. When you take this inward look, don't tiptoe around it. Talking to yourself may be the first step to healing.

- What kind of negative self-talk do you struggle with? What have been some of the reasons for that?
- Who do you know who is struggling? How can you encourage that person today?

**PRACTICE THIS** Think about someone you know who may be struggling with loneliness or depression after the holidays. Find a way to encourage or serve that person today.

"For what will it profit a man if he gains the whole world and loses
his own soul? Or what will a man give in exchange for his soul?
For whoever is ashamed of Me and My words in this adulterous
and sinful generation, of him the Son of Man also will be ashamed
when He comes in the glory of His Father with the holy angels."

**MARK 8:36-38**

**PONDER THIS** Suppose there's a boy who falls in love with a girl, but he doesn't really know how to ask her to marry him. So, he thinks if he just gives her an engagement ring, she'll catch the idea. He has it beautifully wrapped, and inside the wrapping is that velvet box with the satin lining on the inside and a gorgeous ring. He gives it to her and says, "Look at this and tell me what you think." He comes back and says, "What did you think about my present?" She says, "It's beautiful. I love it." And she pulls out the little box. She says, "Look at the hinge. See the little clasp. See how fuzzy it is. And look how soft it is on the inside. Look at that satin." He says, "Yes, but what about what was on the inside?" She says, "You mean that piece of wire and glass? I threw that away, but this is a wonderful box. Thank you so much for it."

It sounds funny, but there are people who are just like that. They don't understand that the body is the box; the soul is the diamond. We pamper the box, and we neglect the diamond that is on the inside. Jesus told us it is a pitiful and bad bargain if a man were to try to exchange his soul even for everything in the world.

- When have you been tempted to invest in things of the world that would keep you from investing in your relationship with God?
- Name a few people you know who prioritize investing in their souls. What difference does that make in their lives?

**PRACTICE THIS** Make a list of different priorities in your life. Look at the list and consider where you are investing in your soul.

For we are His workmanship, created in Christ Jesus for good works,
which God prepared beforehand that we should walk in them.

**EPHESIANS 2:10**

**PONDER THIS** Think of the potential there is in one human soul. It is valuable not only because of what it is but also because of what it can be. You, one day, can be transformed into the likeness of Jesus Christ. Do you believe that? You may not see yourself as God sees you with His creative genius. It has been said that one time, Michelangelo, a great sculptor, said as he looked at a block of marble, "There's an angel in that block, and I'm going to set him free." And he made a magnificent statue. That's what God wants to do for you.

There is a lecture called "Acres of Diamonds" by Russell Conwell, in which he talked about a man who owned a farm in Africa. This man wanted diamonds. So, he sold his farm and went off looking for diamonds. However, the person who bought the land discovered the farm was loaded with diamonds. The seller didn't realize what he had! He was searching for something else. Your heart is on a search. You are standing in acres of diamonds spiritually—the potential that is in you.

- Where do you struggle to see your own potential?
- What would it look like to see your potential as God does?

**PRACTICE THIS** Pray and ask God to remind you of your potential in Him.

Then I saw a great white throne and Him who sat on it, from whose
face the earth and the heaven fled away. And there was found
no place for them. And I saw the dead, small and great, standing
before God, and books were opened. And another book was opened,
which is the Book of Life. And the dead were judged according
to their works, by the things which were written in the books.

**REVELATION 20:11-12**

**PONDER THIS** In the end, Jesus Christ is your Judge—not your opinion of yourself, not some friend, not your mother or your father. Jesus is described in the Bible as a Lamb but also as a Lion. Jesus is both Savior and Judge.

You're going to meet Him as Lamb or Lion, Savior or Judge. Jesus Christ is the unavoidable, inescapable person in your life. You may have cursed Him, you may have mocked Him, you may have ignored Him, but one day I can promise you on the authority of the Word of God that you are going to meet Jesus Christ. He cannot be deceived. He cannot be discredited. He cannot be disputed. His voice is like the sound of many waters. When He speaks, it's like a hundred cascading waterfalls. Can you imagine somebody standing and arguing with Niagara Falls?

This is the One who is sitting on the throne. When we stand before Him on our own power, everything stable is gone. Everything that men have depended upon and looked to is gone. Only in Him do we have a firm foundation.

- How has knowing Jesus as Savior changed your perspective on life and death?
- Who is someone close to you who needs to know Jesus as Savior?

**PRACTICE THIS** Pray for the person you know who needs to know Jesus as Savior. Find a way to talk to or encourage that person today and ask God to give you more opportunities to be a witness for Christ in the future.

# 6

And anyone not found written in the Book of
Life was cast into the lake of fire.

**REVELATION 20:15**

**PONDER THIS** In Revelation, a surprising group standing under the judgment includes those who have been duped by religion. These are church members. They have religion, but they don't have Jesus Christ. They have been baptized. They may have been members of a Bible-preaching, Bible-believing church. The devil would just as soon send you to Hell from that pew as he would the gutter; it makes no difference to him. There are many people who get their names on the church roll but never have their names written in the Lamb's Book of Life. I believe in the church, but the church is not the way to Heaven; the church is a sign that points to Heaven.

One day I planned to go to Forrest City, Arkansas, for a meeting. Suppose you came out on Interstate 40 and saw me sitting on a sign that said Forrest City. You would come to me and ask, "Pastor, what are you doing?" I would tell you, "I'm going to Forrest City. Don't you see the sign that says, 'This way to Forrest City'? I'm sitting on this sign, and I'm on my way to Forrest City." You'd say, "No, Pastor, you don't get there by sitting on a sign. The sign points you to the way. The sign is not the way." The church points you to the way; it is not the way, my friend. The church is only a signpost saying, "Believe in the Lord Jesus Christ."

- What is the difference between putting your faith in a church and putting your faith in Christ?
- When did you choose to follow Jesus? How did that change your life or your plans for yourself?

**PRACTICE THIS** Think of times God has affected your life outside of your church experience. How can you share those experiences with someone else?

Behold what manner of love the Father has bestowed on us,
that we should be called children of God! Therefore, the world
does not know us because it did not know Him. Beloved,
now we are children of God; and it has not yet been revealed
what we shall be, but we know that when He is revealed,
we shall be like Him, for we shall see Him as He is.

**1 JOHN 3:1-2**

**PONDER THIS** Do you want to know how much you're worth? Go to bloody Calvary. See Jesus Christ in agony and blood, dying upon that cross. First Peter 1:18-19 says, "You were not redeemed with corruptible things, like silver or gold... but with the precious blood of Christ, as of a lamb without blemish and without spot." Put your ear on the beating heart of God and hear God say, "I love you, and I want you." Come down lower and see Jesus dying there upon the cross. Why? Because He wants your soul. He paid that price for you! That's how desirable you are to Him.

I know an evangelist named Mike, who often would share how he got saved. He was just throwing his life away like so many kids are today and didn't care about anything. One day, somebody said to him, "Mike, if you had something you really didn't care about and really didn't want and didn't value at all, but somebody else wanted it very much, would you give it to them?" He said, "Sure." Then the person said, "Mike, Jesus wants your soul. He desires you." And somehow Mike's eyes were opened, and he gave his heart to the Lord Jesus Christ. I'm telling you, you are desirable to Him.

- Do you consider yourself desirable to God? Why or why not?
- How does knowing your value to Christ change your relationship with Him?

**PRACTICE THIS** Share with someone today that he or she is valuable to God.

But you, beloved, building yourselves up on your most holy faith,
praying in the Holy Spirit, keep yourselves in the love of God,
looking for the mercy of our Lord Jesus Christ unto eternal life.

**JUDE 1:20-21**

**PONDER THIS** There are some things you can replace. But if you lose your soul, it's an irreversible loss. Jesus said, "What will it profit a man if he gains the whole world, and loses his own soul?" (Mark 8:36). You can't gain the world. If you could gain it, you couldn't keep it. If you could gain it and keep it, it wouldn't satisfy you.

Suppose somebody comes to you and says, "I have an offer for you. I will give you anything and everything you want. Do you want money? You can have it. Do you want pleasure? You can have it. But there's something I want from you. I want your little finger." Would you take him up on that deal? Maybe you wouldn't, but I'm telling you there are millions in this world who'd say, "Sure, it's a deal."

There are so many who are giving far more to gain far less. They are giving their souls, not their eyes, ears, or hands—their souls—and they are not gaining all the pleasures of this world.

- How have you valued building up your faith rather than the things of this world? How have you valued the world over your faith?

- Why do you think it is so easy to get lured in by the world?

**PRACTICE THIS** Think about the people around you. Do they know the value of their souls? Pray for one person you know who is trying to gain the pleasures of the world at the cost of his or her own soul.

"But of that day and hour no one knows, not even the angels
of heaven, but My Father only. But as the days of Noah were,
so also will the coming of the Son of Man be. For as in the days
before the flood, they were eating and drinking, marrying
and giving in marriage, until the day that Noah entered the
ark, and did not know until the flood came and took them
all away, so also will the coming of the Son of Man be."

**MATTHEW 24:36-39**

**PONDER THIS** There is a story of a man who asked another man on the street, "Do you know what the two biggest problems in the world are today?" The man said, "I don't know, and I don't care." The story reflects those two problems: ignorance and indifference. There are some things we cannot and should not be ignorant of and dare not be indifferent to. One of them is the Second Coming of Jesus Christ.

Noah was a preacher. He preached with the wrath of God in the foreground and the ring of hammers in the background. A near contemporary was a man named Enoch. The preaching of these ministers in that day did not penetrate the hearts of the people. Why? The people were marrying and giving in marriage, eating and drinking. Their technology, art, culture, and entertainment distracted them. They had eaten of the fruit of the tree of knowledge and saw themselves as rich and increased with goods and needing nothing.

Can you imagine what the newspaper columnists of our day would have done had they gone out to interview Noah? What a field day they would have had. Our generation has been warned. The last days are going to be marked by solemn preaching and people who will not listen.

- What things distract you from the gravity of God's truth?
- How have you learned to apply what you receive from preaching and from time in God's Word?

**PRACTICE THIS** Identify some distractions in your life and take a fast from them. Share with a friend to help keep you accountable.

And they went into the ark to Noah, two by two, of all flesh in which is
the breath of life. So those that entered, male and female of all flesh,
went in as God had commanded him; and the LORD shut him in.

**GENESIS 7:15-16**

**PONDER THIS** God brought Noah into the ark, and God shut the door. As the
water began to rise, those who'd been laughing at Noah and those who'd been
mocking Noah now began to wonder, "What is this?" After a while, when the
water got up to dangerous proportions, they surely came and began to beat on
the door of that ark and say, "Noah, let us in," but it was too late. God had shut
the door. God shut out the water, and God shut out these people who laughed
and mocked and scoffed. And God shut His people in.

There is an Ark of safety today. His name is Jesus. If you will come to Him and
put your faith in Him, I promise on the authority of the Word of God, He will
change you, He will transform you, and He will give you joy unspeakable and
full of glory. You may ask yourself, "What if it costs me?" Well, when Noah drove
that last nail into the ark, he may have had nothing left, but when he came out
of the ark, he had inherited the Earth.

I'm telling you—it pays to serve Jesus. If you're not saved, you need to get saved.
I mean, get saved, not just become a church member. You need to be born
again. Jesus is the Ark of safety. If you put your faith in Him, He will save you.

- What are some areas where you need a reminder that Jesus is
  your Ark of safety?

- How have you been transformed by Jesus?

**PRACTICE THIS** Remind a fellow Christian who is struggling that Jesus is the
only Ark of safety.

"LORD, make me to know my end, and what is the
measure of my days, that I may know how frail I am."

**PSALM 39:46**

**PONDER THIS** Death is a very real subject but one we often don't take seriously. Man is the only creature who knows he's going to die, and he is desperately trying to forget it. If you mention death in some contexts, people will change the subject like they change the channels with their remote controls. They don't want to talk about death. They don't want to face death. Even though it's something we avoid, reason tells us we're going to die, experience tells us we're going to die, and if you're not prepared to die, you're not prepared to live. No man is ever ready to live until he is no longer afraid to die.

Jesus is the master teacher. He taught that there are three great issues all of us must face: life, death, and eternity. Everything else is a subset of those things.

- How does being prepared to die change the way you live?

- Why is it dangerous to avoid the subject of death?

**PRACTICE THIS** Share with someone a testimony about how being prepared to die has changed the way you live

So teach us to number our days, that we may gain a heart of wisdom.

**PSALM 90:12**

**PONDER THIS** When I was in seminary, I would commute with a young man named Bob. Bob was a tall, sun-crowned preacher, one of the most gifted soul winners I've ever met. Bob said to me, "Adrian, there's an old man who lives near your church. His name is Mr. Bourgeois. He has had a serious heart attack, a number of them, and he only has days to live. Would you go by and tell Mr. Bourgeois how to be saved?" I went to the man and sat down and explained the marvelous, wonderful way a man can be saved by putting his faith in the Lord Jesus Christ. That old man prayed with me, gave his heart to Jesus, and was saved.

Just a few days after that, my friend, Bob, a young man in his 20s, had lunch with his wife, wiped his mouth, put his napkin down on the plate, took a few steps across the living room, gave a gasp, and fell down dead. He had said to me, "Adrian, there's an old man near your church who only has a few days to live." That old man lived for years. It was Bob who only had a few days to live.

You may be thinking, "Well, I'm in good health right now." You don't know what accident you may have on the way home. I'm telling you, if you're not ready to die, you're not ready to live.

- How does the brevity of life give you the urgency to live out your faith?
- Who is someone with whom you feel burdened to share your faith?

**PRACTICE THIS** Plan to meet with someone you know who needs Jesus's hope, and share with that person your hope in Him.

To the pure all things are pure, but to those who are defiled and
unbelieving nothing is pure; but even their mind and conscience are
defiled. They profess to know God, but in works they deny Him, being
abominable, disobedient, and disqualified for every good work.

**TITUS 1:15-16**

**PONDER THIS** Have you ever heard anybody say, "I'm not a Christian because
there are hypocrites in the Church"? That's a sin against reason. Anybody with
a modicum of intelligence knows that is not reasonable. There may be some
Christians who are hypocrites. Judas was a hypocrite.

Some eggs may be rotten, but you've probably had some for breakfast that
weren't the rotten kind. Some money may be counterfeit. Would you burn all
the rest of your money if you saw a counterfeit bill? Imagine saying, "I just don't
believe in hypocrite bills. I'm going to get rid of my money." You know better
than that. It is the hypocrite who proves the validity of the real. Why do people
counterfeit 50-dollar bills? Because of the worth of 50-dollar bills. People don't
make counterfeit gum wrappers.

When you say the Church is full of hypocrites, you know better. I've been
preaching long enough to know the best people on the face of God's green
earth meet on Sunday morning to give Him glory and praise. I'm not going
to let hypocrites keep me out of Heaven and then spend eternity with them
forever in Hell. This is a sin against reason.

- Have you ever been discouraged by seeing hypocrites in the
  Church? How do you respond to the type of logic given in today's
  devotion?
- Who are some people of sincere faith you have learned from?

**PRACTICE THIS** Share with someone today that he or she is valuable to God.

"Do not lay up for yourselves treasures on earth, where moth
and rust destroy and where thieves break in and steal; but lay
up for yourselves treasures in heaven, where neither moth
nor rust destroys and where thieves do not break in and steal.
For where your treasure is, there your heart will be also."

**MATTHEW 6:19-21**

**PONDER THIS** The only thing we know about life after death is what the Bible reveals and what Jesus says. Now one thing that we know is that death is not extinction. Death is not annihilation. There is life after death. "How do you know, Adrian?" Because Jesus teaches it. Your soul will be in existence somewhere when the sun, the moon, and the stars have turned to cinders. Somebody said there is a tombstone, and engraved on that tombstone are these words, "Pause, stranger, as you pass me by. As you are now, so once was I. As I am now, so you will be. Prepare to die and follow me." And someone wrote on that tombstone underneath it, "To follow you, I am not content until I know which way you went." Don't let life pass you by before you consider these things—how your life today will affect the life to come.

- What have you learned about life after death?
- How does knowing about the life to come change the way you live today?

**PRACTICE THIS** Make a list of different things you treasure. Take a moment to consider which of these will fade and which are treasures being stored up in Heaven.

"...So it was that the beggar died, and was carried by the angels to Abraham's bosom. The rich man also died and was buried. And being in torments in Hades, he lifted up his eyes and saw Abraham afar off, and Lazarus in his bosom."

**LUKE 16:19-23**

**PONDER THIS** We're going to die. In this verse, you see what we call the glories of Heaven. When the beggar died, an angel convoy took him to a place called "Abraham's bosom." What does that mean? Abraham was the father of the faithful, the most revered of the Jewish leaders, and the brightest star in the heavenly kingdom for these Jews. To be with Abraham would be a place of incredible honor.

What does it mean to be in "Abraham's bosom?" When people had a banquet in that day, they would not sit around the table as we sit around the table. They would recline. And the best place to recline would be where your head would be near the chest, the bosom, of the host. This man, who'd been feeding on crumbs, was now at a banquet. And not only was he at a banquet, but he was at the very highest place of honor. What Jesus was showing is the great radical change that took place: this man, a beggar, an outcast on Earth, was carried by the angels to Heaven to a place of honor.

Death is not the end. I'm not inviting you to a funeral; I'm inviting you to a feast. That's what our Lord is talking about.

- Have you ever felt rejected by the world? How does it feel to know Jesus has a place of honor for His followers?
- Do you ever look for the approval of people? How does this passage show the things that are most important?

**PRACTICE THIS** Share with someone the joys of Heaven you are looking forward to.

Now when the Pharisees heard it they said, "This fellow does not cast out demons except by Beelzebub, the ruler of the demons." But Jesus knew their thoughts, and said to them: "Every kingdom divided against itself is brought to desolation, and every city or house divided against itself will not stand. If Satan casts out Satan, he is divided against himself. How then will his kingdom stand? And if I cast out demons by Beelzebub, by whom do your sons cast them out? Therefore they shall be your judges. But if I cast out demons by the Spirit of God, surely the kingdom of God has come upon you."

**MATTHEW 12:24-28**

**PONDER THIS** A man may blaspheme God the Father and say, "There is no God." He may blaspheme Jesus Christ and say, "He's a false prophet or a fictitious person." But when the Holy Spirit of God comes, He demolishes those things.

The Holy Spirit of God pulls away the veil of darkness. He opens the eyes of the spirit so that people can see and understand. The Pharisees were not sinning against ignorance; they were sinning against light. When Jesus was on the cross, He could say to those who were crucifying Him, "Father, forgive them, for they don't know what they do" (Luke 23:34). But these men knew what they were doing.

The ministry of the Father is to rule the Universe. The ministry of the Son, in conjunction with the Father, is to save. But the ministry of the Holy Spirit is to open our eyes to give light and to help us to understand. Before I preach, I get on my knees and say, "Oh, Holy Spirit of God, open eyes. Help people to understand. Help them know You today." It's the Holy Spirit that opens understanding. When men and women stand before God to be judged, they're not going to be judged primarily by the sin they committed but by the light they rejected.

- Have you ever prayed for the Holy Spirit to open your eyes? How did you experience answers to this prayer?
- What are some matters in your life for which you need the Holy Spirit to open your eyes?

**PRACTICE THIS** Write down some of the things you need God's direction in and pray for the Holy Spirit to open your eyes about what to do.

Brethren, my heart's desire and prayer to God for Israel is that they may be saved. For I bear them witness that they have a zeal for God, but not according to knowledge. For they being ignorant of God's righteousness, and seeking to establish their own righteousness, have not submitted to the righteousness of God. For Christ is the end of the law for righteousness to everyone who believes.

**ROMANS 10:1-4**

**PONDER THIS** Think of the person you love most. What is your deepest desire for that individual? What do you desire for those you love most? Your greatest desire for them is extremely important because it shows what you value. For example, parents, do you desire an education for your children? Is that your greatest desire? If that's all you desire, you're going to raise clever devils. That's all. Do you desire culture for your children? Now, we're trying to refine young intellects and add culture. But if that's your heart's desire, if culture is your hope, all you're doing is making the world a better place to go to Hell from. Is that your desire? You may say, "Well, I want them to be materially well off. I want them to have sufficiency." What difference will that make if they have it all and then die and rise in judgment to face a God they do not know?

You see, Jesus came not as a great philosopher, not as an educator, not as an economist, not as a social worker; Jesus came as a Savior because man's greatest need is salvation. And the desire you ought to have for all your loved ones is salvation.

- Who are the people you love most?
- What is your desire for the people you love?

**PRACTICE THIS** Consider what it would look like for you to express the desire for your loved ones to know Jesus.

"I have been crucified with Christ; it is no longer I who live, but Christ lives in me; and the life which I now live in the flesh I live by faith in the Son of God, who loved me and gave Himself for me."

**GALATIANS 2:20**

**PONDER THIS** Imagine there's a wedding. The vows have been said. The cake has been cut. Tom and Susie are in the car. They're driving off. Susie looks over to Tom and says, "Tom, would you please take me home?" He says, "Susie, I can't take you home. We're going on our honeymoon. And then I'll take you home." Susie says, "No, Tom. I don't mean that home. I mean my home. I want you to take me back to my mother. I'm glad that you're my husband, I know that you love me, and I want you to know I'm grateful to be your wife. I'll try to come to see you on weekends, and if I get sick or need anything, I'll call you, but Tom, I'm going back to my old way of life."

That doesn't make a lot of sense, does it? Have you ever heard anybody say, "Now, Lord Jesus, I take You as my Savior. Thank You. That's done. Now I'm going back to my old way of life. Oh, yes, Lord, I'll come and see you a few times on weekends. And, Lord, if I need anything or if I get sick, I'll call on You."? That is the kind of religion that is filling Hell. People have never really made the authentic confession that Jesus Christ is Lord.

- Have you recognized and submitted to Jesus Christ as your reigning Lord? Has that changed your life?
- What former ways of life are you tempted to hold onto?

**PRACTICE THIS** Think of someone you know whose life has been changed by Christ. Ask that person to share his or her testimony.

Thomas said to Him, "Lord, we do not know where You are going, and how can we know the way?" Jesus said to him, "I am the way, the truth, and the life. No one comes to the Father except through Me."

**JOHN 14:5-6**

**PONDER THIS** What will you do with Jesus? This is the most important question.

It is a present question, and it is a personal question. It is not about what somebody else is going to do with Jesus. Very personally, you are going to decide what you're going to do with the Lord Jesus Christ. It's a very pertinent question; your destiny hangs on your answer. It is a pressing question; you will answer. You may say, "Nope, I'm not going to answer that question." Oh, yes, you will. You will answer the question one way or another. You say, "I'm not going to decide." You just decided not to decide and that was your decision. It is inescapable and unavoidable.

Everybody who lives will accept Him or reject Him, confess Him or deny Him, crown Him or crucify Him. Nobody can be neutral. You will do something with the Lord Jesus Christ.

- What will you do with your relationship with Jesus today?
- How would your life change if you asked yourself this question every day?

**PRACTICE THIS** Pray and ask God if there is someone you need to ask this essential question.

Pilate said to them, "What then shall I do with Jesus who is called Christ?" They all said to him, "Let Him be crucified!" Then the governor said, "Why, what evil has He done?" But they cried out all the more, saying, "Let Him be crucified!" When Pilate saw that he could not prevail at all, but rather that a tumult was rising, he took water and washed his hands before the multitude, saying, "I am innocent of the blood of this just Person. You see to it." And all the people answered and said, "His blood be on us and on our children." Then he released Barabbas to them; and when he had scourged Jesus, he delivered Him to be crucified.

**MATTHEW 27:22-26**

**PONDER THIS** It is not enough to tip your hat to Jesus; you must bow the knee. It is not enough to say, "I find no fault in Him," and think you're all right for doing so.

The thing Pilate did that convicted him, the verdict that condemned him, was that he attempted to remain neutral. He thought he could simply wash his hands of the whole matter.

What he thought was, "I'm washing my hands of this whole affair. I am not saying yes, and I'm not saying no. It is your decision. I am neutral!" You can't be neutral about Jesus. When Pilate said, "I am neutral. I will not make a decision"—that was the worst decision Pilate ever made. Because not to decide is to decide. Jesus said, "He who is not with Me is against Me." (See Matthew 12:30.)

An ocean full of water could not have washed the sin from Pilate's hands. And when the gavel fell in Pilate's court, another gavel fell in Heaven. Pilate was condemned when he allowed Jesus to be condemned. You cannot be neutral concerning the Lord Jesus Christ. To be neutral is to be against Him.

- Have you ever been tempted to stay neutral on matters of faith? Why or why not?

- Who do you know who is neutral on the matter of Jesus? How can you pray or encourage someone to make a decision?

**PRACTICE THIS** Take time to pray for a loved one or neighbor who desires to be neutral on matters of faith. Ask God to show you how to share His love with that person.

He said to them, "But who do you say that I am?" Simon
Peter answered and said, "You are the Christ, the Son of
the living God." Jesus answered and said to him, "Blessed
are you, Simon Bar-Jonah, for flesh and blood has not
revealed this to you, but My Father who is in heaven."

**MATTHEW 16:15-17**

**PONDER THIS** The first trial of the Lord Jesus was a mockery of justice. I'm going to put Jesus on trial again today. And I'm going to ask you to decide on a pertinent, personal, present, and pressing decision. I'm going to ask you to answer the question, "What do you think of Christ?" You're the jury. Look at the Word and see the strong testimony about who Jesus is. Look at Simon Peter, a fisherman who said, "You are the Christ, the Son of the Living God." Consider Martha, who hosted Jesus many times and observed Him in all sorts of situations. Martha said, "I believe that You are the Christ, the Son of God" (John 11:27).

What about the testimony of Jesus' enemies? Why did the Pharisees want Jesus crucified? Because, they said, "This Man receives sinners." (See Luke 15:2.) Aren't you glad He did? What about the centurion? He helped drive those scalding nails into Jesus' quivering palms. He watched Him die and said, "Truly this was the Son of God!" (See Matthew 27:54.)

In a very real sense, Pilate represents every man, woman, boy, and girl on the face of the Earth. We are each faced with the same question: What will I do with Jesus? As Jesus was before Pilate, Jesus is before you today. What will you do?

- How has your decision to follow Jesus changed the way you live?
- What kind of testimonies have you heard about Jesus from others?

**PRACTICE THIS** Write down a testimony about who you have seen Jesus to be.

Therefore be imitators of God as dear children. And walk in love, as Christ also has loved us and given Himself for us, an offering and a sacrifice to God for a sweet-smelling aroma.

**EPHESIANS 5:1-2**

**PONDER THIS** What did God the Father say about who Jesus is? He said, "This is My beloved Son, in whom I am well pleased" (See Matthew 3:17.) God the Father showed us who Jesus is through His actions. When they nailed Jesus up on that cross and put Him in that cold, dark tomb, they said, "He is worthy of death! Crucify Him!" Almighty God reversed the decision of the court and raised Him from the dead. He is shown to be the Son of God with power by the resurrection from the dead. (See Romans 1:4.)

I have believed this good news and lived for this good news. Have you? The early apostles believed it. Many of them died for their faith. Men may live for a lie; few men will die for a lie. Men tell lies to get them out of trouble, not into trouble.

Now it's time for you to consider what you will do with Jesus. Will you crown Him or crucify Him? Will you acknowledge Him or reject Him? Will you receive Him or deny Him? You will decide, and how you live will be evidence of that decision. You cannot wash your hands as Pilate did, and you cannot be neutral.

- What does it look like to live for the good news of Jesus?
- How do you acknowledge Jesus in your everyday life?

**PRACTICE THIS** Consider and journal about what it would look like to grow in how you acknowledge Jesus every day.

By faith we understand that the worlds were framed
by the word of God, so that the things which are seen
were not made of things which are visible.

**HEBREWS 11:32**

**PONDER THIS** Did you know in the Bible the existence of God is never explained; the existence of God is never argued? God is simply presented. The Bible just says to believe.

Have you ever had anybody come up and ask you, "Can you prove there's a God?" When they ask me, I say, "No." Then I say, "Can you prove He doesn't exist?" And if they are honest, they will have to say no. We can neither prove nor disprove God. So the skeptic says, "You just live by faith. You're just believers." I say, "You live by faith also. You're a believer also. I believe there is a God; you believe there is no God." I accept by faith that God exists. They accept by faith that God does not exist. To take this world apart looking for God would be like taking a piano apart looking for a song. You can't do it.

Unbelief in God is not really a matter of the mind, it is a matter of the heart. Now that doesn't mean there's not any evidence on our side. If you have seen creation, you are pointed to a Creator. That's evidence, but not proof. Our faith is rooted in evidence and goes beyond the evidence. Faith is necessary for spiritual wisdom. By faith we understand.

- How has your life changed through growing in faith in Jesus?
- In what areas of your life do you struggle to believe in God?

**PRACTICE THIS** Pray and be honest with God about the areas you struggle to have faith. Ask Him to grow your faith in those areas.

Therefore we also, since we are surrounded by so great a cloud of witnesses, let us lay aside every weight, and the sin which so easily ensnares us, and let us run with endurance the race that is set before us, looking unto Jesus, the author and finisher of our faith, who for the joy that was set before Him endured the cross, despising the shame, and has sat down at the right hand of the throne of God.

**HEBREWS 12:1-2**

**PONDER THIS** In a race, a runner doesn't run while looking back at the other people. Runners lose seconds if they turn their heads any other way except facing the goal. Likewise, you must keep your eyes on the goal. Jesus puts you in the race. He sustains you in the race. And He is the goal that you're running for. It is not great faith in God that you need; it is faith in a great God that you need. You need to quit trying to have great faith and start learning who Jesus is. The more you see Jesus, the more you understand Jesus, and the more your faith will grow.

Suppose I wanted to cross a major bridge, and I'm standing on one side, afraid that the bridge can't hold me up. So, I try to make myself believe the bridge can hold me up. I could try to work up my faith, or I could just observe the bridge. I could see cars and people going over the bridge; then the belief grows naturally. As I look at the bridge, faith is the byproduct of seeing and understanding that the bridge holds heavier weights than me. Faith is the byproduct of seeing and understanding Jesus Christ. Look to Jesus. Understand who the Christ of the Scripture is. Get in the Word of God. Look to Jesus as the author and the finisher of your faith. And lay aside the sin that dims your view of Him.

- What are some things you know about Jesus? How has that changed your relationship with Him?
- When have you struggled to keep your eyes on the goal of Jesus?

**PRACTICE THIS** Write down some things you look at instead of your goal of Jesus. Write down what you hope to find in these things when they distract you from Him.

"Ask, and it will be given to you; seek, and you will find; knock,
and it will be opened to you. For everyone who asks receives, and
he who seeks finds, and to him who knocks it will be opened."

**MATTHEW 7:7-8**

**PONDER THIS** Why do we pray? To invite God to be a part of our lives so we can delight ourselves in the Lord. The Bible says there in 2 Corinthians 6:1a that we are, "Workers together with Him." God loves us so much that He gives us the privilege of participating in His kingdom work through prayer.

God can work without our prayers, but we cannot work without God, and it is prayer that leads us to depend upon Him. God does not want us to live lives independent of Him. If God simply blessed us without our asking, what would that do? That would teach us to live life independently from God. But Jesus said, "If you abide in Me, and My words abide in you, you will ask what you desire, and it shall be done for you" (John 15:7). God wants you to abide with Him. That's the reason He has taught us to pray; to invite Him to take control of our lives.

The devil cannot keep God from answering. So, what will he do? He will endeavor to keep you from asking. But our Lord in today's passage says, "Ask, seek, and knock."

- What kind of things do you pray about? What things do you not pray about?
- Who do you know who lives as an example of someone who abides in Christ? How do you observe them doing this?

**PRACTICE THIS** Consider some things you do not pray about enough. Bring those matters to God in prayer today.

Let no one deceive himself. If anyone among you seems to be wise
in this age, let him become a fool that he may become wise

**1 CORINTHIANS 3:18**

**PONDER THIS** Why would we worship? That's what God wants of you. Say to yourself, "God wants me to worship." We become like what we worship. That's the reason idolatry is such a sin. First, the man molds the idol, and then the idol molds the man. We become like what we worship. That's true in the negative sense, but it's also true in the positive sense. The more you worship God, the more you will become like God.

When you worship God, you increasingly become like what you worship, and God's fire will be in you. As you contemplate the Lord, as you worship the Lord, as you keep your heart open to the Lord, you will be changed to be more like the Lord Jesus Christ.

Consider this question: Do other people see Jesus in you? Answer this sincerely in your heart. Are you being changed day by day into the glory of our Lord and Savior, Jesus Christ?

- When was a season in your life when you were being changed day-by-day into the image of Jesus? What has changed? What has stayed the same?

- What does it look like to worship in your day-to-day life?

**PRACTICE THIS** Write down some ways to worship God in your everyday life. Ask a brother or sister in Christ to give you some more ideas of how you might worship God every day.

But God, who is rich in mercy, because of His great love with which
He loved us, even when we were dead in trespasses, made us alive
together with Christ (by grace you have been saved), and raised us
up together, and made us sit together in the heavenly places in
Christ Jesus, that in the ages to come He might show the exceeding
riches of His grace in His kindness toward us in Christ Jesus.

**EPHESIANS 2:4-7**

**PONDER THIS** If you are in Christ Jesus, where does this passage say you are seated? In heavenly places. You are in Christ. When God raised Christ, He raised you. Jesus by death destroyed him that had the power of death, and now He is seated in the heavenly places, far above all principalities and powers that ever were, are, or will be. He is there living, risen, and victorious. Guess who's there with Him? You are!

Has Jesus ascended? Yes. Have you ascended? Yes! Does Jesus have all power? Yes! Do you have all power? The word *power* means "authority." It doesn't mean you can fly or walk on water. Were demons subject to Jesus? Yes. Are they subject to you? Yes!

If you're not living in dominion, it is not because the devil is so powerful. Satan has no power over you. Jesus said, "I give you authority over *all* the power of the enemy." You may say, "Then why don't I have it?" Paul wrote this to remind us of what we have in the Lord Jesus Christ. Remember what you have in Him!

- How should knowing this truth about who you are in Christ change the way you will live today?
- Who are some brothers and sisters in Christ you know who need to be reminded of who they are in Him?

**PRACTICE THIS** Encourage your brothers and sisters in Christ about who they are in Him.

"But the hour is coming, and now is, when the true
worshipers will worship the Father in spirit and truth;
for the Father is seeking such to worship Him."

**JOHN 4:23**

**PONDER THIS** I once had the pleasure of attending a father-daughter banquet with my daughter, Janice, and we were in the program for the evening. Janice stood up first and spoke of what her father meant to her. I could not tell you how my heart was blessed, how deeply moved I was, and how grateful I was to hear my child speak not only privately to me, but openly and publicly of her love and devotion to her father. That's the way God's great heart is. It gives Him pleasure when we worship. A father wants love.

Now, I've got some good news for you. Every Father's Day little children wonder, "What can I get for daddy? What can we give daddy?" You could give him some slippers, or you could give him a tie, but you know what your daddy wants? Love! What can you give to God today? You say, "Well, I can't sing like these people sing. I can't preach like so-and-so. I can't do this. I can't do that." There is nobody who can love God better than you can, and that's what God wants more than anything else. Isn't that great?

- Have you ever felt inadequate to love and worship God? Why or why not?
- How do you express your love for God?

**PRACTICE THIS** Make an intentional effort today to express your love for God in a special way.

Jesus said to her, "Woman, believe Me, the hour is coming when you will neither on this mountain, nor in Jerusalem, worship the Father. You worship what you do not know; we know what we worship, for salvation is of the Jews."

**JOHN 4:21-22**

**PONDER THIS** What is the highest good? What is the ultimate privilege? Here Jesus said it so clearly: we're to love God.

We are to love Him thoughtfully with all our hearts. A full heart is no excuse for an empty head. Serve the Lord with knowledge and wisdom. Love Him in spirit and in truth. Then we love Him practically with all our strength—everything we do. Whatever we do in word or deed, we do to the glory of God. (See Colossians 3:17.)

What is worship? It's giving God glory. The Bible says to serve your masters, according to the flesh, as if they were Jesus, for you serve the Lord God. (See Ephesians 6:5.) Your workplace can be your temple of devotion, your lampstand of witness, as you worship God with all your strength. That's what Jesus was telling this woman. She said, "Do we worship here, or do we worship there?" Jesus said, "Woman, you worship in spirit and in truth." There is no place that is not a holy place. There is no ground that is not sacred ground. There is no time that should not be a time of worship.

- Where in your life is it hardest for you to worship God?
- What would it look like to worship God as you work throughout your day?

**PRACTICE THIS** Write down one way you can commit to worshiping God as you work in your home, at your job, or in any other place He has called you for this season.

Where do wars and fights come from among you? Do they not come
from your desires for pleasure that war in your members? You lust
and do not have. You murder and covet and cannot obtain. You fight
and war. Yet you do not have because you do not ask. You ask and
do not receive, because you ask amiss, that you may spend it on
your pleasures. Adulterers and adulteresses! Do you not know that
friendship with the world is enmity with God? Whoever therefore
wants to be a friend of the world makes himself an enemy of God.

**JAMES 4:1-4**

**PONDER THIS** Sometimes our prayers are utterly selfish rather than God-centered. That's one reason we don't get our prayers answered. But do you know what enmity with God means? It's talking about warfare. When James mentioned adulterers and adulteresses, he wasn't talking literally; he was talking spiritually. Christ is the bridegroom and we're the bride. And if we want anything that the bridegroom does not want, we are flirting with this world, and we are taking away our love from our Lord and Savior the bridegroom. To love this world is spiritual adultery, and it is enmity, warfare, with God. Don't have a girlfriend called "This World," if you are a Spirit-filled man. And if you're a Spirit-filled woman, don't have a boyfriend called "This World." That is spiritual adultery. Many times, we ask God for things in this way. We ask God to underwrite our worldliness. We ask God to underwrite our carnality.

Whenever you pray about anything and the answer doesn't come, ask yourself this question: Are my motives pure? Am I earnestly, sincerely, with all my heart, seeking the will of God? And sometimes the answer, therefore, may be simply denied.

- When have you prayed with selfish intentions?
- What does it look like to earnestly seek the will of God with all your heart?

**PRACTICE THIS** Read Psalm 51:10. Take some time to pray and ask God where there has been selfishness in your heart.

Therefore do not be like them. For your Father knows
the things you have need of before you ask Him.

**MATTHEW 6:8**

**PONDER THIS** Have you ever asked God for something and didn't get it, but later your eyes were opened and you thanked God for that unanswered prayer? This is a silly illustration, but when I was a kid, I saw an old car that was being sold for $125, and I prayed for God to give me the money to get it. God didn't answer my prayer. Somebody else got that car, the motor fell out of it, and I had to thank God that He did not answer that prayer. You see, prayer may be specifically denied. It may be strategically delayed, and it may be significantly different than you expected.

On a more serious note, I once fasted and prayed for something and did not receive an answer from God. One day, God spoke to me. He said, "Adrian, I heard your prayer a long time ago. You're asking me to do something that I'm not going to do. You're asking me to reach in and change somebody's heart against that person's will, and I don't operate that way. But Adrian, I know the need of your heart. I know what you want. I know what you need. And your prayer is heard." As I look back, I see how clear that was and how great our God is. If God doesn't give us what we ask, He will give us something better and sweeter than we ask, if we ask Him in the wonderful name of Jesus.

- When in your life have you wrestled with unanswered prayers?
- Who can you remind of God's love and of His ability and faithfulness to answer prayer.

**PRACTICE THIS** Encourage someone you know who is wrestling with unanswered prayer. Ask your friend how he or she is doing and really listen. Then remind that person that God hears and will do exactly what is needed!

"I know your works, that you are neither cold nor hot. I could
wish you were cold or hot. So then, because you are lukewarm,
and neither cold nor hot, I will vomit you out of My mouth."

**REVELATION 3:15-16**

**PONDER THIS** Are you moderate about your love for Jesus? God have mercy on you. Does your religion make the Lord nauseous? He would rather have you outright against Him—absolutely cold—than have you pretending to be on His side and not zealous about it. He said, "I could wish that you were either cold or hot," just don't be lukewarm. You say, "That doesn't make sense to me. It would be better to be lukewarm about it than to be cold." No. The cause of Christ has been hurt by lukewarm Christians—Sunday morning benchwarmers who claim to be on the Lord's side but don't love Him and don't live for Him. The problem is we can't reach the goal if we're stumbling over our own players. Jesus said, "I wish that you were either hot or cold. But now that you're lukewarm, I'm going to spew you out of My mouth." And then He says in Revelation 3:19, "As many as I love, I rebuke and chasten. Therefore be zealous and repent." There is the zeal that displays the grace of God. "The grace of God that brings salvation has appeared to all men" (Titus 2:11), and because of that, we're to be zealous of good works. Yes, we're saved by grace, but we should never be nonchalant about it.

- How would others describe your faith? Are you hot, cold, or lukewarm?
- Who do you know who lives a life zealous for Jesus?

**PRACTICE THIS** Speak to someone you know who exemplifies what it looks like to live on fire for Jesus. Ask that person to share his or her testimony.

And as they went, they entered a village of the Samaritans, to prepare for Him. But they did not receive Him, because His face was set for the journey to Jerusalem. And when His disciples James and John saw this, they said, "Lord, do You want us to command fire to come down from heaven and consume them, just as Elijah did?" But He turned and rebuked them, and said, "You do not know what manner of spirit you are of. For the Son of Man did not come to destroy men's lives but to save them." And they went to another village.

**LUKE 9:52B-56**

**PONDER THIS** There is a zeal that is ugly in service to the Lord. You can get so zealous in serving the Lord that you run ahead of God. It's just as bad to run ahead of Him as it is to run behind Him. There's enough time in every day to gracefully do everything God wants you to do. Jesus said, "Come aside by yourselves to a deserted place and rest a while" (Mark 6:31a). Some people think that to deny yourself, you must be somber. Jesus wasn't somber; Jesus was a man of joy. Jesus went to parties. Little children sat on His lap. There's an extremism that is foolish and fruitless. I'm talking about misguided zeal. In this passage, Jesus was dealing with the Samaritans. Now you know the Samaritans and the Jews had quite a rivalry going. The disciples spoke to Jesus and said, "Let's get these Samaritans, Lord. We're going to bring down fire on these people." But notice Jesus rebuked them.

What am I saying? There ought to be a burning, blazing, passionate, emotional love for the Lord Jesus Christ, a zeal that displays grace. But God keeps us from a zeal that distorts grace and makes us fanatics. Do you know what a fanatic is? Somebody who's lost his direction and doubled his speed. Churches today are full of these people. It's the grace of God that we need.

- Have you ever been tempted to defend yourself the way the disciples did? What was that like?

- How does Jesus' response challenge you?

**PRACTICE THIS** Think about a time you took matters of God into your own hands. Repent, and consider what it would mean to live like Jesus in those moments.

Though I speak with the tongues of men and of angels, but have
not love, I have become sounding brass or a clanging cymbal. And
though I have the gift of prophecy, and understand all mysteries
and all knowledge, and though I have all faith, so that I could
remove mountains, but have not love, I am nothing. And though
I bestow all my goods to feed the poor, and though I give my
body to be burned, but have not love, it profits me nothing.

**1 CORINTHIANS 13:1-3**

**PONDER THIS** A little boy was reading the Bible, and he saw some pictures and some listings of angels. He read there about the cherubim and the seraphim and he asked his daddy, "Daddy, what is the difference between the cherubim and seraphim?" Suppose your little boy asks you that question, would you know? Well, this daddy didn't know, but he said, "Son, we'll look it up." He got down some commentaries, and he found that cherubim comes from a Hebrew word that means "knowledge," and seraphim comes from a Hebrew word that means "flame." This commentary went on to say that it was commonly believed or supposed that the cherubs, therefore, were angels that excelled in knowledge, and the seraphs were angels that excelled in love. And the little boy thought about that and then said, "Daddy, when I die, will I be a seraph? I'd rather love God than know everything."

Love excels knowledge. Love excels faith. Faith is wonderful. Without faith, you can't be saved, but what Paul is saying is if you have enough faith that you can remove mountains, and yet you can't remove malice, what good is it? If your heart is headquarters for hate but you could remove mountains, what good would it be?

- When has someone expressed God's love clearly to you? How did that impact you?
- How has God's love changed you? How has that changed how you love others?

**PRACTICE THIS** Express God's love to someone today through encouragement, service, prayer, or a thoughtful gift.

Love suffers long and is kind; love does not envy; love does
not parade itself, is not puffed up; does not behave rudely,
does not seek its own, is not provoked, thinks no evil; does not
rejoice in iniquity, but rejoices in the truth; bears all things,
believes all things, hopes all things, endures all things.

**1 CORINTHIANS 13:4-7**

**PONDER THIS** We hear people say, "Love is blind," but love isn't blind. Love sees more, but the difference is that we still forgive. Love forgives seventy times seven. Love does not give a person what he or she deserves; it gives a person what he or she needs.

A little girl was heard praying, "Lord, make all the bad people good and make all the good people nice." Wouldn't it be great if all the good people were nice? Love enables you to be patient; it's long-suffering. Love enables you to be kind, and love enables you not to envy. Do you want to take a test and see whether or not you're an envious person? Do you rejoice in the success of other people? I'm not talking about the success of somebody who is in a completely different field or social circle than you. I'm talking about one of your peers. Can you rejoice when somebody else has success? Do you cringe when somebody else is praised? If you do, dear friend, you need to load up on love.

- When has someone loved you when you did not expect it?
- Who do you envy or struggle to love?

**PRACTICE THIS** Extend Christ's love to someone who is difficult for you to love.

By this we know love, because He laid down His life for us. And
we also ought to lay down our lives for the brethren. But whoever
has this world's goods, and sees his brother in need, and shuts
up his heart from him, how does the love of God abide in him?

**1 JOHN 3:16-17**

**PONDER THIS** Knowledge puffs up, but love fills up. Through Christ's love, you can be humble. Not only does love enable you to be humble, but love also enables you to be courteous. Do you know what courtesy is? Love in little things. Love that says please, and love that says thank you. Love steps back and gives the other first place. We can talk about love in great flowering and swelling words, but our homes, the places we work, and the places where we worship would be much sweeter places if we'd learn to be courteous.

Don't you think it's time we started putting an emphasis on our responsibilities to other people? Christ's love enables you to be unselfish, humble, and courteous.

- How has someone's humility, unselfishness, and courtesy had an impact on your life?
- What would it look like to prioritize these things in your life when you are tempted to react based on your emotions?

**PRACTICE THIS** Consider selfishness and discourtesy in your life. Pray, repent, and pursue peace with the people you've hurt.

"Hear, O Israel: The LORD our God, the LORD is one! You shall love the LORD your God with all your heart, with all your soul, and with all your strength. And these words which I command you today shall be in your heart. You shall teach them diligently to your children, and shall talk of them when you sit in your house, when you walk by the way, when you lie down, and when you rise up."

**DEUTERONOMY 6:4-7**

**PONDER THIS** The marriage relationship is meant to be the most intimate of all human relationships. The word *intimate* comes from the Latin word *intimus* which means "inmost." Marriage is where we share the inmost part of our natures with another person. When we don't build our homes on God's definition of intimacy, we see that homes unravel and fall apart.

Somewhere years ago, I read about a city that had a landfill. After it was filled, an enterprising entrepreneur bought it from the city authorities. He went out there and began to haul dirt on top of the garbage. After he had covered it with dirt, he laid it out into a subdivision, and it became a beautiful site for homes. Young couples moved in and bought those homes, and it was a wonderful community. Little children were riding around on their tricycles. Everything was fine for a number of years until the walls in those houses began to sag, roofs began to crack, and the subsoil gave way. After a while families moved out, and it was deserted. The community was built on garbage, and it could be hidden for a little while, but the truth became evident.

This is what happens to us often—we try to build our homes on garbage. We don't understand the truth of God's Word. One wise man said, "When the bottom falls out, maybe you ought to examine the foundation." This is a question that matters: What did God intend for the family?

- What are some things that influenced your family?
- What would it look like to have a family built on Christ's foundation?

**PRACTICE THIS** Pray for five families you know, and ask God to build their families on His foundation.

Husbands, love your wives, just as Christ also loved the church
and gave Himself for her, that He might sanctify and cleanse her
with the washing of water by the word, that He might present her
to Himself a glorious church, not having spot or wrinkle or any
such thing, but that she should be holy and without blemish.

**EPHESIANS 5:25-27**

**PONDER THIS** Do you know what my assignment from God is? My assignment from God is to love Joyce as Christ loved the Church. And how does Jesus love the Church? The verse says that He loved it this way, "[He] gave Himself for her, that He might present her to Himself a glorious church, not having spot or wrinkle or any such thing." Do you know what spots are? That's defilement. Do you know what a wrinkle is? It's an inward scar. But many husbands have failed to love as they ought.

My chief assignment from God is to make Joyce a more radiant, beautiful Christian. If you are a married man, that is your chief assignment also—take it seriously.

The bottom line is that you cannot have a Christian home without Christians, any more than you could have a cherry pie without cherries. And if you want God in your home, then you've got to give your heart to God and be transformed by Him. Through Him, you can truly know His love and extend it to others.

- How has the love of Christ changed the way you love others?

- Where is God calling you to love others in a specific way this week?

**PRACTICE THIS** Pray and ask God to show you someone to whom you can extend His love. If you are married, do something special to extend God's love to your spouse.

For as many of you as were baptized into Christ have put on Christ.
There is neither Jew nor Greek, there is neither slave nor free, there
is neither male nor female; for you are all one in Christ Jesus.

**GALATIANS 3:27-28**

**PONDER THIS** I want to ask you a question: Who is better, the man or the woman? The answer is "Yes." A man is infinitely superior to a woman at being a man, and a woman is infinitely superior to a man at being a woman. God made us different so that He might make us one. Never forget it. Neither is superior to the other, but we are different.

You know Joyce and I are a lot alike, but Joyce and I are also very different. We have this idea that the differences we see divide us, but it is actually the opposite—it's these differences that unite us. God made us different so that He might make us one. When we look, there are definitely some differences between men and women, and these are more than mere psychological proclivities. These are there by divine design.

- What does it look like to value unity the way God does?
- Do you look at differences as a good or bad thing? Why?

**PRACTICE THIS** Pray and ask God to help you see differences the way He does, as part of His design for the purpose of unity in Him.

And the Lord God said, "It is not good that man should be alone;
I will make him a helper comparable to him." Out of the ground
the Lord God formed every beast of the field and every bird of the
air, and brought them to Adam to see what he would call them.
And whatever Adam called each living creature, that was its name.
So Adam gave names to all cattle, to the birds of the air, and to
every beast of the field. But for Adam there was not found a helper
comparable to him. And the Lord God caused a deep sleep to fall
on Adam, and he slept; and He took one of his ribs, and closed up
the flesh in its place. Then the rib which the Lord God had taken
from man He made into a woman, and He brought her to the man.

**GENESIS 2:18-22**

**PONDER THIS** In the garden, Adam named the animals, but he was evidently looking for a mate. He had a certain loneliness about him, and none of the animals seemed to fit. God saw his need and made Adam this woman He called Eve. When Adam saw her, what did he say? It loses something in translation. He says, "This is now bone of my bones and flesh of my flesh" (Genesis 2:23a). Now, what did he mean by that? What he was saying was, "She is not another animal; she has a skeletal structure, and she's a person like me. 'This is bone of my bones.'" He's been looking at all the animals, and they're so different, and then he looks at her and he says, "I like that. This is bone of my bones; this is flesh of my flesh. She is like me." If you want to know what God's pattern for the home is, right here we see it. God made for Adam someone like him. He not only liked her because she was like him, but he also liked her because she was not like him. God brought together both things in perfect harmony.

- How well was God's design for unity in marriage modeled in the home in which you grew up? How can you improve the unity in your home now?

- What are some ways you celebrate similarities and differences?

**PRACTICE THIS** Write a list of reasons that you are thankful for God's design.

And the tongue is a fire, a world of iniquity. The tongue is so
set among our members that it defiles the whole body, and
sets on fire the course of nature; and it is set on fire by hell. For
every kind of beast and bird, of reptile and creature of the sea,
is tamed and has been tamed by mankind. But no man can
tame the tongue. It is an unruly evil, full of deadly poison.

**JAMES 3:6-8**

**PONDER THIS** I want you to think about the awesome power of communication. Jesus is the example of this. Jesus spoke the truth; He is called the Word. His life is full of grace and truth. Jesus taught us that real communication comes out of the heart. Jesus said, "Out of the abundance of the heart the mouth speaks" (Luke 6:45b). If you want to know what's in the heart, listen to the words.

There is a saying that goes, "What's down in the well comes up in the bucket." Harsh words, a harsh heart. Negative words, a negative heart. Overly reactive words, an unsettled heart. Boastful words, an insecure heart. Filthy words, a dirty heart. Critical words, a bitter heart. Encouraging words, a happy heart. Gentle words, a loving heart. Truthful words, an honest heart. If you want to know what's in the heart, listen to the words.

- What do your words reveal about what's in your heart?
- How has your relationship with Jesus changed the way you communicate with others?

**PRACTICE THIS** Think of someone you struggle to communicate with. Make a step toward them in love and peace this week.

Nevertheless let each one of you in particular so love his own wife
as himself, and let the wife see that she respects her husband.

**EPHESIANS 5:33**

**PONDER THIS** What is a man's greatest desire? He wants to be admired; he wants to be respected. She is a lover, but he is an achiever. God gave woman a nurturing instinct, but God told man "to tend and keep" the garden. (See Genesis 2:15.) God equipped him mentally to do that; God gave him that tough exterior. The man wants to be admired by the woman. I want Joyce to admire me. I get more of a blessing when Joyce admires me and says, "Adrian, you are wonderful." She gets a blessing when I am romantic, loving, and tender toward her.

When a woman tells a man a problem, do you know what the average man will do? He'll try to fix it. She doesn't want you to fix it. Joyce was at the airport in Knoxville, and she missed a plane. She called me and said, "I just missed the plane." I said, "Well, go to another counter." She said, "I did that; I'm telling you, I just missed the plane." She did not want me to fix it. Trying to fix it didn't allow me to hear her; she wanted sympathy. Men, your wives don't always want you to fix it; they just want you to hug them and love them. They want love, but what does a man want? A man wants admiration. We can serve one another when we understand and celebrate our differences.

- Do you view differences with others as positive or negative? Why?
- How can knowing your differences change the way you serve others?

**PRACTICE THIS** Consider how you can grow in respect or love for your spouse if you are married. If you are not married, consider how you can grow in understanding how to serve those around you.

Now, therefore, you are no longer strangers and foreigners, but
fellow citizens with the saints and members of the household
of God, having been built on the foundation of the apostles and
prophets, Jesus Christ Himself being the chief cornerstone...
**EPHESIANS 2:19-20**

**PONDER THIS** Which is better: male or female? Neither is better. We are just different. When they built the San Francisco bridge, the engineers built the bridge so that all the parts inter-fit, but they all swayed. In the middle of that suspension bridge, that one-mile span, it will sway as much as twenty feet. It's concrete and steel; it's all bolted and welded together. There's flexibility but also strength. The towers go down to bedrock, and all of those cables connect everything to those two great towers. There is strength in flexibility; it is not a weakness. What keeps that bridge up? Two things. Number one, the foundation. Number two, the flexibility. Both of those components are necessary for the bridge to be effective.

Now, what should be the two great towers for your home? One: love for God and love for one another. That's the bedrock. Two: the flexibility that keeps your bridge from falling down. Never forget the power of flexibility in your family. Neither male nor female is better. We are different, but our differences don't have to be our weaknesses—they can be our strengths when we have flexibility.

- How have you made the love of God and love for one another a bedrock in your life and family?
- When are you most tempted to demand your own way instead of being flexible?

**PRACTICE THIS** Speak to a Christian couple you admire. Ask this husband and wife how they keep love for God and love for others as their bedrock and how they exercise flexibility in their family.

Let nothing be done through selfish ambition or conceit,
but in lowliness of mind let each esteem others better
than himself. Let each of you look out not only for his
own interests, but also for the interests of others.

**PHILIPPIANS 2:3-4**

**PONDER THIS** One of the many reasons we experience failure to communicate is self-centeredness. What is the biggest problem in relationships? Selfishness. We want to be the king or queen on the throne of our own lives.

We say we have our rights, but Jesus, the Lord of glory, "did not consider it robbery to be equal with God, but made Himself of no reputation." (See Philippians 2:6-7.) He laid down His life for the Church, which is His bride. Self-centeredness is a hindrance to good communication. Most arguments are not over problems—they're about ego. There are no problems too big to solve, just people too small to solve them. The problem is, we're full of rotten pride. Rather than attacking the problem, we attack one another because we are selfish by nature, and we're so full of pride we want to be right. But if both husband and wife would center on the problem rather than trying to prove who's right or wrong, then we would have communication.

- When has selfishness gotten in the way of your communication?
- What would it look like to look to the interest of others?

**PRACTICE THIS** Intentionally serve another person in relationship this week.

So then, my beloved brethren, let every man be
swift to hear, slow to speak, slow to wrath.

**JAMES 1:19**

**PONDER THIS** I have an occupational hazard; I am a preacher, and I like to talk. As a result, I'm not necessarily a good listener, but I am learning. We all need to learn to listen.

When you listen, you encourage others to talk. If another person has the idea that you're not listening, that person is not going to want to talk. When you listen, you encourage people to talk. Well, what good does that do? It helps you understand. You cannot understand somebody you're not listening to. And when you understand your mate, it follows as night follows day that understanding will bring you closer together. You're going to achieve intimacy. You don't have to be a rocket scientist to understand that.

The reason many of us don't listen is, number one, we're defensive. Our ego is there. We don't want to hear; we don't want anybody to tell us anything. Number two, we assume we already know what others are going to say, and we finish their sentences for them before they ever get to the end. Number three, while they're talking, we're thinking about what we're going to say and how we're going to answer. Instead of listening, we're preparing our own speeches in response. The Bible says we need to learn to listen.

- When do you struggle to listen to others?
- How have you been impacted when someone took the time to listen to you?

**PRACTICE THIS** Ask someone how he or she is doing today and practice really listening.

With it we bless our God and Father, and with it we curse
men, who have been made in the similitude of God.
Out of the same mouth proceed blessing and cursing.
My brethren, these things ought not to be so.

**JAMES 3:9-10**

**PONDER THIS** The old rabbis used to say God gave us two ears that are out, exposed, and easy to be seen, but God put our tongue behind some iron bars, guarded and inside to show that we ought to listen twice as much as we speak.

Sometimes, we want to be the judge, the jury, and the executioner. We want to play the blame game and blame our mates. It goes all the way back to the Garden of Eden when Adam wanted to blame Eve. We assign guilt. We say, "It's all your fault; you should be ashamed." Listen, if you find yourself saying words like, "You always," or "You never"—that's destructive. Don't ever begin the sentence with "You-this" or, "You-that," because you're playing the judge, and that's not your role. The Bible says, "Love is kind." Rather than saying, "You always," or "You never," try, "I feel," "I need," or "It seems to me." The Bible says we're to guard our tongues. (See Proverbs 21:23.) When you listen, listen carefully. When you speak, speak wisely.

- When have your words been hurtful to someone else?
- How have you been affected by the hurtful words of others?

**PRACTICE THIS** Think about someone you may have hurt recently with your words. Repent and make peace.

And He said, "My Presence will go with you, and I will give you rest."
**EXODUS 33:14**

**PONDER THIS** There's an often-repeated illustration about the bookmark some of us have in our older Bibles. It's an embroidered bookmark; on one side is just a mass of tangled threads, but on the other side it says, "God is love." Now some just look at it from the back, and they only see that tangled mass of threads. That is often like our faith—we don't see the ways of God—that God is love—and it all looks like a mess to us. But our ways and God's ways are so different.

Peter and James were both put in prison. They were servants of the Lord Jesus, apostles of Christ, arrested and put in prison for preaching the Gospel. Do you know what happened to James? His head was cut off. Do you know what happened to Peter? He was delivered miraculously from the same prison. (See Acts 12.)

How are we to explain that? If all you see are the works of God, you will be hopelessly confused and push the panic button all the time. You will never rest until you know God intimately. To know God intimately is the way of tranquility. Nothing will bring rest to your troubled soul like an intimate knowledge of God. If all you see is what God does in the world, you will be one nervous Christian. Change comes when we come to know Him intimately.

- When was a time you were confused by the ways of God?
- How has God's presence been comforting to you in a time of trouble?

**PRACTICE THIS** Think about how you spend time with God now and consider how you might seek to know Him more intimately.

"You shall love the LORD your God with all your heart, with all your soul, and with all your strength. And these words which I command you today shall be in your heart. You shall teach them diligently to your children, and shall talk of them when you sit in your house, when you walk by the way, when you lie down, and when you rise up."

**DEUTERONOMY 6:5-7**

**PONDER THIS** Marriage was made for communication. Adam said this is now bone of my bone and flesh of my flesh. If you take that passage and go all the way to Ephesians 5, you'll find out that the Bible also uses that as an analogy for Christ and the church. A husband and his wife are to communicate a principle. They are to be a picture of the Church and the Lord Jesus Christ. Did you know the greatest sermons preached on Earth are not necessarily preached from pulpits, but from homes like yours? The greatest testimony of the Lord Jesus Christ is a Christian home. Christianity in the Early Church went from house to house. That does not mean somebody went down a street knocking on every door. What that means is our homes are to give praise to Him. You see, it's not your marriage; it's His marriage. It's not your home, it's His home. They're not your children; they belong to Him. Marriage is to communicate praise to our great God. Your home is to be the center of God's glory.

- How do you treat the people in your household? Does it reflect the heart of Jesus?
- How can you grow in loving the people of your household and showing them who Jesus is?

**PRACTICE THIS** Write out the hopes you have for your family and loved ones, then pray and surrender your desires for them, asking God to show them who He is.

"Be angry, and do not sin": do not let the sun go down on your wrath.

**EPHESIANS 4:26**

**PONDER THIS** James 1:19 says we are to be "slow to wrath." That means we should not get upset easily or be disturbed quickly. The Amplified Bible Classic Edition says it this way: "...be quick to hear, slow to speak, *slow to take offense and to get angry*" (emphasis added).

The Bible describes those with uncontrolled tempers in several ways. Ecclesiastes 7:9b says, "Anger rests in the bosom of fools." Don't go explaining it away with excuses. You are a very foolish person if you're angry.

Proverbs 16:32 says, "He who is slow to anger is better than the mighty, and he who rules his spirit than he who takes a city." If you don't learn to control your anger, it will bring you into all other kinds of sins. And Proverbs 29:22 says, "An angry man stirs up strife, and a furious man abounds in transgression." That's the reason the Bible says, "...be swift to hear, slow to speak, slow to wrath." When you get angry, it's like throwing a rock into a wasp nest. You're going to stir up things that you wish you never had.

- When are you most prone to anger? How do you act in those times?
- How have you learned about the danger of reacting in anger?

**PRACTICE THIS** Write down the moments you are most prone to react in anger. Repent and ask God to equip you to live as a person of peace.

That we should no longer be children, tossed to and fro and carried
about with every wind of doctrine, by the trickery of men, in the
cunning craftiness of deceitful plotting, but, speaking the truth in
love, may grow up in all things into Him who is the head—Christ...

**EPHESIANS 4:14-15**

**PONDER THIS** Don't practice avoidance, and don't practice appeasement. It's a very unhealthy marriage when one mate always gives in to have peace and appease the other. When one mate gets his or her way most of the time and seems to dominate, your marriage is in serious trouble. One man said, "I like to go to the seashore, my wife likes to go to the mountains, so we compromise and go to the mountains." If that's the kind of marriage you have, it's going to end up on the rocks.

One of these days those smoldering rags in your heart will burst into an open flame, and your home will be engulfed. And if it doesn't erupt into a raging fire because you keep your feelings stuffed down inside you, you're going to be a self-pitying person. You will be living—though you may not separate—with an emotional divorce.

Don't practice avoidance or appeasement; instead, do as Ephesians 4:15 says and "speak the truth in love."

- What is your tendency in relationships: dominating or appeasing?
- What does it look like to speak the truth in love?

**PRACTICE THIS** Think through the last few arguments you have had. Consider where you need God's help to grow in love during those times.

For He established a testimony in Jacob, and appointed a law in
Israel, which He commanded our fathers, that they should make
them known to their children; that the generation to come might
know them, the children who would be born, that they may arise and
declare them to their children, that they may set their hope in God,
and not forget the works of God, but keep His commandments.

**PSALM 78:5-7**

**PONDER THIS** Children don't make a rich man poor; they make a poor man rich.
The rich man can't take his money to Heaven, but I'm taking my kids to Heaven.
I'm taking my grandkids too. We're going to Heaven. This is our wealth. How is
our faith to be carried on? From generation to generation.

When my first boy was born, I was a student in college. He wasn't happenstance;
he was planned. But thank God for the happenstance—they're planned also.
We wanted to begin our family, and we did, and God gave us a boy. We named
him Steve, after Stephen in the Bible. When I looked at that little red face, I
saw my wife, kissed her, and thanked her for going down into the valley of the
shadow of death to bring life into the world. Then I dropped to my knees, and I
wept. I said, "Oh God, if I never amount to much, if I fail as a pastor if I don't know
how to preach if I am never heard of—oh God, make me a good daddy. Make
me a man of God that my children can look up to."

- How have you invested in creating a legacy of faith, whether you
  have children or not?
- Who has left a legacy of faith with you?

**PRACTICE THIS** Think about three people you can invest in and pray for to
continue the legacy of faith you have received.

That the older men be sober, reverent, temperate, sound
in faith, in love, in patience; the older women likewise,
that they be reverent in behavior, not slanderers, not
given to much wine, teachers of good things....

**TITUS 2:2-3**

**PONDER THIS** God's way is for a woman to leave a legacy. Today's passage says older women have a ministry from God to teach the younger women. It says here very clearly that the aged women are to teach the younger women. That is God's plan.

Through the years, we have had a very wonderful program in our church— it's called Woman to Woman. The older women minister to and disciple the younger women because many don't have mentors to disciple them. God's Word says older women are to teach these young women. If we miss God's call on our lives, we're failing God and missing a blessing. Don't neglect to pass on the legacy of faith.

- Who have you passed your faith on to? How have you been a mentor to someone?
- Who has mentored you? How did that make a difference in your life?

**PRACTICE THIS** Pray for the person you mentor, or ask God who you could mentor (or who might mentor you) in this season.

But as He who called you is holy, you also be holy in all your
conduct, because it is written, "Be holy, for I am holy."

**1 PETER 1:15-16**

**PONDER THIS** Here's what Scripture says older women are to teach younger women: "...older women similarly are to be reverent in their behavior, not malicious gossips nor addicted to much wine, teaching what is right and good" (Titus 2:3). Notice here that it says they are to be holy in their behavior. As I studied this, I learned this means they are to have an aura of holiness about them. It literally infers they are to have the fragrance of holiness. It has the picture of the priest who has gone into the sanctuary to minister, and when he comes out, the sweet perfume of incense is still in his garments. And as you breathe in, you feel His presence. You can tell that person has been in the holy place. That's the idea of becoming holy. Have you known people like this? I have. Just to be in their presence is like being in a holy place. They have the fragrance and the beauty of Jesus Christ in their lives.

- Who do you know who has "the fragrance of Jesus"?
- How has God's presence in your life changed your "fragrance"?

**PRACTICE THIS** Encourage someone you know who has the aroma of Jesus.

And He answered and said to them, "Have you not read that
He who made them at the beginning 'made them male and
female,' and said, 'For this reason a man shall leave his father and
mother and be joined to his wife, and the two shall become one
flesh'? So then, they are no longer two but one flesh. Therefore
what God has joined together, let not man separate."

**MATTHEW 19:4-6**

**PONDER THIS** Marriage is supreme above any other earthly commitment. Parents are not the supreme commitment. We're to honor our parents, but the Bible teaches that a man is to leave father and mother and cleave unto his wife.

Children are not the prime commitment. We're to love our children and care for our children, but we make a tragic mistake if we pour all our devotion into our children but not into our spouses; the children, sooner or later, will leave the home. Mate to mate is a higher relationship in the Bible than child to parent. That's what God's Word teaches.

Business life is not the supreme commitment. Many of you are in danger of sacrificing your home on the altar of your business. Many business people are expected to give supreme loyalty to their businesses. One man was told by his company that he had to transfer and go to another place. His wife thought that would be upsetting. He said, "Well, she'll just have to get used to it. If she wants to stay with me, she ought to realize that my job is important. I can always find another wife." Do not neglect the primary earthly commitment you made.

- Are you married? How can you invest in that primary commitment?
- Is there a married couple you feel called to serve? How can you serve, love, and encourage this week?

**PRACTICE THIS** If you are married, make an intentional effort to invest in this primary commitment. If you are not married, ask God to put a couple on your heart that you can love and serve in a way that encourages the marriage commitment.

Children, obey your parents in the Lord, for this is right. "Honor your
father and mother," which is the first commandment with promise:
"that it may be well with you and you may live long on the earth."

**EPHESIANS 6:1-3**

**PONDER THIS** The Bible says in Exodus 20:12a, "Honor your father and your
mother." What does the word *honor* mean? It means your parents are not to be
taken lightly. They are to be given weight in your life.

One of the main ways you can honor them is by showing respect. Leviticus
19:3a says, "Every one of you shall revere his mother and his father." That does
not mean to tremble in their sight; it means to have respect and never speak
disrespectfully to your parents. Leviticus 20:9 says, "For everyone who curses
his father or his mother shall surely be put to death. He has cursed his father
or his mother. His blood shall be upon him." In the Old Testament, under the
theocracy, if a child were to curse his father or his mother, it was a capital crime.
The Bible is clear. You may say, "Well, my parents are not worthy of respect." But
only perfect children can demand perfect parents. Adolescence and middle
age are both difficult times. Parents go through stages too, but you're to respect
and honor your parents as God has commanded.

- When has it been most difficult for you to honor your parents?

- What does it look like to show someone respect even when you
  don't agree with that person (or may even have to keep your
  distance for reasons of safety and well-being)?

**PRACTICE THIS** Ask God for forgiveness for the times you have not treated your
parents with honor. Seek to honor them today in the way you speak to them
and the way you speak about them to others.

Drink water from your own cistern, and running water
from your own well. Should your fountains be dispersed
abroad, streams of water in the streets? Let them be only
your own, and not for strangers with you. Let your fountain
be blessed, and rejoice with the wife of your youth.

**PROVERBS 5:15-18**

**PONDER THIS** God gave us sex not only for procreation but for fellowship, communion, joy, comfort, and mutual love. In the Bible, when a husband and wife would come together sexually, it was said that they knew one another. What does that mean? It means that sex is a form of communication that cannot be put into words. It is a way of saying "I love you" that cannot be said any other way. God's law in Scripture is not trying to keep sex *from* you; God is keeping sex *for* you. Did you get that? Sex is a wonderful, beautiful gift from God.

If you had a piece of art from Rembrandt or Van Gogh, chances are you wouldn't have that hanging on your family room wall. It would be in a vault somewhere. And God has protected sex because it is so intrinsically beautiful and wonderful. God is not negative concerning the sexual life; He is very positive concerning sex rightfully given. Sex is like the sod in your yard—it's beautiful there, but take a shovel full and put it on your living room floor, and it's just dirt. In its place, it is right. Out of its place, it is so wrong.

- Have you ever had a tough time trusting that God's law was for your good? What was that like?
- How has God's law been a blessing in your life?

**PRACTICE THIS** Think about the instructions in Scripture that you wrestle with the most. Ask God to help you in those areas.

"A new commandment I give to you, that you love one another;
as I have loved you, that you also love one another. By this all will
know that you are My disciples, if you have love for one another."

**JOHN 13:34-35**

**PONDER THIS** Let me give you some words to remember to help you keep your marriage on track. The first one is *decision*. Make a decision that you're going to live for God. God will not force His will on you. Listening to sermons will not change who you serve. (See Joshua 24:15.) Give your heart to the Lord. The next word is unless you decide to obey the Word of God. Choose...this day on whom you will *depend*. It is not enough to decide because you do not have the strength in your own power to live for God. But God can deliver you if you will depend on Him. The third word is *devotion*. Begin to love the Lord with all your heart and all your soul, and love your wife as yourself. After this decision and after this dependence, let God pour His love through you. You are to love each other, not if you feel like it, but because God commands it. Love for one another comes primarily from Almighty God. Fourth is *development*. Continue to feed your love daily. You must nurture your love. It is a growing thing. It's like a flower that needs to be cultivated. It needs to be protected, and its full beauty can be developed through life.

- When have you had to depend on God in order to love someone else?

- What does it look like to make an intentional effort to love another person?

**PRACTICE THIS** If you are married, find an intentional way to nurture your marriage. If you are not married, find an intentional way to love someone else the way Jesus loves.

Behold, children are a heritage from the LORD, the
fruit of the womb is a reward. Like arrows in the hand
of a warrior, so are the children of one's youth.

**PSALM 127:3-4**

**PONDER THIS** What is my responsibility as a dad? My responsibility is to shape, sharpen, and shoot arrows at the enemy. As arrows are in the hand of a mighty man, so are the children of one's youth. My highest ambition is not to be primarily a good pastor or a good preacher; it's to be a good husband and a good father. If I had to choose between my profession and my family, I'd choose my family. There are many pastors and preachers in the world, but my kids only have one dad.

As a matter of fact, the Bible says that if a man doesn't practice it at home, he won't be able to do it outside the home either. (See 1 Timothy 3:4-5.) A pastor ought to be one who has his family under his spiritual leadership. The archer of these arrows must be strong: "Like arrows in the hand of a warrior." We're not talking about physical strength here because some of us could not qualify. We're talking about spiritual strength, and any can qualify. Be strengthened in the Lord so that you can pass on the legacy of faith.

- Who passed down a legacy of faith to you?
- Who do you have the opportunity to share your legacy of faith with?

**PRACTICE THIS** Consider ways to pass on your legacy of faith to another and take a specific action this week that moves toward that goal.

Train up a child in the way he should go, and
when he is old he will not depart from it.
**PROVERBS 22:6**

**PONDER THIS** Your family may hear people preach about God, but the home is the real classroom. How will your family members see God at work in your home? First, they'll see God in your worship. They'll watch you when company comes to see whether you miss church. They'll watch your priorities in your worship. They'll see the way you spend your money. They'll watch how you use your time. Let them see God as a vibrant reality in your life.

Our kids know we're not perfect, but our kids need to know God is number one. If I were to bring one of your children up here and ask, "What is the priority of your parents?" What would that child say? Let your children see God at work in your home. The next step is to cover your family members constantly with prayer. If you are the archer, and the children are the arrows, the bow is prayer. That's what sends them forth. A parent without prayer is like an archer with an unstrung bow. You need to pray for your children regularly.

- What priorities have you observed in people you have looked up to spiritually?
- Who regularly prays for you? How has that impacted your life?

**PRACTICE THIS** Take some time to pray for your children, your grandchildren, or the people you mentor.

Brethren, my heart's desire and prayer to God for Israel is that they may be saved. For I bear them witness that they have a zeal for God, but not according to knowledge. For they being ignorant of God's righteousness, and seeking to establish their own righteousness, have not submitted to the righteousness of God. For Christ is the end of the law for righteousness to everyone who believes.

**ROMANS 10:1-4**

**PONDER THIS** John Paton was a missionary in the South Sea Islands, and he was with a tribe that did not have a Bible. So, he took on the work of translating the Bible into the language of the tribe. When he got to the word *believe* he asked, "What is the word for belief?" The people gave him the word for intellectual belief, as in, "I believe that two and two equal four." He said, "No, that's not the word I want." He said, "I want the word for belief that means trust, confidence, reliance upon." And he kept asking but they couldn't give him the word.

One day as he was working on this translation, a man came in while Paton was sitting in a chair. Paton put his whole weight on the chair, with his feet off the floor, and asked, "What am I doing?" The local gave him a word that means "to lean your whole weight upon," which he put in the Bible translation for reliance upon the Lord Jesus Christ. When we say, "Lord Jesus, I just cast myself upon You," that is not just an intellectual belief; it is a deep reliance.

- How has your faith been marked by a deep reliance upon Jesus?
- What is the difference between intellectual belief and deep reliance?

**PRACTICE THIS** Think about an area of your life in which you may be depending more on intellectual belief than deep reliance on Jesus. Pray about those things. Determine to lean your whole weight upon Jesus.

**2**

> For with the heart one believes unto righteousness, and
> with the mouth confession is made unto salvation. For the
> Scripture says, "Whoever believes on Him will not be put to
> shame." For there is no distinction between Jew and Greek,
> for the same LORD over all is rich to all who call upon Him. For
> "whoever calls on the name of the LORD shall be saved."
>
> **ROMANS 10:10-13**

**PONDER THIS** I've been walking with the Lord now since I was a teenage boy. I'll tell you this: I've failed Him sometimes, but He has never failed me. His resources have been there for me every time I've called on Him. I'm not talking about financial resources, though He has done that. I'm talking about the life of God that's in my heart. He has met my need.

There is a hymn that says, "Friends all around us are trying to find what the heart yearns for by sin undermined. I have the secret. I know where 'tis found. Only in Jesus, true pleasures abound." He is rich unto all who call upon Him, not only some but anyone who wants to be saved. Paul told those who were very religious, who had a zeal for God but not according to knowledge, that they needed to be saved. There's nobody so good he need not be saved, and there's nobody so bad he cannot be saved. That's what it's all about.

- When was a time that God met your need?
- Have you believed you were too good to need to be saved or too bad to be saved? What brought you to surrender to Jesus?

**PRACTICE THIS** Make a list of your needs right now and ask God to meet those needs.

**3**

Therefore we also, since we are surrounded by so great a cloud of
witnesses, let us lay aside every weight, and the sin which so easily
ensnares us, and let us run with endurance the race that is set before
us, looking unto Jesus, the author and finisher of our faith, who for
the joy that was set before Him endured the cross, despising the
shame, and has sat down at the right hand of the throne of God.

**HEBREWS 12:1-2**

**PONDER THIS** Some people don't have faith because they have their eyes on
everything other than the Lord Jesus Christ. Don't look at others; look to Jesus.
Don't look at yourself; look to Jesus. Don't look at circumstances; look to Jesus.
Don't look at Satan; look to Jesus. Look away from everything else. That's literally
what the Greek word means when it says, "Looking unto Jesus." It literally means
"looking away from everything else and looking to Jesus." Faith is "Forsaking all,
I trust Him." The object of your faith must be God. Your faith is no better than
its object.

Don't put faith in faith; put faith in Jesus. The devil used to pull that trick on
me. He used to ask, "Adrian, how do you know that you really believe enough?"
After a while, I learned how to turn the tables on him. I'd say, "You know, devil,
you're right, my faith is weak, but Jesus is wonderful. I'm not putting my faith in
my faith. I'm putting my faith in Jesus." Jesus never said, "Look at your look." He
says, "Look to Me, and be saved, all you ends of the earth" (Isaiah 45:22a)! Don't
look at your look and don't put faith in faith—put faith in Jesus. Faith in faith is
positive thinking. Faith in Jesus is salvation.

- Have you ever doubted your faith? What was that like?
- What is the difference between putting your faith in faith and
  putting your faith in Jesus?

**PRACTICE THIS** Make a list of things that you may be looking to instead of Jesus.
Repent and ask Jesus to help you look to Him completely.

For to you it has been granted on behalf of Christ, not
only to believe in Him, but also to suffer for His sake.

**PHILIPPIANS 1:29**

**PONDER THIS** You can have natural faith in the natural realm; we all live by natural faith. You're putting faith in the chair that you're sitting in right now. When you go to a restaurant, you're putting faith in the cook.

But biblical faith is in the supernatural realm. You don't generate that. God gives it, so you don't work it up; it comes down. In 2 Peter 1:1, Peter talks about those who have obtained precious faith. People cannot believe in God unless God enables them to believe.

The only way you can believe in God is to hear from God, and God must enable you to believe. The instrument God uses to enable you to believe is His Word. Faith is not a leap in the dark; it's a step in the light. You hear from God. But without a word from God, you have no basis for faith. There are some people today who say, "You name it and claim it." But here is the fact of the matter: you can't claim it unless God names it. He is the Author of our faith.

- Where do you turn when you have doubts in your faith?
- Have you ever asked God to help you grow in your faith? What was that like?

**PRACTICE THIS** Share with a friend some areas of faith you struggle with. Ask that friend to share about how God has grown his or her faith in Him.

How then shall they call on Him in whom they have not
believed? And how shall they believe in Him of whom they
have not heard? And how shall they hear without a preacher?
And how shall they preach unless they are sent? As it is
written: "How beautiful are the feet of those who preach the
gospel of peace, who bring glad tidings of good things!"

**ROMANS 10:14-15**

**PONDER THIS** Faith is not man's way of getting the will of man done on Earth; faith is God's way of getting God's will done in Heaven. So many of us think that faith is something that we can use for ourselves. Romans 10:12 says, "For there is no distinction between Jew and Greek, for the same Lord over all is rich to all who call upon Him." God's will is for you to be saved.

The preacher doesn't originate his own message. No, I am to be a messenger boy with beautiful feet, running with glad tidings. I have been sent where God says, "Go tell them this."

We have workers at our church who buy things for the church, like cleaning supplies, paper goods, snacks, and so on. We don't just say, "Go buy whatever you think you want or whatever you think we need." There is a requisition, a purchase order, something that is given so that they come back with the right stuff. The objective of someone who goes to the supply store with a purchase order is to get what the leader says is needed. Faith is God's way of getting the things He wants to be done through us. Have we asked Him what He wants for you or have you assumed you know His plan?

- Is God calling you to share the Good News about Him with someone?
- When have you taken matters into your own hands instead of seeking direction from God?

**PRACTICE THIS** Pray and seek God to find out who He would have you encourage or share your faith with today.

## 6

> I say then, have they stumbled that they should fall? Certainly not!
> But through their fall, to provoke them to jealousy, salvation has
> come to the Gentiles. Now if their fall is riches for the world, and
> their failure riches for the Gentiles, how much more their fullness!
>
> **ROMANS 11:11-12**

**PONDER THIS** Paul became the apostle to the Gentiles, and you and I are reading from a Jew who wrote to us the Book of Romans. We're blessed by the mysterious plan of God. But God said that came about in a strange way when the Jews turned from the Gospel and the Gentiles were blessed. In effect, God is saying in this Scripture: "If I keep my Word to the Gentiles, how much more, then, will I keep My Word to Israel and bring her people back to Me?" Remember that Israel was not to be just simply a reservoir through which God poured His blessings, but it was a pipeline through which God dispersed His blessings. In Genesis, God said to Abraham, "In you all the families of the earth shall be blessed." (Genesis 12:3c). Abraham is the tree, and we who are Gentiles have simply been grafted in. We're the wild olive. If God can take unbelieving pagans and make believers out of them, how much more can He bring Jews to their true Messiah?

- How does it affect you to think of the way God has brought you into His family? How has that changed your life?
- What friends have you prayed for who need salvation and reconciliation with God?

**PRACTICE THIS** Consider those you know who are far from God. Get to know them and their stories, and seek to share how your faith has changed your life.

Oh, the depth of the riches both of the wisdom and knowledge
of God! How unsearchable are His judgments and His ways
past finding out! "For who has known the mind of the Lord? Or
who has become His counselor? Or who has first given to Him
and it shall be repaid to him?" For of Him and through Him
and to Him are all things, to whom be glory forever. Amen.

**ROMANS 11:33-36**

**PONDER THIS** None of us will ever fully understand everything about God. How do I know this? The Apostle Paul didn't know. He essentially said, "Who can understand this? Who has been God's counselor? His ways are past finding out." We should quit trying to fully understand His ways and begin to live by the Word of God and what God has revealed to us.

It's not up to you to synthesize these things; it's not up to you to put these things together. You just simply believe. When the Bible says, "Whoever desires, let him take the water of life freely" (Revelation 22:17c), believe it. And when the Bible says God wants everyone to be saved, believe it. (See 1 Timothy 2:4.) And when the Bible says Christ died for the whole world, believe it. (See 1 John 2:2.)

- What matters of faith have you struggled to wrap your brain around?
- When have you taken God at His Word?

**PRACTICE THIS** Write down some of the things of faith that you don't understand. Ask God to help you trust Him with those things.

Lift up your eyes on high, and see who has created these
things, who brings out their host by number; he calls
them all by name, by the greatness of His might
and the strength of His power; not one is missing.

**ISAIAH 40:26**

**PONDER THIS** It's the Lord Jesus who fuels the sun with its power. It's the Lord Jesus who veils the moon with its beauty. It's the Lord Jesus who guides the planets. There's no natural law. It's the laws of God that nature obeys.

Joyce and I took a vacation some years ago on a little island in the Bahamas. There was no television and no radio—just a little place on the beach; we loved it. There was a dock out in front, and at nighttime Joyce and I would just go down and get flat on our backs on the dock and look up at the stars. We would just lie there and talk and marvel at the stars in the Universe.

You see, Jesus is the producer of creation. Jesus is the preserver of creation. By Him all things exist. And Jesus is the purpose of creation. Colossians 1:16 says, "All things were created through Him and for Him." The Universe came from Him, the Universe is sustained by Him, and everything comes back to Him. People ask, "What's the world coming to?" It's coming to Jesus, "For of Him and through Him and to Him are all things" (Romans 11:36b).

- When was a time you marveled at God's work in creation? How did that impact you?

- How does the truth that God is reconciling all things to Himself encourage you?

**PRACTICE THIS** Go outside or look out your window and spend time praising God for all He has done in creation and for how He is reconciling all things to Himself.

For of Him and through Him and to Him are all
things, to whom be glory forever. Amen.

**ROMANS 11:36**

**PONDER THIS** What is the origin of effectual prayer? Its roots are in the purpose of God. The prayer that gets to Heaven starts in Heaven. "For of Him and through Him and to Him are all things." Prayer is God's way of getting Heaven's will done on Earth, not man's way of getting man's will done in Heaven.

Why has God allowed us to pray? Have you ever thought about that? Prayer is so mysterious. God knows what we need before we ask Him, so why should I ask God for what He already knows I need? Could God do it without our praying? He will not do it without our praying, and if we don't pray, we will not have, for the Bible says, "You do not have because you do not ask" (James 4:2d).

But God has given us the privilege of working with Him. God, in His administration of the Universe, has called us laborers together with Him. When we pray, we have the privilege of working with God. And through prayer we also bond with Him. If we didn't pray, many of us would never think about God. Many of us would take His blessings for granted. But God wants us to be perpetually dependent upon Him, so He teaches us to pray.

- What aspects of prayer have you struggled with?
- How has prayer grown your relationship with God?

**PRACTICE THIS** Take some intentional time in prayer to focus on God and His will, which is found in His Word.

I beseech you therefore, brethren, by the mercies of
God, that you present your bodies a living sacrifice, holy,
acceptable to God, which is your reasonable service.

**ROMANS 12:1**

**PONDER THIS** Sacrifice is personal. You present yourself. I can't do it for you; you can't do it for me. You don't need to ask, "Lord, what would You have Adrian do?" But each one of us must say, "Lord, today, I present myself." It is personal.

In the Old Testament, a sacrifice was an animal slain and put on an altar. Are you willing to present yourself as a sacrifice today? Many of us don't know God because we aren't willing to die to ourselves. When you die, you have no more rights. Your wife, your husband, your children, your car, your home, your ambitions, your education, and your business all belong to Him. God doesn't want you to take Him into your business as your partner. He's your boss. He owns it; it is His. You can't have half a sacrifice. God will not accept half a sacrifice. You are to present yourself as a living sacrifice, holy and acceptable unto Him.

- When have you given your life to God as a sacrifice? What does that require of you?
- What are some things that hold you back from living as a sacrifice to God daily?

**PRACTICE THIS** Talk to a friend in the faith today about the things that are holding you back from making the commitment as a living sacrifice.

For we are God's fellow workers; you are
God's field, you are God's building.
**1 CORINTHIANS 3:9**

**PONDER THIS** Why has God allowed us to pray? Have you ever thought about that? Prayer is so mysterious. What is the purpose of prayer?

God has given us the privilege of working with Him. God in His administration of the Universe has called us to be laborers together with Him. We work together with God as we work with one another, and we work with God in administrating the Universe. God wants to move through His people. Why would He do it that way? I've often used the illustration of flying an airplane. I don't know how to fly an airplane, but there have been times when I've been up with the pilot and he would say to me, "Do you want to fly this airplane?" I'd say, "Sure." So, he'd turn the airplane over to me. He was sitting there alongside me, of course, and he had his hands on his controls. I had mine on the other controls and was flying the airplane. I want to make it very clear that he could do it without me. However, I couldn't do it without him, but there's the joy of that fellowship as he says, "I'm going to let you help me fly this airplane." That's the way God wants to work with us through prayer.

- Have you ever thought of yourself as a laborer with Christ? How does that change the way you see your purpose in the day-to-day?
- What would it look like to pray as a laborer with Christ?

**PRACTICE THIS** Pray with a friend for God to work in your community, church, town, and beyond for His glory.

For of Him and through Him and to Him are all
things, to whom be glory forever. Amen.

**ROMANS 11:36**

**PONDER THIS** God is in the business of getting glory for Himself, and the reason many of our prayers are not answered is that we are not interested in the glory of God. We're interested in our own personal gain. When you get interested in the glory of God, you're going to see prayers start being answered. James said, "You ask and do not receive, because you ask amiss, that you may spend it on your pleasures." (James 4:3) We're to ask God for the glory of God.

This is why we pray in the name of Jesus. We are to ask in His name that the Father may be glorified in the Son. (See John 14:13.) Why do we pray in the name of Jesus? That God will be glorified. That's what it means to pray in the name of Jesus.

- In prayer, are you more likely to ask something of God or offer Him praise? Why?

- When have you started a prayer with praise to God? How did that change your attitude as you prayed?

**PRACTICE THIS** Spend time offering thanksgiving to God.

And do not be conformed to this world, but be transformed
by the renewing of your mind, that you may prove what
is that good and acceptable and perfect will of God.

**ROMANS 12:2**

**PONDER THIS** I want people to see Jesus in me. Don't you want people to see Jesus in you? The little boy said to his father, "Dad, is Jesus bigger than I am?" Dad said, "Well, yeah, son, I guess He is." He said, "Well then, if Jesus is in me, He'll stick out, won't He?" He sure will if you'll let Him! The inner nature of a Christian is Jesus.

When there comes transformation, then there comes revelation. When you're changed by Christ, you gain the mind of Christ. Why did God renew your mind? So, you could think with it. After he talks about renewing your mind, Paul essentially says, "Think, think, think! Don't be afraid to use your mind. You have the mind of Christ." The will of God is found between your ears when you get right with God.

When you present yourself to Him as a living sacrifice, you're transformed, you get the mind of Christ, you can use the mind of Christ, and you're able to make assessments that you could never make before. You think not with human rationality, not with human intellect, not with human intuition, but with divine guidance because you have the mind of the Lord Jesus Christ.

- Have you been transformed by Jesus? How has that changed the way you think?

- Think about your old ways. How did you think before you were transformed by Jesus?

**PRACTICE THIS** Share with someone your testimony about how Jesus transformed your life.

Let every soul be subject to the governing authorities. For
there is no authority except from God, and the authorities
that exist are appointed by God. Therefore whoever resists
the authority resists the ordinance of God, and those
who resist will bring judgment on themselves.

**ROMANS 13:1-2**

**PONDER THIS** The Word of God and the Book of Romans speak very clearly about the matter of Christian citizenship.

Paul says, "Let every soul be subject unto the governing authorities." He is literally talking about the civil magistrate, the governmental leaders. Let every soul be subject unto the civil magistrate. "For there is no authority except from God," that is the rulers, the leaders, the magistrates that be, "are appointed of God." Now you might think of your minister as an ordained minister, but have you ever thought of your governor as an ordained governor? "Therefore, whoever resists the authority resists the ordinance of God."

Who was the authority when Paul wrote this? Caesar. The Roman government was in power. The Christians were disenfranchised. They had no political power. Still, even in that time, Paul wrote that if you resist these authorities, you're resisting God because it is God who set them up.

- Why do we often struggle with authority?
- How can you show respect to your God-appointed leaders?

**PRACTICE THIS** Ask a friend who knows you well about your attitude toward authority. Give that person space to speak some critique as well as encouragement.

For because of this you also pay taxes, for they are God's
ministers attending continually to this very thing. Render
therefore to all their due: taxes to whom taxes are due, customs
to whom customs, fear to whom fear, honor to whom honor.

**ROMANS 13:6-7**

**PONDER THIS** Jesus paid His taxes; you ought to pay your taxes. As a matter of
fact, there's a wonderful story from when it was time for Jesus to pay His taxes.
(See Matthew 17:24-27.) He told Peter (paraphrased), "Go cast a hook in the sea.
Take the first fish that comes up and look in his mouth; you'll find a coin." Jesus
said, "I'm a citizen of another world, but I'm doing this lest I should offend." Now,
ever-increasing taxes are a burden, but we are to pay for our government. We're
to render all their dues, custom to whom custom, and so forth. Jesus said, "Give
to Caesar the things that belong to Caesar." And Jesus said, "Render to God
the things that belong to God." (See Matthew 22:15-22.) To God is our highest,
greatest allegiance, but God has also called us to submit to the governing
authorities He has put in place.

- Have you ever considered paying your taxes as a way to be
  obedient to God? Why or why not?
- How does following Jesus' instruction in this area help you to
  better trust Him with all your life?

**PRACTICE THIS** Pray for the money that you are paying in your taxes; ask God to
use it for His purposes and help you give it honestly.

Let us walk properly, as in the day, not in revelry and drunkenness, not in lewdness and lust, not in strife and envy. But put on the Lord Jesus Christ, and make no provision for the flesh, to fulfill its lusts.

**ROMANS 13:13-14**

**PONDER THIS** In these verses, Paul called us to put on Jesus Christ as Lord. He is my Master; I am His slave. Is Jesus Christ your Master? He is if you put Him on. Put on the Lord Jesus Christ.

Jesus means Savior. The name *Jesus* means "Jehovah saves." Not only do you put on the Lord Jesus as Master for direction, but you put on the Lord Jesus as Savior for deliverance. It's a vile world out there, and as you go out, you must be clothed. You need someone who can deliver you, dress you in the robes of righteousness, protect you, cleanse you, and keep you clean. Put on the Lord Jesus Christ where you're dressed in His righteousness alone because he is Lord and Savior.

The word *Christ* means "Messiah" or "king." He is the one who rules over me and teaches me how to rule in this life because He is the Messiah, He is the king, He is Lord of lords and King of kings. We are to wear Jesus like a suit of armor, the armor of light.

- What is your morning routine? What reminds you to put on Christ Jesus as Lord?
- How has your life changed since giving God authority over your life? Where do you need to give Him further authority?

**PRACTICE THIS** Consider what it looks like to put on the Lord Jesus Christ. Consider how you can practice that daily.

"And the glory which You gave Me I have given them,
that they may be one just as We are one."

**ROMANS 13:13-14**

**PONDER THIS** Jesus wants unity in His Church. One thing that gives Joyce and me great joy is seeing our children love one another. We pray for our children and grandchildren. We want them to love Jesus, love us, and love one another. Likewise, God wants you to love your brothers and sisters in Christ, all His children.

Unity is the delight of the saved. There's nothing more heartbreaking than to be in a church where there's division. There's nothing more glorious than to be part of a church in which you have sweet fellowship and oneness of spirit. What a fellowship and what a joy divine!

Unity is the dread of Satan. Satan gets very nervous when God's people dwell together in unity because this makes us a winning team. The celebrated basketball coach, John Wooden of UCLA, was asked, "What does it take to make a winning team?" He said, "Get the players in condition. Teach them the fundamentals of the game. Teach them to play together as a team." Isn't that simple? That's exactly what it takes to make a great church. Get in condition, get right with God, learn the fundamentals of the game, learn what being a Christian is all about, and then live in unity for the Lord Jesus Christ.

- When have you struggled to pursue unity in your church? Why?

- What are some steps that you can take toward pursuing unity in your church now?

**PRACTICE THIS** Reach out to one person for the sake of pursuing unity and reconciliation as needed.

The king's heart is in the hand of the LORD, like the
rivers of water; He turns it wherever He wishes.

**PROVERBS 21:1**

**PONDER THIS** We are to pray for our government. First Timothy 2:1-3 says, "Therefore I exhort first of all that supplications, prayers, intercessions, and giving of thanks be made for all men, for kings and all who are in authority, that we may lead a quiet and peaceable life in all godliness and reverence. For this is good and acceptable in the sight of God our Savior." You may ask the question, "Should I pray for my leader if he's wicked?" If that is the case, you should pray all the more for him. Why? Because God can change a ruler, remove a ruler, and overrule a ruler. Pray for those who are in authority.

One of the mightiest rulers in the Old Testament was a king named Nebuchadnezzar. Nebuchadnezzar ruled over ancient Babylon. Daniel was in the court of Nebuchadnezzar, and Daniel told Nebuchadnezzar where the king's power came from. In Daniel 2:37, God said through Daniel to Nebuchadnezzar, "You, O king, are a king of kings. For the God of heaven has given you a kingdom, power, strength, and glory." Nebuchadnezzar was not a godly king. He was so full of himself that God brought judgment on Him. God set him up, and God brought him down. We can pray for even the most wicked leaders, asking our heavenly Father to deal with them rightly.

- Have you ever struggled to pray for those in leadership? Why or why not?

- What would it look like to pray fervently for leaders even when you do not agree with them?

**PRACTICE THIS** Do some research and find out the names of your local, state, and national government leaders if you don't know them. List their names and pray for them in their roles.

But sanctify the Lord God in your hearts, and always be
ready to give a defense to everyone who asks you a reason
for the hope that is in you, with meekness and fear.

**1 PETER 3:15**

**PONDER THIS** We are called to preach to the people in our country. God's people dare not be silent. We dare not identify the Christian faith with the Democrat or the Republican Party. We need to be free to tell people in both parties to repent and get right with God.

We should be civil, but we can't be silent. Nathan warned David. Elijah preached to Ahab. Eleazar warned Jehoshaphat. Daniel preached to Nebuchadnezzar. Moses warned Pharaoh. John the Baptist preached to Herod.

Would you pray for the people in America right now? And remember, when you're praying for those in America, you're praying for yourself, too. *Lord, help us, we deserve judgment, but we need mercy. Bring people in this nation to You.*

Whether America survives or not, there is another kingdom and another King. His name is Jesus. And you need to render to God the things that are God's. Your life belongs to God, and you need to give it back to Him. Jesus died for you on the cross. You are invited to live reconciled with Him through faith and to invite others in your country, state, nation, and beyond to be reconciled with Him as well.

- With whom you have been nervous to share your faith?
- When have you seen people share the hope they have with conviction and meekness?

**PRACTICE THIS** Seek opportunities to share your faith with at least one other person this week.

The king's heart is in the hand of the Lord, like the rivers of water;
He turns it a stumbling block or a cause to fall in our brother's way.

**ROMANS 14:13**

**PONDER THIS** Unity is a matter of lordship, liberty, and love. Romans 14:15 says, "Yet if your brother is grieved because of your food, you are no longer walking in love. Do not destroy with your food the one for whom Christ died." Let me tell you what love will do in a church. Love will keep your brother from stumbling.

Love says, "I'm not going to give him a reason to stumble." There are certain things in life that I don't do, not because I think they would hurt me, but because I think they may hurt someone else who observed me. We are called not to cause another person to stumble.

Love does not give a reason for sorrow. The point of Romans 14:15 is this: *I don't need to do anything that would break your heart; even if I could argue, I have every right to do it.* Paul was saying, "Don't destroy your brother with your rights." The word *destroy* here actually means "to overthrow or ruin." Don't mar another person's well-being through personal preference.

- Have you ever abstained from something because you knew it was a stumbling block for someone else?

- What has been a stumbling block for you? How could you share this with others who might help you guard against it?

**PRACTICE THIS** Share with a trusted Christ follower some of your stumbling blocks and ask him or her to support you as you seek to avoid those things.

Now may the God of patience and comfort grant you to
be like-minded toward one another, according to Christ
Jesus, that you may with one mind and one mouth
glorify the God and Father of our Lord Jesus Christ.

**ROMANS 15:5-6**

**PONDER THIS** The purpose of the Church is to give Jesus Christ glory and honor, to make Him known to our neighbors and to the nations, and to move believers in Him toward maturity and ministry. The Church exists to help you grow up so that you can serve.

There is no such thing as an inactive Church member. That's an impossibility. Every Church member is active. Either we're building up, or we're tearing down. Either we're a part of the team and helping, or we're not a part of the team and hurting. In Matthew 12:30, Jesus said, "He who is not with Me is against Me, and he who does not gather with Me scatters abroad." Every member of the Church is gathering or scattering. Every member of the Church is working with the Lord Jesus or working against Him.

Let me say again, nobody is excluded. If you are reading this, this message is not "to whom it may concern"—it is to you. It has your name and address on it, and God wants you to serve and minister. You've been called into the ministry.

- Do you consider yourself part of the ministry of your church? Why or why not?

- Who is an active member of your church that has made an impact on your life? How can you seek to influence others similarly?

**PRACTICE THIS** Write down different ways you have been impacted by people who tried to build up your church. Consider what you have done to contribute to that effort.

Now may the God of hope fill you with all joy and peace in
believing, that you may abound in hope by the power of
the Holy Spirit. Now I myself am confident concerning you,
my brethren, that you also are full of goodness, filled with
all knowledge, able also to admonish one another.

**ROMANS 15:13-14**

**PONDER THIS** There's never been a greater time to preach the Gospel of Jesus Christ. The great revivalist Vance Havner said, "Too many are willing to sit at God's table but not work in His field. ...God has a place and purpose for you, somewhere for you to be and something for you to do. You never will be happy elsewhere, nor can you please God anywhere but there."

Remind yourself today and say out loud: "I have been called into the ministry. I am saved to serve. God, make me a servant. God, make me a minister." God has called you. Think what will happen if all of us really begin to minister. We'll turn the world upside down and inside out for Jesus Christ. We could change the world for Jesus if we each understood we've been saved to serve. God has called you into the ministry. You don't just sit in church to soak and sour but to serve.

- Where have you served in your church?
- What have been some of your hesitations about serving God?

**PRACTICE THIS** If you aren't yet serving, contact someone on staff at your church and ask him or her how you can serve in your church.

For as the body is one and has many members, but all the members
of that one body, being many, are one body, so also is Christ.

**1 CORINTHIANS 12:12**

**PONDER THIS** In Scripture, there are many ways that the Church is described. For example, the Church is described as the bride of Christ. He is the Bridegroom, and we are the bride. The Church is described as His building, not a physical building, but a spiritual building with Christ as the foundation and us as living stones. The Church is described as a flock of sheep. We're the sheep of His pasture, and Jesus is the Good Shepherd who leads His flock. Finally, the Church is the body of Christ. He is the head, and we're the members. Whether it be a bride, a flock, or a building, all these illustrations of the Church speak of community. None speaks of individualism. It speaks of togetherness. We're in this together. The Bible teaches we are members, one of another.

Now if people say, "I believe in Jesus, but I don't believe in the Church," there is a lot they don't understand. Jesus and the Church are not identical, but Jesus and the Church are inseparable, like a bride and a groom, a head and a body, a foundation and a building, or a shepherd and a flock. All of these go together. So don't say yes to Jesus and no to the Church. When you say that, you are missing a major part of the heart of God. Love for Jesus and love for what Jesus loves are inseparable.

- When have you struggled to love the Church? Why can this be difficult?
- How have you been blessed by the Church?

**PRACTICE THIS** Find a way to practically love and serve others in your church.

"I have been crucified with Christ; it is no longer I who live, but Christ lives in me; and the life which I now live in the flesh I live by faith in the Son of God, who loved me and gave Himself for me. I do not set aside the grace of God; for if righteousness comes through the law, then Christ died in vain."

**GALATIANS 2:20-21**

**PONDER THIS** How is the world going to know the Lord Jesus Christ? Through His body. Through us. That's kind of frightening, isn't it? When you think about it, how is this world going to know the Lord Jesus Christ? God is spirit, and a spirit is invisible. My spirit, the real me that lives inside this earthly body, is invisible. Jesus lives in His body, which is the Church, and Jesus is manifested by His body. We are here to tell our communities what Jesus Christ is like. We are to manifest the Lord Jesus. In a body, there is a manifested person. The Church is the visible part of the invisible Jesus, and Jesus is the invisible part of the visible Church. As His body, we manifest the life of the Lord Jesus Christ.

Now, there's only one who's ever lived the Christian life. Do you know what His name is? It's Jesus. If Jesus' life is being lived behind my pulpit, it'll be Jesus in Adrian doing it. It won't be Adrian; it'll be Jesus in me. If Jesus is manifested in your home, it'll be because Jesus is manifesting Himself through you. If you try to imitate Jesus in your own power, all you will be is a cheap imitation.

- Who has been a manifestation of Jesus in your life?
- How do you seek to make Jesus visible in your life?

**PRACTICE THIS** Call the person that has been a manifestation of Jesus to you. Encourage him or her regarding the impact this person has made on your life.

> If the whole body were an eye, where would be the hearing? If the
> whole were hearing, where would be the smelling? But now God has
> set the members, each one of them, in the body just as He pleased.
>
> **1 CORINTHIANS 12:17-18**

**PONDER THIS** Now my body is not supposed to have any plans of its own. I would be afraid of my body if it had plans of its own. My body is to serve me; I'm not to serve it, and it's only to serve me at my command. Suppose I woke up this morning, and my hand somehow had the ability to speak and say, "Good morning, Mr. Rogers. I have some plans today. I'm going to scratch your ear, I'm going to shave you, I'm going to take a pen and write some words for you, and I'm going to shake some hands for you." I'd say, "I don't want you to have any plans of your own. Just be there." I would be afraid of that thing!

So many times, we're telling Jesus what we're going to do for Him. He doesn't want us to do anything for Him. Does that surprise you? He wants to do something through you. Your body is here to minister to you! Our purpose as followers of Jesus is to hear what the head says and to do it. That's what we're here to do. And therefore, we must listen to what our Lord is saying. We are to minister to Him.

The best ability is availability. That's it. Are you available? Are you responsive to Him? A body has a ministering purpose. The body is to minister to the purpose of the person who lives in it.

- When have you told God what you were going to do for Him?
- How have you made yourself available to be used by God?

**PRACTICE THIS** Think about a time recently when you told God what you were going to do. Repent and ask God to help you trust His purpose for you.

For by one Spirit we were all baptized into one body—
whether Jews or Greeks, whether slaves or free—and
have all been made to drink into one Spirit.

**CORINTHIANS 12:13**

**PONDER THIS** The motivating power of Jesus' body is the Holy Spirit. The Holy Spirit is to be the life of the Church. Without the Holy Spirit, there is no power in the Church! There is a difference between an organism and an organization. The Church is organized, but it is not an organization; it is an organism. An organization does not necessarily have life. There are so many wonderful organizations, but none like the Church. The life of God is to be in us.

Granted, you can get a group of people together, get a beautiful building, get a man who can speak well, get them organized around some causes, and call it a church, but it may not be the Lord's Church. It may be a wonderful organization. But there's a distinct difference when the Spirit of Almighty God is working and moving among His people. There is a spiritual dynamic in the Church. Just as my human spirit is the life of my body that is motivating me right now, the Holy Spirit of God is the life of the Church. There is a song that says, "All is vain unless the Spirit of the Holy One comes down." The Church is not a corporation with Jesus as the president. It is a body with Jesus as the head.

- How have you seen the Holy Spirit at work in your church?
- When have you seen the Holy Spirit alive in other members of your church?

**PRACTICE THIS** Pray for your church and ask God to make His Holy Spirit alive in your local church body.

For you can all prophesy one by one, that all may learn and
all may be encouraged. And the spirits of the prophets
are subject to the prophets. For God is not the author of
confusion but of peace, as in all the churches of the saints.

**1 CORINTHIANS 14:31-33**

**PONDER THIS** I want my life to count for Jesus. I'm tired of sitting around, drawing breath, drawing a salary, and fighting to live while I live to fight. Do you want your life to count? Are you content to only sit around and endure until you die? One of these days soon we're going to give an account.

God has called you to serve Him, and God has equipped you to serve Him. God has given you at least one spiritual gift and possibly more.

As you use these gifts, remember that real revival doesn't put you out of control; real revival brings you under the control of the Holy Spirit. God is the One who gives direction according to His Word. Your life is to be used for His purpose.

You are to take His gifts, discover them, develop them, and deploy them for Jesus.

- What would it look like to make your life count for Jesus by using His gifts in your life?
- How is the fruit of the Spirit evident in your life?

**PRACTICE THIS** Write down the spiritual gifts you see reflected in yourself. Write another list of the ones you would like to learn more about.

There are diversities of gifts, but the same Spirit. There are differences of ministries, but the same Lord. And there are diversities of activities, but it is the same God who works all in all. But the manifestation of the Spirit is given to each one for the profit of all.

**1 CORINTHIANS 12:4-7**

**PONDER THIS** When Joyce and I got married, we got all kinds of gifts, as do many couples when they get married. It's a custom. These gifts might include waffle irons, blenders, toasters, can openers, and coffee makers. All these items have different functions. But they all must be plugged in; they don't operate without power. It's the same power that operates them all, but they all have different functions and different capacities. That is what Paul is saying about the body of the Lord Jesus Christ. We have different capacities and different functions, but it is the same Spirit. We're all plugged into Him. What you need to do is to plug in your spiritual gift. Your ministry is your place of service, but God is the source of life for us all; He is the source of power for every gift.

God doesn't want us all to be alike. We're not a congregation of clones. God makes us different. Unity is not uniformity—everybody doing the same thing. Unity comes from the life of the Spirit within. We all share the same Holy Spirit, and we all have unique gifts to be used for His glory.

- When have you sought to use a spiritual gift in your own strength—without relying on the Holy Spirit?
- How have you pursued unity in your church? How can you do so further?

**PRACTICE THIS** Think about someone you have had a difficult time getting along with in your church. What would it look like to have unity of the Spirit with that person? Pursue unity in one practical way this week.

Love suffers long and is kind; love does not envy;
love does not parade itself, is not puffed up.
**1 CORINTHIANS 13:4**

**PONDER THIS** A woman once told a preacher, "You have brought me to a saving faith in Jesus Christ." And the preacher said, "I'm grateful for that. I like to know how God uses me. What was it I preached that brought you to Christ?" She said, "It was nothing you preached. I was standing around when somebody criticized you to your face, and I watched you respond to that person with kindness. I knew that what you had was real."

Love is kind. There are many people who are religious but not necessarily kind. That's the reason a little girl prayed, "Lord, make all the bad people good and all the good people nice." Love enables us to be patient. It enables us to be kind. It enables us not to envy. Envy and love don't dwell in the same heart. Do you know how to see if you have love or not? If somebody else is being blessed and you rejoice, then you have love. If you cringe when other people are being praised, there's no love in your heart. Proverbs 14:30 says, "A sound heart is life to the body, but envy is rottenness to the bones."

- When have you felt justified to be unkind to someone else?
- What causes you to envy others?

**PRACTICE THIS** Assess where envy might live in your heart. Submit this before the Lord and ask Him to lead you to love others.

Love...does not behave rudely, does not seek its own, is not provoked,
thinks no evil; does not rejoice in iniquity, but rejoices in the truth;
bears all things, believes all things, hopes all things, endures all things.

**1 CORINTHIANS 13:4-7**

**PONDER THIS** Love is not irritable. Do you have a hair-trigger temper? Are you a person who easily flies off the handle or is easily irritated?

Years ago, when I was working my way through school, there was a deacon in our church who hired me to work for him. I thought he was one of the most wonderful men I'd ever known. I worked with this man, and on one occasion, I saw this man I greatly respected get so angry. He picked up a tool and threw it all the way across the room, muttering something that I would not want to repeat. I was so hurt because I'd looked up to him. He was a leader in our church, and I was just a young person. I thought how sad that this man was so easily provoked.

We all have our faults. There have been those moments when I have taken my eyes off the Lord and gotten provoked, and the Holy Spirit has reminded me, "Adrian, the reason you did that is because that's what you were full of." What spills out is what you're full of. We need to learn to drown insults in a river of love. One of the precious virtues of love is that it is not irritable.

- How easily are you irritated? What are specific things that set you off?
- How has someone's patience made an impact on your life?

**PRACTICE THIS** Ask someone you are close with to keep you accountable for times you are easily irritated. Resolve to drown insults you receive in a river of love.

I beseech you therefore, brethren, by the mercies of
God, that you present your bodies a living sacrifice, holy,
acceptable to God, which is your reasonable service.

**ROMANS 12:1**

**PONDER THIS** Have you ever said to God: "I am here. You can have all there is of me. I present myself as a sacrifice. All my plans, my goals, my so-called possessions—I sacrifice them to You, Lord"? Does that seem strange to you? If we are honest with ourselves, there are so many of us who want to take Christianity and tack it onto our regular lives. We want to hold onto our lives and our rights.

A sacrifice in the Old Testament was killed; it had no more plans of its own. On the altar, they had two hooks and those hooks would be put into that sacrifice that was to be burned to hold it on the altar. Do you know what will hold you on the altar? Discipline and devotion will hold you there as a living sacrifice, but most of us don't want those flesh hooks.

Many will say, "I don't want to get bound down. I would teach a class, join a church, and make a pledge to the love offering, but I don't want to get bound down. I want to be free." No. This is a sacrifice. And what happened to an Old Testament sacrifice was this—it was consumed; it was burnt up. You do not truly worship God until you are consumed.

- If you are honest with yourself, what are the things you aren't willing to give up to follow Jesus?

- Do discipline and devotion to Jesus have a prominent place in your life? Why or why not?

**PRACTICE THIS** Speak to a person you know who has sacrificed a lot to follow Jesus. Ask that person to share insights about discipline, devotion, and living sacrificially.

> But the manifestation of the Spirit is given
> to each one for the profit of all.
> **1 CORINTHIANS 12:7**

**PONDER THIS** There was a lady who took a first aid course. Later she said, "I am so glad I took my course in first aid. Out in front of my house, there was a terrible car accident. An old man, driving a car, went up the curb and hit an oak tree. He was thrown out of the car. When I got there, this man was in terrible condition, and the scene was gruesome. It was horrible!" Then she said, "I remembered my first aid. I remembered if I would put my head between my knees I wouldn't faint." That's the kind of theology that many have today, which is really "me-ology." Many people are only thinking about themselves.

Your spiritual gift is given to profit the entire body. We are to, as the hymn says, "Rescue the perishing, care for the dying, weep o'er the erring one, lift up the fallen, tell them of Jesus the mighty to save." That's why you have a spiritual gift. The gift is designed so that you might be a blessing to your entire church. God wants you to be a blessing to your church and make the church a blessing to your community and your community a blessing to the world.

- When have you sought to use your gifts purely for your own benefit? Why is this easy to do?
- How have you seen someone else use his or her spiritual gifts to bless the Body of Christ?

**PRACTICE THIS** Encourage someone you know to use his or her spiritual gifts to bless the Body of Christ. Tell that person how he or she has impacted your life through obedience to Jesus.

**2**

For to one is given the word of wisdom through the Spirit, to another
the word of knowledge through the same Spirit, to another faith by
the same Spirit, to another gifts of healings by the same Spirit, to
another the working of miracles, to another prophecy, to another
discerning of spirits, to another different kinds of tongues, to another
the interpretation of tongues. But one and the same Spirit works
all these things, distributing to each one individually as He wills.

**1 CORINTHIANS 12:8-11**

**PONDER THIS** God brings us together as a body. Some are eyes, some are ears, and some are feet. We all have different gifts, and yet those gifts are to be put to work in the body of our Lord and Savior, Jesus Christ.

Do you want to know what your spiritual gift is? You will discover your spiritual gift in the context of the Body of Christ. I had no idea that God would call me into ministry. Once upon a time, a person in my church invited me to be the youth week pastor. This was an opportunity for youth to fill the roles of the church and learn where they were gifted and how the church operated. I was scared when I received this invitation, but I got up and preached, and after, I received words of encouragement and affirmation on my gift of preaching. We find our spiritual gifts by operating in the Body of Christ. You are a gifted child. God doesn't want you just to sit in the church pew. You have a spiritual gift with which to serve Him.

- Have you ever been invited to serve in an area in your church that you had never considered for yourself? How did that experience help you grow?

- What have you learned about yourself and your gifts as you have been part of your church community?

**PRACTICE THIS** Speak to a spiritual leader in your church and ask that person where your church may need you to serve. Ask him or her for help in identifying your spiritual gifts.

Then Joseph said to his brothers, "I am Joseph; does my father still live?" But his brothers could not answer him, for they were dismayed in his presence. And Joseph said to his brothers, "Please come near to me." So they came near. Then he said: "I am Joseph your brother, whom you sold into Egypt. But now, do not therefore be grieved or angry with yourselves because you sold me here; for God sent me before you to preserve life."

**GENESIS 45:3-5**

**PONDER THIS** People are not saved until they see the sovereignty of God and recognize themselves as people who deserve judgment. There is no conversion without conviction. Sometimes people come forward to join churches like they're doing God a favor, but they have never been terrified by their sin and realized the weight of their sin that nailed Jesus to the cross. I don't think anyone has ever been saved until he or she has seen himself or herself as a Hell-deserving sinner. If you have little children, and you wonder if they are ready to be saved, I don't think it's good to berate them and say, "You're a no good, unworthy sinner." But the time will come when, through Bible teaching, they will come under a conviction of sin, and then they're going to be ready for a Savior. Don't just simply ask a little child, "Do you believe in Jesus?" Little children will believe whatever you tell them to believe. That's not the point. Has that child understood sin in the sight of a righteous and holy God? If he or she has, then that child is ready for a Savior. The same is true for adults—there must be conviction of sin before there is conversion.

- When did you realize the gravity of your sin? What was that like?
- What happens when we forget the weight of our sin? How does that affect our walk with Jesus?

**PRACTICE THIS** Reflect on the weight of your sin, and take time to praise Jesus for your conversion.

Then you will call upon Me and go and pray to Me, and I will
listen to you. And you will seek Me and find Me, when you
search for Me with all your heart. I will be found by you, says
the LORD, and I will bring you back from your captivity; I will
gather you from all the nations and from all the places where
I have driven you, says the LORD, and I will bring you to the
place from which I cause you to be carried away captive.

**JEREMIAH 29:12-14**

**PONDER THIS** Do you know the great privilege of being saved? It is not about merely having our sins forgiven, having provision, having a future, or having a missionary charge: through reconciliation, we can have a relationship with Jesus. Jesus is real to me. I talk to Him often. He is a dear friend. Did you know God wants you to talk with Him? God is a God of love, and what good is love if there's not someone to love and someone to love back? That's why God created us. God didn't make you only to serve Him. If He only wanted servants, He has angels. God made us so that He could love, talk, and share with the creation made in His image.

Joyce and I will call our son David in Spain. International phone calls cost, but it's worth it. When we speak to him, we like to hear about everything, not just the big things but also the small, incidental things. Sometimes you might get the idea that God doesn't want to hear from you about small things, but He does because He loves you. Do you think you're a bother to Him? Do you think our son is a bother to us when we share little things together? No, that's the joy that He loves us enough to share those small things as well as the big things. Can you think of anything that's really big to God? There's nothing really big to Him.

- How often do you talk to God? What do you talk to Him about?
- When is it hardest for you to talk to God?

**PRACTICE THIS** Consider when you struggle to speak with God. Ask God to grow your communication with Him in those times.

A friend loves at all times, and a brother is born for adversity.

**JEREMIAH 29:12-14**

**PONDER THIS** There was a publication that ran a contest for a definition of *friendship*, and there were some great entries. One of them was, "A friend is somebody who multiplies our joys and divides our grief." Another was, "A friend is somebody who understands our silence." Those things are true of friendship, but here's the one that won the prize: "A friend is someone who comes in when the whole world goes out."

We need friends! We need friends who will strengthen us with their prayers, bless us with their love, and encourage us with their hope. A friend is on the scene when you need him or her. A friend is somebody wise enough to leave you alone when needed. A friend is there to help you celebrate when there's something to celebrate.

A friend is somebody who sharpens. Proverbs 27:17 says, "As iron sharpens iron, so a man sharpens the countenance of his friend." A good friend will sharpen you, but a false friend will blunt and dull your life. Our English word *friend* relates to the word *freedom* because a friend is somebody who sets you free to be all that you can be. A friend is somebody who encourages you and knows how to speak the word that will draw you out and lead you on.

- Who has been a good Christian friend to you?
- How have you been sharpened by that friend?

**PRACTICE THIS** Reach out to a friend who has been there for you and sharpened you. Tell your friend about the impact he or she has made on your life.

Who has believed our report? And to whom has the arm of
the LORD been revealed? For He shall grow up before Him as a
tender plant, and as a root out of dry ground. He has no form or
comeliness; and when we see Him, there is no beauty that we
should desire Him. He is despised and rejected by men, a Man
of sorrows and acquainted with grief. And we hid, as it were, our
faces from Him; He was despised, and we did not esteem Him.

**ISAIAH 53:1-3**

**PONDER THIS** When you think about God coming to Earth through Jesus, you
might expect He would come in a jeweled chariot. But how did He arrive? He
was born as a baby in Bethlehem—a small, insignificant town. You might expect
He would have been raised in a royal court, but He was raised as a carpenter's
son in another obscure, hated village called Nazareth. You might expect that
Jesus would come with wealth, opulence, and power, but He walked about in
sandal shoes with no home and no place to lay His head.

The natural eye looks at Jesus and asks, "What's so great about Him?" If we
started to talk about His life completely, we would never be able to finish. There
are so many miracles. He went about doing good and showed great love in
the way that He lived. He was not without sorrow, but He was without sin. The
virtuous life of the Lord Jesus is nothing glamorous at first glance, but it is full
of glory and worthy of praise.

- What are some things that come to mind when you think about
  who Jesus is?

- What does Jesus's life on Earth teach you about humility? Where
  do you struggle with humility?

**PRACTICE THIS** Think about someone you have seen exhibit humility and service.
Ask that person to share how he or she got to that point.

And so it is written, "The first man Adam became a living being." The last Adam became a life-giving spirit.

**1 CORINTHIANS 15:45**

**PONDER THIS** I read of four men who were climbing the Matterhorn—that majestic mountain in Switzerland—together. There were two guides and two tourists. To complete this climb, they had to be tied together. Climbing up the mountain, there was a guide, then a tourist, a guide, and then a tourist. They were going up that steep icy slope, and the last man tied to the rope put his foot down on the ice, slipped, and swung over the side. The man who fell was tied to the second man, who was the guide and a skilled Alpine climber, but he was dragged over. When he went over, he pulled the next man over.

When the lead guide felt the tug on the rope, he knew what was happening, and he dug his cleats in, put his pickax into the ice, strained his muscles, and held for all he could. These other three men were dangling, but they finally got their feet back on, and all four of them went up the mountain together. Using this account as a theological picture, the first man who slipped was Adam, but the last man who held was Jesus. We're all tied together but thank God for that last man, the Lord Jesus Christ, who has survived for us.

- When have you felt like you fell away in life? How did Jesus save and restore you?
- How does knowing Jesus' strength change the way you interact with the challenges in life?

**PRACTICE THIS** Consider one area of life where you feel like you are slipping. Call out to God for His help and ask Him to remind you of the strength you can have in Jesus, even when the situation seems grim.

Behold, I tell you a mystery: We shall not all sleep, but we shall all be changed—in a moment, in the twinkling of an eye, at the last trumpet. For the trumpet will sound, and the dead will be raised incorruptible, and we shall be changed.

**1 CORINTHIANS 15:51-52**

**PONDER THIS** A woman and her two children were in their garden enjoying a beautiful day when a big bee sat on the little boy and stung him. The little boy began to cry, and the sting began to swell. Then the bee began to buzz around the little girl, and she was terrified. By this time the little boy had quieted down, and the mother said to the little girl, "Darling, don't be afraid. Come over here and let me show you something. Look closely at your brother's arm. Do you see the stinger that's there? When that bee stung little brother, he left his stinger." Did you know that a bee does that? He can't sting but one time. She continued, "Now sweetheart, that bee can't hurt you because he left his stinger in little brother. He may buzz, and he may frighten you, but he can't hurt you."

The sting of death was taken by Jesus Christ. Death cannot hurt you. Death may frighten you, but Jesus has taken the sting out of death and the gloom out of the grave.

- What feelings arise for you when thinking about the reality of death?
- How does the hope of Christ lead us to grieve differently, even though we're sad someone has died?

**PRACTICE THIS** Pray and tell God any reasons you are afraid of death. Take some time to look up and reflect on Scripture passages that speak to the hope followers of Jesus have after death.

**9**

Therefore, my beloved brethren, be steadfast, immovable,
always abounding in the work of the Lord, knowing
that your labor is not in vain in the Lord.

**1 CORINTHIANS 15:58**

**PONDER THIS** There is a reason Paul wrote about the mysteries of what is to come and the hope we have because death has lost its sting. He had an application in mind, not just information. He said, "Therefore, my beloved brethren, be steadfast." You can have stability. Don't get blown around. Stay in there. Seek stability in Christ, be unmovable in the hope you have in Him, and you will have fervency—"always abounding in the work of the Lord."

If you believe Jesus Christ is coming again, what should you do? Go live for Jesus. Occupy your time by loving others like He does until He comes. Get your head out of the clouds of prophecy and get your feet on the pavement of soul-winning. The great proof that you believe the prophecies of the Bible to be true is you follow God's instruction. There needs to be stability. There needs to be fervency. The labor you are doing for the Lord is not in vain.

- Have you ever lived as if your service to Jesus didn't really matter?
- Who have you shared your faith with? What was that experience like?

**PRACTICE THIS** Take some time to pray and consider who you can express Jesus' love to today. Take action to share the hope of Jesus with that person.

To Titus, a true son in our common faith: Grace, mercy, and peace
from God the Father and the Lord Jesus Christ our Savior.

**TITUS 1:4**

**PONDER THIS** A Christian who doesn't share the Gospel of Christ is like a bus driver who won't drive a bus or a barber who won't cut hair. Jesus said, "You shall be witnesses to Me." (See Acts 1:8.) The question is, do you have any spiritual children? Is there anyone you have passed your legacy of faith on to? Not only was Paul a spiritual father, but he was a grandfather because now Titus was winning others to Christ. Spiritual impact can be passed on to many generations.

On April 1, 1885, there was a man named Kimball who went into a shoe store where there was a shoe clerk he had a burden for. The shoe clerk's name was Dwight. Mr. Kimball went in, and he stuttered and stammered, but he told Dwight about Christ. There in the shoe racks, this young 19-year-old clerk bowed his head and gave his heart to Jesus and became Mr. Kimball's spiritual son. That young man gained a heart to share Jesus. He lived in Chicago and began to gather boys and girls for Sunday school to tell them about Christ. His name was Dwight L. Moody. This uneducated shoe clerk began to preach and hold great crusades; thousands came to know Christ through his ministry. What about you? Who is your spiritual parent, and who are your spiritual children?

- Who has influenced you in your faith?
- Who have you been pouring into as you walk with Jesus? Who do you need to begin to do this with?

**PRACTICE THIS** Write a note of gratitude to specific people who have been influential in your walk with Jesus.

Where is boasting then? It is excluded. By what law? Of works?
No, but by the law of faith. Therefore we conclude that a
man is justified by faith apart from the deeds of the law.

**ROMANS 3:27-28**

**PONDER THIS** The denial of grace is legalism. Many Christians are prone to legalism. One person might preach Jesus Christ and Him crucified, a message that calls people to believe in the Lord Jesus Christ and be saved, that you are saved by grace through faith alone. But it does not take long for someone else to come to that new believer with a lot of rules, rituals, and laws to follow. If a new believer is insecure in the liberty he or she has in Jesus, that person will go back into the playpen of legalism because it is easier.

Don't let anybody make a legalist out of you. You are not saved by keeping laws or by ritual. You're not saved by anything other than the grace of God. A person who tries to be saved or sanctified by rules is like a person trying to get out of quicksand. The more he struggles, the more he sinks. Ten thousand rules will not make you one bit more like Jesus.

- When have you focused more on following legalistic rules than on the grace of God?
- How have you extended God's grace to others recently?

**PRACTICE THIS** Make a list of the differences between legalism and grace. Do you approach people with legalism or grace? What needs to change?

...being confident of this very thing, that He who has begun a good work in you will complete it until the day of Jesus Christ.

**PHILIPPIANS 1:6**

**PONDER THIS** Once you are saved, you come out of law school, and you get into grace school. Unlike law school, grace school never closes. The teacher never fails to show up and you're continually being taught.

In salvation, there is nothing to earn, but there is much to learn. Do you know what discipleship is? It simply means learning. A disciple is a learner. You're learning to live as you should. That's the reason none of us has a diploma yet. There's not one of us who can say, "I have graduated from grace school." We are being discipled by the grace of God, and He's still working on us.

John Newton wrote the song many of us know and love: "Amazing Grace." John Newton also wrote, "I am not what I ought to be, I am not what I want to be, I am not what I hope to be in another world, but still I am not what I once used to be, and by the grace of God I am what I am." You see, He's still working on us, and we are growing in the grace and knowledge of our Lord and Savior, Jesus Christ.

- What are some lessons in grace you have learned?
- How have you prioritized learning the things of God over the rules of man?

**PRACTICE THIS** Think about when you first became a Christian. Make a list of some of the lessons of grace you have learned since then.

> Likewise, exhort the young men to be sober-minded, in all
> things showing yourself to be a pattern of good works; in
> doctrine showing integrity, reverence, incorruptibility.

**TITUS 2:6-7**

**PONDER THIS** I got a letter from a person the other day, and I know the person meant well. The letter said, "Pastor, I enjoyed the message on grace. It was so good when you took the offering, and you said, 'Because of the grace of God, we give.' I'm so glad you didn't mention tithing because that is Old Testament law." This letter grieved me because the person had missed the point. Because I'm saved, that doesn't mean I don't want to give to the level of the tithe; it means I want to give more.

The Bible says the righteousness of the law is fulfilled in us. It's not that we say, "Now that I'm saved by grace, I'll live by a lower standard." No, we live by a higher standard because we have the love of Jesus on the inside.

The Law says, "Don't commit adultery." Grace doesn't mean you can. The Law says, "Don't steal." That doesn't mean I can. (See Exodus 20:14-15.) Instead, the righteousness of the law is fulfilled in us. William Henry Griffith Thomas once said, "I will not work my soul to save, for that work my Lord has done; but I will work like any slave, for the love of God's dear son."

- What are some of the laws of Scripture that you struggle with?
- Since you became a follower of Jesus, how has your attitude toward good works changed?

**PRACTICE THIS** Write down the laws or teachings of Jesus you struggle with most. Ask God to transform your heart in those areas so that you can serve Him with gladness.

For the grace of God that brings salvation has appeared to all
men, teaching us that, denying ungodliness and worldly lusts,
we should live soberly, righteously, and godly in the present
age, looking for the blessed hope and glorious appearing of
our great God and Savior Jesus Christ, who gave Himself for us,
that He might redeem us from every lawless deed and purify
for Himself His own special people, zealous for good works."

**TITUS 2:11-14**

**PONDER THIS** God's grace leads Him to give to us where there is no merit. God's grace leads Him to give to us when there are many demerits. And God's grace leads Him to give at great cost to Himself. Anybody, any place, any time, no matter how wicked or how vile, can come to Him in repentance and faith and be gloriously, instantaneously, radically, dramatically, and eternally saved by His grace. There is not one thing to earn, but there is much to learn.

Our passage says, "For the grace of God...has appeared to all men, teaching us" how to live "soberly, righteously, and godly in" this present world. The devil does not want you to hear the message of grace. But if he cannot deny grace, he will try to distort grace. He would have you believe that after you have received grace, it doesn't make any difference how you live. Grace does more than free us from sin; it frees us to live for God and follow His Son, Jesus, through the power of the Holy Spirit.

- What has changed about your life since you became a Christian? What has remained the same? What still needs to change?

- Who do you know that needs the grace of God?

**PRACTICE THIS** Share with another person how God's grace has transformed your life.

For the grace of God that brings salvation has appeared to all men.

**TITUS 2:11**

**PONDER THIS** In the past, when a general went to war and won a great victory, he would often take a part of the prize of the battle. He would get a treasure and bring it back home as a trophy for himself—his special possession.

The Bible says in the ages to come, you and I will be trophies of God's grace. We are His special possession. The Captain of our salvation went to bloody Calvary, defeated Satan, and paid the sin debt. He then redeemed unto Himself a special people. That's what grace bought. We're purchased. We're purified. We're special. We're different. Grace brought salvation, it taught sanctification, and it sought service.

Jesus did not bathe this world with His blood to have you serve the world of the flesh. What has grace sought? He gave Himself for us that He might redeem us from all iniquity and purify for Himself a special people zealous of good works. "O to grace how great a debtor daily I'm constrained to be!" That's what it's all about.

- How has your relationship with Jesus changed the way you live? Why is this always necessary?
- What is an area where you still struggle to choose to serve Christ?

**PRACTICE THIS** Take some time for self-reflection and pray about an area where you may still be serving the desires of your flesh.

**16**

For by grace you have been saved through faith, and
that not of yourselves; it is the gift of God.

**EPHESIANS 2:8**

**PONDER THIS** When I was a young Christian, I would often fail. The same old words sometimes would come out of my mouth. That fiery temper would come back. There was a battle going on that lasted about two years.

During those two years, I began to listen, and the grace of God began to teach me some things. On a walk one night, I prayed, "Oh, God, I'm so miserable. I don't know whether I'm lost and the Holy Spirit has me under conviction, or I'm saved, and the devil's trying to make me doubt it." Have you ever been there? I continued, "I just don't have peace, God, and I want to get it settled tonight. You remember when I went forward in that church, and I was sincere, but God, I've been riding a roller coaster up and down and I want it stopped. With every fiber of my being, I trust you to save me. I'm not depending on myself. I don't look for a sign, and I don't ask for a feeling; I stand on Your Word. You died for me; You paid my sin debt. I receive You now once and for all as my Lord and Savior." After that prayer, a river of peace began to flow in my heart, and it's still flowing. What made that possible? It is the grace of God that brings salvation.

- What are some things you've needed to surrender to God even after becoming a Christian?

- How has God's grace transformed your life?

**PRACTICE THIS** Share with someone about how God's grace transformed something in your life.

**17**

...who gave Himself for us, that He might redeem us
from every lawless deed and purify for Himself His
special own people, zealous for good works.

**TITUS 2:14**

**PONDER THIS** You need to learn to resist the pull of the world. We all feel that pull of the world. The Bible says, "Therefore let him who thinks he stands take heed lest he fall" (1 Corinthians 10:12). What temptation pulled on Lot in Genesis 13? It was the money, pleasure, and social life available to him from the world. Lot had no prayer. He wasn't seeking God. There wasn't a thought for the welfare of his children.

Often, young people are told, "Make all the money you can, just so you make it honestly." And we say, "Well, a man has to live." No, he has to die. And after he dies, he has to face God. First John 2:16 says, "For all that is in the world—the lust of the flesh, the lust of the eyes, and the pride of life—is not of the Father but is of the world." Lot saw the lust of the flesh, Sodom with its pleasures. He saw the lust of the eyes, Sodom with its possessions. There was the pride of life, Sodom, with its philosophy. Now, Lot's sin was not a sin only the rich have. You can be poor and covetous. You can have nothing and still feel the pull of the world. This world flirted with Lot. He was enticed. He became a friend of the world and committed adultery against God. Those same forces that worked on Lot are working on you and me day by day. Resist the pull of the world.

- Where do you feel the pull of the world most strongly?
- How do you respond when you feel the pull of the world?

**PRACTICE THIS** Speak to an accountability partner about the areas where you feel the pull of the world. Pray together about those things.

## 18

For we ourselves were also once foolish, disobedient, deceived,
serving various lusts and pleasures, living in malice and envy,
hateful and hating one another. But when the kindness
and the love of God our Savior toward man appeared...

**TITUS 3:3-4**

**PONDER THIS** We're blessed because God loves us. That's grace. God doesn't love us because we're valuable; we're valuable because God loves us. That's what the Gospel is all about.

Those of you trying to work your way to Heaven, how are you going to do it? You don't have any righteousness. There is nothing you can do that will take away what you've already done. It is not subtraction. There is nothing you can stop doing; you'll still be missing reconciliation with God. What I'm trying to say is sin is sin, and it must be atoned for. If you try anything other than the grace of God, it will never work.

I read somewhere about a man who fell out of a rowboat into the Niagara River. The river was flowing toward the falls, and they tried to save him, so they threw him a rope. He held the rope for a while, but then he saw a log coming past and let go of the rope to grab hold of the log. No matter what else you hold onto, if you are not linked by the rope of grace to the heart of God, you're going to perish. Salvation is not by works of righteousness, but according to His mercy—He saved us.

- When have you valued your good works too highly?
- How have you tried to sustain your faith by your own strength? Why is this impossible?

**PRACTICE THIS** Write down some "good works" you have done recently. Surrender those things to God.

Not by works of righteousness which we have done, but according to his mercy he saved us, through the washing of regeneration and renewing of the holy spirit, whom he poured out on us abundantly through jesus christ our savior, that having been justified by his grace we should become heirs according to the hope of eternal life.

**TITUS 3:5-7**

**PONDER THIS** When I played high school football, there was a game when it was pouring rain, and there was water standing on the field. During the game, just by happenstance, a pass was intercepted by our defensive tackle. Now, he was not the pass-intercepting type. We blocked every opposing team member to get him down the field, and he scored on that play. I roomed with him that night, and all night long, he talked about those brilliant moves and how he went down the field. I'd hate to be in Heaven with people talking about how they got themselves to Heaven. The Bible says it's "not of works, lest anyone should boast" (Ephesians 2:9). We're going to Heaven by the grace of God, and all glory, praise, and honor goes to Him. What is the grace of God? It is the sovereign love of the Father, and it is the supernatural work of the Spirit.

He also regenerates us—we're sanctified through Him. You may have been an adulterer. You may have been sexually perverted. You may have been a thief or an extortioner. But when you get saved, you are washed whiter than snow in the precious blood of Jesus Christ.

- When have you bragged or been tempted to brag about your good works?
- When have you felt like you couldn't measure up to the standard of God's law?

**PRACTICE THIS** Consider which side you tend toward, bragging about your own good works or feeling ashamed because you can't measure up to the law. Ask God to correct your thinking.

**20**

Stand fast therefore in the liberty by which Christ has made us
free, and do not be entangled again with a yoke of bondage.

**GALATIANS 5:1**

**PONDER THIS** It is "by grace you have been saved through faith, and that not
of yourselves; it is the gift of God" (Ephesians 2:8). You can't beg it, you can't
buy it, you can't borrow it, you can't steal it, and you can't earn it. It is the grace
of God; salvation was bought by Christ on the cross. When Christ finished, it
was accomplished. You cannot deplete it, and you can't add to it—it is the
supernatural work of God. It is the grace of Christ. He is the subject of the Gospel.
It is about Him: the death, burial, and resurrection of Jesus Christ.

You may say, "Well, I believe the plan of salvation." You can believe the plan
of salvation and go straight to Hell because you're not saved by the plan of
salvation. You're saved by the Man of salvation. It's not a creed. You may say, "I
believe if you live right, you'll go to Heaven." Paul said if righteousness comes by
the law, then Christ is dead in vain. (See Galatians 2:21.)

Do you know why there is so much religious mayhem in the world today?
People have met creeds, not Christ. They've entered into codes of living but
not Christ. They've joined churches without meeting Christ. Salvation is not
believing something; it is receiving Someone. Jesus is just not a good way to
Heaven; He's the only way to Heaven.

- What are some other things you can think of that people put
  their faith in instead of Jesus?

- What are you tempted to put faith in over Jesus?

**PRACTICE THIS** Pray for a friend or loved one who has not put his or her faith in
Jesus. Confess any ways you need to turn back to Jesus or turn to Jesus for the
first time.

"I have been crucified with Christ; it is no longer I who live, but Christ lives in me; and the life which I now live in the flesh I live by faith in the Son of God, who loved me and gave Himself for me. I do not set aside the grace of God; for if righteousness comes through the law, then Christ died in vain."

**GALATIANS 2:20-21**

**PONDER THIS** Under legalism, you're a slave to yourself. Under criticism, you're a slave to others. Under legalism, you're a slave to circumstance, but the grace of God will set you free from all that. It's all centered on the cross of Jesus Christ. The cross is our statue of liberty; it is the cross that tells us of our freedom. The cross sets us free from legalism because every demand of the law was paid with the precious blood of Jesus Christ. The cross sets us free from criticism. You can criticize me, but I know who I am, and He loved me enough to die for me.

Because you died with Christ, the law has no more demand on you. It is an exchanged life. He gave Himself for us so that He might give Himself to us. He inhabits our humanity. The life I now live, I live by the faith in the Son of God who loved me and gave Himself for me.

- Why is Jesus worthy of our full trust every day?
- How would life look different if you truly lived with full faith in the Son of God each day?

**PRACTICE THIS** Make a list of your daily activities and responsibilities. Next to each listed item, note how it might look different if undertaken by faith in the Son of God.

**22**

But when the kindness and the love of God our Savior toward man
appeared, not by works of righteousness which we have done,
but according to His mercy He saved us, through the washing of
regeneration and renewing of the Holy Spirit, whom He poured
out on us abundantly through Jesus Christ our Savior."

**TITUS 3:4-6**

**PONDER THIS** What is present grace? It's the love of the Father; it's the washing of regeneration and renewing of the Holy Spirit. He makes you new, and He keeps renewing. This means continuous action. Day by day, moment by moment, He keeps us, He renews us, He restores us, and He refreshes us. His mercies are new every day. He doesn't just forgive us and then say, "That's it." This is the grace of God. It is the sovereign love of the Father. It is the supernatural work of the Holy Spirit and the saving death of the Son.

Throughout our lives with Jesus, the Holy Spirit just drops little gems into our hearts. He sees our fears, and He sees our tears. A jewel of joy, a pearl of peace—they are gifts for today, but we will get the full legacy later. Right now, we have the earnestness of the Spirit. He is giving little tokens and little down payments, and there will be future glory. We're going to inherit all things. Aren't you glad you are saved? Think of your past guilt. Think of your present grace. Think of your future glory with the Lord Jesus Christ. This is the amazing grace of God. When you receive Jesus, you receive the eternal life that's in Him. You can't have that life without Jesus. Through Him, you will be forgiven, transformed, and receive future glory.

- When was a moment you felt worn out in your faith? How did God renew you?
- Who do you know who is in a difficult season and may need some spiritual renewal?

**PRACTICE THIS** Pray for and serve the person you know who needs spiritual renewal.

> ...that having been justified by His grace we should
> become heirs according to the hope of eternal life.

**TITUS 3:7**

**PONDER THIS** I want you to see our future glory through Jesus. Titus 3:3 speaks of our guilt. Titus 3:4-6 speaks of grace. And Titus 4:7 speaks of glory. "That having been justified by His grace, we should become heirs according to the hope of eternal life." That's talking about what is coming. That is talking about our future. We are heirs of God and joint heirs of Jesus Christ (Romans 8:7). Do you know what a joint heir is? A joint heir means we share in the same way. We are heirs of God. We inherit all things. The best is yet to come.

Now, the Bible calls the Holy Spirit that we have right now the down payment. He is the earnest of our inheritance. Do you know what the word earnest means? If you're going to buy something large, like a house, you give earnest money. It's the start of what is to come. The Holy Spirit in your heart is the earnest money. You'll get the full legacy later. You don't have it all now; it is future glory. That's the reason we remember this world is not our home. We're just pilgrims, passing through to a future glory that awaits us.

- In your walk with Jesus, do you experience hope for what is to come? Why or why not?
- How have you shared the hope of Jesus with others?

**PRACTICE THIS** Write down some things that make you dread the future, then write down reasons from Scripture that give you hope for the future.

...knowing this, that our old man was crucified with
Him, that the body of sin might be done away with,
that we should no longer be slaves of sin.

**ROMANS 6:6**

**PONDER THIS** When Jesus died, the old Adrian died. Calvary doesn't just deal with my sin. Jesus didn't just take my sin to the cross. He took me to the cross. You see, if He had simply died for my sin, that would still leave me. And I'm the problem. The cross does not merely deal with my sin; it deals with me—the source of my sin.

This is a simple and profound truth. When we follow Jesus, our old man is crucified with Him. When He died, He died for me; therefore, I died with Him on that cross. Dr. Robert G. Lee, the former pastor of Bellevue Baptist Church, once went to the Holy Land and to the place called Calvary. It was the first time he'd ever been to Israel, and the guide asked this question, "Have any of you ever been here before?" Dr. Lee raised his hand. The guide said, "When was that?" He said, "Two thousand years ago." Through Jesus, there was a very real way he was there at Calvary. I was there. You were there. Jesus Christ died on that cross for our sins, and we died with Him. He dealt with the penalty of sin but also with the power of sin.

- How does it change your perspective to recognize that your old self died with Jesus?
- What are some things about your old self that you are still tempted to hold onto?

**PRACTICE THIS** Pray and thank God for dealing with you and your sin on the cross.

Likewise you also, reckon yourselves to be dead indeed to sin,
but alive to God in Christ Jesus our Lord. Therefore do not let sin
reign in your mortal body, that you should obey it in its lusts.

**ROMANS 6:6**

**PONDER THIS** In the matter of spiritual victory, it is not your ability that counts. It is not your responsibility; it is your response to Jesus' ability. *Your responsibility is your response to His ability.* You can't do it without Him. He will not do it without you. You must yield.

I heard about the driver of a little pickup truck; he jumped out on the interstate and never slowed down to look and see if someone was coming. He nearly caused an accident, so the driver of a big eighteen-wheeler pulled over, leaned out the window, and said, "Hey, didn't you see that sign?" The man said, "What sign?" The trucker said, "The sign that said YIELD." The man responded, "Well, I opened the window and yelled as loud as I could."

You cannot yield half-heartedly; you are to yield with all your heart. I'm going to sum it up and tell you something that has absolutely gripped my heart. When temptation comes, you must yield, and you will yield. That much is settled. The only question is, which way will you yield? Will you yield to Satan or to Christ? That's the only question. When temptation comes, you must yield. You must, and you will. Choose today to yield to Jesus.

- What does it look like to yield to Jesus in your life?
- What is something you like to have control over? How can you yield to Jesus in this area?

**PRACTICE THIS** Ask a spiritual mentor how he or she seeks to continually yield to Jesus.

"For I am the least of the apostles, who am not worthy to be
called an apostle, because I persecuted the church of God.
But by the grace of God I am what I am, and His grace toward
me was not in vain; but I labored more abundantly than they
all, yet not I, but the grace of God which was with me."

**1 CORINTHIANS 15:9-10**

**PONDER THIS** Perfectionism is a thief. It promises rewards, but it steals joy. Why? Because perfection is an unattainable goal.

If you get the idea that God is going to accept you based on your performance, that is a trap. Think about it. If you believe God is going to accept you based on your performance in your quiet time, Bible study, giving, and witnessing, then you will never know if you've done enough. You will never truly feel accepted.

If we could achieve perfection, we wouldn't need a Savior. If you're a perfectionist, you'll end up angry with God because things don't work out just right. Everything in life is not neat; something is going to happen that's going to make you a little angry with God. Or maybe you're going to be afraid of God.

We get the idea that God is up in Heaven judging us. He's sort of a hard-nosed teacher or parent saying, "David gets a C. Bob did terrible. Scotty did all right, but he sure could do better." This is our idea of God, and we'll never be able to live up to the demands He has on us that we have made for ourselves. We began in the Spirit when we were saved, but now we're trying to prove to God just how good we can be.

- What comes to mind when you think about who God is?
- In what areas do you put high standards on yourself?

**PRACTICE THIS** Identify the areas in which you wrestle with perfectionism and repent.

Let your gentleness be known to all men. The Lord is at hand. Be
anxious for nothing, but in everything by prayer and supplication,
with thanksgiving, let your requests be made known to God;
and the peace of God, which surpasses all understanding,
will guard your hearts and minds through Christ Jesus.

**PHILIPPIANS 4:5-7**

**PONDER THIS** There is a zeal that is divisive, destructive, and deadly. You can take a hammer and build a house with it, or you can cause someone harm with it. Anything taken to an extreme can become bad. We need to learn the difference between zeal and moderation. Let your moderation or your gentleness be known unto all men. Zeal and moderation are not enemies; they're friends.

That doesn't mean we compromise our beliefs, but we need to learn to live by grace. The cause of Christ has been hurt by misguided zeal many times. When Jesus was in Samaria, the Samaritans were mistreating the Lord Jesus Christ. James and John were with Jesus, and they became very zealous for Jesus. They said to Him in Luke 9:54, "Lord, do You want us to command fire to come down from heaven and consume them, just as Elijah did?" But Jesus turned, and rebuked them, and said, "You do not know what manner of spirit you are of. For the Son of Man did not come to destroy men's lives but to save them" (Luke 9:55-56). The manner of spirit they had was that of a misguided zealot. They saw the way the Samaritans were living, and they said, "Lord, let's get them." The cause of Christ has sometimes been hurt far more in the house of its friends than in the house of its enemies.

- What is an issue that easily riles you up? How can you guard against misguided zeal?

- When have you been tempted to take justice into your own hands?

**PRACTICE THIS** Talk to another Christian who knows you well and ask where you tend to have misguided zeal. Ask your friend to keep you accountable for submitting those things to God.

## 28

For you have need of endurance, so that after you have
done the will of God, you may receive the promise.

**PHILIPPIANS 4:5-7**

**PONDER THIS** *Endurance* means the ability to bear up under trials and
difficulties. Many people fail to receive because they fail to endure. This is really
the language of athletics. For a time, I ran track, and I would run distance races.
In those distance races, if you run a mile and you're a hundred yards ahead but
you quit running, you're going to lose the race, no matter what.

Now, what is patience? Patience is more than waiting. It is more than passive
resignation to trials. The word *patience* from the Bible does not have a good
English synonym. The word in the Greek language literally means "to abide
under." It has the idea of steadfastness. It has the idea of constancy. It has the
idea of staying in power. Patience is the bridge between doing the will of God
and receiving the promise.

You need patience so that you might inherit God's promises. Remember
yesterday's provision. He saw you through then, and he'll see you through again.
Remember, it is not patience that solemnly waits in the dark; it is patience
that gloriously anticipates the dawn. And then, rest in tomorrow's promise. I
encourage you to take hold of the Word of God and never let it go.

- How have you actively pursued God when you needed to be
  patient?
- When you think about the future, do you most often look
  with joy or despair? Why?

**PRACTICE THIS** Consider areas of your life in which you need to practice pursuing
God as you are patient.

But without faith it is impossible to please Him, for he
who comes to God must believe that He is, and that He
is a rewarder of those who diligently seek Him.

**HEBREWS 11:6**

**PONDER THIS** God wants us to be diligent. When I was growing up and playing with my friends, we would sometimes ring a doorbell and run away. The person would come to the door, and there'd be nobody there. I think sometimes we do that with God. Too often, before God ever gets there to answer the prayer, we're gone.

Some of our prayers are easily offered and soon forgotten. No wonder we don't inherit the promise. Some of our prayers are wandering generalities rather than specific requests. This means many of us could not even remember what we've prayed for—whether or not God has answered our prayer.

God wants us to be diligent *and* devoted. The writer says we are to diligently seek *Him*. Often, we are seeking the blessing rather than seeking the Lord, the Blesser. We are called to seek His face, who He is. We're not to only seek His hand, the things we can receive from Him. We are to hold onto God, even when the promise does not seem to come right away.

- How difficult do you find it to be diligent in prayer?
- What is the difference between seeking God's face and merely seeking His hand? Why is it important to make the distinction between the two?

**PRACTICE THIS** Consider your recent prayer requests; evaluate what you have been seeking from God and how diligent you have been in seeking *Him*.

Therefore do not cast away your confidence, which has great
reward. For you have need of endurance, so that after you
have done the will of God, you may receive the promise.

**HEBREWS 10:35-36**

**PONDER THIS** Every person who has walked with God very far knows God has seen you through dark times. The passage is basically saying, "Remember and don't throw in the towel. Don't cast away your confidence!" After God has brought you through things, you initially say, "I will never ever doubt God again." Have you said that? But later, you find yourself doubting God again.

One time, Joyce looked at me and said, "Adrian, you're so wonderful. If I ever criticize you about anything, I want you to remind me of what I'm saying right now about how wonderful you are." And you know, I've had to remind her many times. We forget sometimes just how good our God is. Then we get into difficulties and trials and God brings us through, and we say, "Thank You, Jesus. I'll never forget." But then another trial comes, and we do forget.

The first thing you do when you want to hold onto a promise is remember yesterday's provision. God took care of you yesterday, and He will be with you in the future.

- When have you witnessed God's faithfulness? When have you forgotten God's faithfulness?
- How can you make an active practice of remembering God's faithfulness?

**PRACTICE THIS** Encourage someone you know who is struggling to remember God's past faithfulness.

Hear, O Israel: The Lᴏʀᴅ our God, the Lᴏʀᴅ is one! You shall love the Lᴏʀᴅ your God with all your heart, with all your soul, and with all your strength. And these words which I command you today shall be in your heart. You shall teach them diligently to your children, and shall talk of them when you sit in your house, when you walk by the way, when you lie down, and when you rise up.

**DEUTERONOMY 6:4-7**

**PONDER THIS** We are to love God supremely. We're to love Him with sincere love, with all our hearts. Jesus spoke of people who honored God with their words, but He said, "But their heart is far from Me." (See Matthew 15:8.) Do you know what your children need to see in your home? They need to see sincere love. They need to see in you a burning, passionate, emotional sincerity when it comes to the things of God. Kids can spot a phony a mile away, and they know whether or not you love God with all of your heart. And it is the phoniness of parents, by and large, that turns kids off to the things of God.

There was a young Jewish boy who lived with his father in Germany. His father was a successful merchant. They had moved from Germany to England. Having always practiced Judaism, the boy was surprised to see his father join a Lutheran church. That boy asked, "Dad, why did you join a Lutheran church?" And the father said, "Well, son, we, we live in a different place now, and there are so many Lutherans in this particular place in this particular town. It is good for business." At that moment, that boy, who had a deep interest in religion, lost it all. Kids can spot a phony. You're to love God with a sincere love.

- What does it look like to be phony in your faith?
- What does it look like to love God with a sincere love?

**PRACTICE THIS** Speak to someone you have seen love God with a sincere love; ask for a word of encouragement or insight on what motivates that person to live with sincere faith.

---

**2**

---

Blessed are those who keep His testimonies,
who seek Him with the whole heart!

**PSALM 119:2**

**PONDER THIS** Deuteronomy 6:5 says, "You shall love the LORD your God with all your heart, with all your soul, and with all your strength." Your soul is yourself. The whole self, the total self, needs to be given over to God. There should be no area in your life that is off-limits to God. How are you going to teach your children there is one Lord? They are to see in you that one love. They are to see in you a sincere love and a selfless love for our Lord.

Do you know how I can measure any person pretty well? I only need to see two things. I'm talking about your calendar and your bank account. Where are you putting your time? Where are you putting your money? You're to love God selflessly.

Strong love is also required. You're to love God with all your might—every inch, every ounce, and every nerve. He's not just talking about physical strength. He's talking about whatever strength you have emotional strength, financial strength, intellectual strength. Love Him selflessly. Love Him strongly.

- Which one do you struggle with more: loving God selflessly or strongly?
- What areas have you made "off limits" to God?

**PRACTICE THIS** Pray about what areas you consider off limits to God and surrender those things to Him.

"You shall not make for yourself a carved image—any likeness
of anything that is in heaven above, or that is in the earth
beneath, or that is in the water under the earth..."

**EXODUS 20:4**

**PONDER THIS** A woman came to her pastor and said, "Pastor, when should I begin the spiritual training of my child? When he's five years old?" Pastor said, "No." "When he's three years old?" "No." "When he's three months old?" He said, "No." "Well, when shall I begin?" The pastor said, "With his grandparents." The faith that was first in your grandmother and now in your mother and now in you. (See 2 Timothy 1:5.) Don't you want your children to love God? Show them by example how you worship. It is so important that we teach our families to worship.

Do you worship the one true God? Do you worship Him in spirit and truth? Do your children know that you love Him more than anything else? I've got four kids, and one thing they know is their dad is not perfect. They know it. But I'll tell you something else they know. All four of them will tell you that dad is not a phony—he loves God. They know that God is number one in my life. The best thing you can do for your kids is not to give them a college education or leave them a legacy but to teach them to worship God.

- What does a life of worship look like for you?
- Who have you seen exemplify a life of worship before God? How has that impacted you?

**PRACTICE THIS** Tell someone who truly lives a life of worship before God how he or she has impacted you.

"You shall not take the name of the LORD your God in vain, for the LORD will not hold him guiltless who takes His name in vain."

**EXODUS 20:7**

**PONDER THIS** Sometimes we're such hypocrites. We sing, "My Jesus, I love Thee. I know Thou art mine. For Thee all the follies of sin I resign." Do you sing that and still keep sin in your heart? We sing, "Take my silver and my gold; not a mite would I withhold." And yet we hold onto our possessions with all our might. We sing, "Faith of our fathers, holy faith; we will be true to Thee till death," and think nothing of skipping church if a good excuse comes up. We sing, "All to Jesus I surrender. All to Him I freely give." If you don't mean that, you are taking the name of God in vain. You can do it with profanity. You can do it by frivolity. You can do it through hypocrisy.

But in the negative, there is a positive. When we learn to take His name in victory, we'll certainly be afraid to take His name in vanity. Colossians 3:17 says, "And whatever you do in word or deed, do all in the name of the Lord Jesus, giving thanks to God the Father through Him." That's taking His name in victory.

- When have you used God's name in vain?
- What is something you could do to take the name of God in victory?

**PRACTICE THIS** Write down a list of things you do in a day, then consider what it would be like to do those things in Jesus's powerful name.

**5**

> "Honor your father and your mother, that your days may be
> long upon the land which the Lord your God is giving you."
>
> **EXODUS 20:12**

**PONDER THIS** Don't get the idea that you must be a perfect parent. You're not a perfect parent, and your children are not perfect children.

God gave each of your children a will. I don't have goals for my children; I have desires for them. Do you know who I have goals for? For myself. Why? Because I can't control my children, I can control myself by God's grace. So, my desire is that I will have godly children; my goal is that I will be a godly dad. Do you understand the difference? With God helping me, I will be a godly dad.

I want to relieve you from the burden of perfectionism—from thinking if your child fails, it's because you weren't perfect. If their success depends upon your perfection, they won't ever succeed; they will fail because no one is perfect.

- Have you ever felt overwhelmed by the desire to be a perfect parent or perfect person?
- How does Jesus's work on our behalf relieve the pressure for us to be perfect?

**PRACTICE THIS** Encourage some parents you know in a tangible way, whether by a word of encouragement or a thoughtful gift.

## 6

Now the works of the flesh are evident, which are: adultery,
fornication, uncleanness, lewdness, idolatry, sorcery,
hatred, contentions, jealousies, outbursts of wrath, selfish
ambitions, dissensions, heresies, envy, murders, drunkenness,
revelries, and the like; of which I tell you beforehand, just
as I also told you in time past, that those who practice
such things will not inherit the kingdom of God.

**GALATIANS 5:19-21**

**PONDER THIS** There are all kinds of false idols, each one we need to be aware of and guard against. For example, you can make an idol of yourself. When we do that, we go from theology to me-ology. We worship the creature instead of the Creator. Anything or anyone that you love more, fear more, and serve more than God is an idol.

Others have made a god of money. The reason some won't come to church is they say, "All they want down there is my money." But the truth of the matter is that kind of attitude can be a sign of greed. Jesus said, "You cannot serve God and [money]." (See Matthew 6:24.) Either God is God, or money is god. And there are many who worship money.

There are some who worship the family. You will make a terrible mistake if you put your family before your relationship with Jesus. Jesus said, "He who loves father or mother more than Me is not worthy of Me" (Matthew 10:37a). The best thing you can do for your family is not to put them first. Joyce doesn't mind being second place in my heart, and she is second; God is first. I love her so much more because God is the first place in my heart and in my life. Don't make a god of your family.

- Where are you most tempted to devote yourself to someone or something else more than to God?
- What would it look like to give God first place in your heart?

**PRACTICE THIS** Put into practice one habit that will help you remember to keep God first place in your heart.

"God is Spirit, and those who worship Him
must worship in spirit and truth."

**JOHN 4:24**

**PONDER THIS** We become like what we worship. It is so important that we have a proper conception of God. We must understand who God is and what God is like. Therefore, God has absolutely forbidden the making of anything material as an object of worship. Why? Because God is not a material God; He is spiritual. That is His essence. God is spirit and to worship Him, we must worship Him in spirit and truth. What material thing can represent spirit? God is like a circle whose center is everywhere and whose circumference is nowhere. How would you make the image of a God like that? You cannot do it. So, we are forbidden from making anything material to show what God is like.

We communicate love for God with our worship. How are you teaching your children about the worship of God? The greatest thing you can do for your children is teach them to worship. How you worship will go on down to your children, your grandchildren, and your great-grandchildren. The way you worship has a result that will last long after you are gone.

- What have you learned from the way in which your mothers and fathers in the faith worshiped?
- How do you worship God on a regular basis? Think outside the boundaries of Sunday morning service alone.

**PRACTICE THIS** Identify one way you can worship God with your family and implement that this week.

---

**8**

---

Therefore comfort each other and edify one
another, just as you also are doing.

**1 THESSALONIANS 5:11**

**PONDER THIS** Wise encouragement is better than lavish praise. Children need encouragement.

I once planted some flowers. They were beautiful, but after a little while, they started to wilt. So, I went and got the hose and sprinkled them. When I woke up the next morning, they were beautiful again. Children need encouragement, like plants need water. They need it repeatedly. You need to catch them doing something right and let them know through your encouragement that you believe in them. Let your speech affirm them.

What is the difference between encouragement and praise? Praise tells a child, "I get approval when I do good. If I will do good, then they will approve of me. When my performance is good, the approval rate goes up. When my performance is bad, then my acceptance goes down, and my self-image goes down with it." Praise says, "You are great because you did something." There's nothing wrong with praise, but I'm saying that encouragement is twice as strong as praise. Encouragement looks at a child and values that child, not primarily for what the child can do, but for who the child is. Encouragement says, "You can do it. Thank you. I'm so grateful for you."

- When have you been impacted by a word of encouragement?
- Who are some people you can encourage today?

**PRACTICE THIS** Encourage someone close to you today.

## 9

Let us therefore be diligent to enter that rest, lest anyone
fall according to the same example of disobedience.

**HEBREWS 4:11**

**PONDER THIS** When I stand under the sun outside, I can see my shadow. The light is up there, the shadow is down there, and I am there in middle. Have you ever seen a dog chasing the shadow of a bird on the ground? He's chasing the shadow, but the bird is up there. When people try to keep the covenant Sabbath according to the Old Testament, they are only chasing shadows. The Sabbath was a shadow of the Lord Jesus Christ. The substance is Christ. The Sabbath is the shadow that pointed to the substance. Don't miss Jesus! That's the reason Jesus said in Matthew 11:28, "Come to Me, all you who labor and are heavy laden, and I will give you rest." He is your rest. He has made you a new creation. He is now sitting at the right hand of the Father. It is done. It is finished. It is paid in full. The Lord Jesus is our finished rest.

The reason we gather for worship on Sunday is because Jesus broke the bonds of death and came out of the grave upon the first day of the week! Revelation 1:10 calls the first day of the week, "the Lord's Day." The Sabbath was never called the Lord's Day in the Old Testament, but the new creation Calvary Sabbath is called the Lord's Day.

- How has Jesus given you rest in Him?
- What changes when you think about Sunday as the Lord's Day, not just a general day to rest?

**PRACTICE THIS** Intentionally plan a restful and worshipful Lord's Day this week.

## 10

This is the day the LORD has made; we will rejoice and be glad in it.

**PSALM 118:24**

**PONDER THIS** If we're not under the Old Testament laws of the Sabbath, how do we keep the Lord's Day? What are the regulations for keeping the first day of the week? I cannot give you any rules because the Bible does not give any. Be careful that you don't try to take the Old Testament rules concerning the Sabbath and apply them to Sunday, the Lord's Day. That doesn't mean we've forgotten the Ten Commandments, which say, "Remember the Sabbath day to keep it holy" (Exodus 20:8). We simply see its ultimate fulfillment as it applies to the Church of the Lord Jesus Christ. Is it a holy day? Absolutely—because it is the Lord's Day! But it's a day of love and not legalism.

So, is it alright to watch television on Sunday? Is it alright to go to a ball game on Sunday? Could I play softball on Sunday? Could I go out on a boat on Sunday? Could I go to the grocery store if we're out of milk on Sunday? Good questions, but I'm not the one to answer them. It's not my day. It's the Lord's Day. Ask Him, "Lord, how can I honor You on this day? How can I take this day and give You glory, reverence, and praise so at the end of that day I can say 'Lord that was Your day'"?

- What is your typical Sunday routine?
- What would change if you were to ask God how to spend your day?

**PRACTICE THIS** Ask God to guide you in how to spend the Lord's Day so that it honors Him.

"The thief does not come except to steal, and to kill,
and to destroy. I have come that they may have life,
and that they may have it more abundantly."

**JOHN 10:10**

**PONDER THIS** Life is God's wonderful gift. Therefore, we should enjoy life and choose life. Jesus is the great Life-Giver. Satan is the great life-destroyer. When Jesus referred to "the thief," He was not talking about a thief in the general sense; He was talking about Satan. Satan came to steal and destroy; Jesus came to give life.

Our Lord said if we allow hatred in our hearts, we have transgressed against Him. First John 3:15 says, "Whoever hates his brother is a murderer, and you know that no murderer has eternal life abiding in him." This includes mental murder. Is there somebody you hate? You may say, "I'm not overtly evil." Do you hate anybody? Is your heart a headquarters for hate? Any kind of hate is not from Jesus, the Author of life.

- When are you most prone to hate? What people or groups of people make you the angriest?
- Where have you seen the damage of hate in your life?

**PRACTICE THIS** Pray and repent from the habits of hate in your life.

And He answered and said to them, "Have you not read that
He who made them at the beginning 'made them male and
female,' and said, 'For this reason a man shall leave his father and
mother and be joined to his wife, and the two shall become one
flesh'? So then, they are no longer two but one flesh. Therefore
what God has joined together, let not man separate."

**MATTHEW 19:4-6**

**PONDER THIS** Marriage has the highest priority. The highest priority of human relationships is not parent to child or child to parent but husband and wife to one another. Therefore, we as parents must be preparing our children to leave us. We must come to a place where the eagles stir the nest to send out those children so they can have homes of their own.

Now, the baby eagle doesn't want to leave the nest. It's so comfortable there. The mother eagle comes with little bits of fish or big fat juicy worms to feed that little eagle, but there comes a time when that eagle must fly and get out of the nest. It would be easy to do everything for the bird and never really teach that baby eagle how to fly. What a mistake!

Marriage deals with more than simply a sexual union, though that is included. It means one flesh physically, emotionally, and spiritually. Two become one. Marriage is a romance, and in the first chapter, both the hero and the heroin die, and they become one new person. This does not end when you have children; you are still one, and you need to prioritize that relationship, preparing for the day your child will be sent out.

- What are some relationships that have a high priority in your life?
- How can you pour into the next generation, preparing them to leave the nest?

**PRACTICE THIS** If you are married, prioritize your spouse today. If you are not married, ask a couple you know if there is a way you could serve and pray for their family.

## 13

Jesus said to him, "I am the way, the truth, and the life.
No one comes to the Father except through Me."

**JOHN 14:6**

**PONDER THIS** Jesus gives spiritual life. When He said, "I am the way," He meant, "Without Me there is no going." When He said, "I am the truth," He meant, "Without Me there is no knowing." And when He said, "I am the life," He meant, "Without Me, there is no growing. I give supernatural, spiritual life." Christians are not just nice people trying to do better who have accepted some creed or some code. They are new creatures regenerated supernaturally by Jesus Christ, who transforms them by sending His Spirit into their hearts and giving them supernatural life.

Jesus, who gives physical and spiritual life, also gives eternal life. John 10:10 says, "I have come that they may have life, and that they may have it more abundantly." In verses 27-28 of that same chapter, Jesus said, "My sheep hear My voice, and I know them, and they follow Me. And I give them eternal life, and they shall never perish; neither shall anyone snatch them out of My hand." Jesus is the author of physical life, spiritual life, and eternal life. What does eternal life mean? It speaks of the quality of life and quantity of life. He adds years to life and life to the years.

- How has Jesus provided spiritual life for you?
- How can you share your testimony about the abundance of life Jesus gives?

**PRACTICE THIS** Talk to a friend about how Jesus has provided abundant life for you.

"But seek first the kingdom of God and His righteousness,
and all these things shall be added to you."

**MATTHEW 6:33**

**PONDER THIS** Part of choosing life is presenting spiritual life. I have four children on Earth and a little boy in Heaven. My children are a long way from perfect, but they all love God. When my son, Steve, was a teenager, I watched him and noticed I didn't see the beauty of Jesus in his life, though he'd walked down the aisle and made a profession of faith. I said, "Steve, get in the car with me. Let's go for a ride. Let's go out and walk in the woods." During that day together, I said to him, "Son, daddy has got to know that you know Jesus."

We talked, and out there in the woods, we kneeled and prayed. During our conversation, he assured me, "Daddy, I love Jesus." From then on, I started to notice him showing it through his life. One day I prayed, "Lord, if any of my children are not saved, I don't want to go to Heaven without all my children." I didn't say anything to my wife, Joyce, or the children about it. But the next Sunday, when I gave the invitation, my oldest daughter, Gayle, came down the aisle, and she said, "Daddy, I don't believe I've ever really and truly been saved. I want to be saved." I believe that was directly related to that prayer. Families need to choose spiritual life.

- Whose spiritual health do you regularly pray for?
- How can you choose spiritual life through your daily routines?

**PRACTICE THIS** Pray for any family members who don't seem to show fruit of the Spirit in their lives or who have wandered away from their faith.

Let us therefore come boldly to the throne of grace, that we
may obtain mercy and find grace to help in time of need.

**HEBREWS 4:16**

**PONDER THIS** I have some tips for getting your marriage back on track: first, decide to live for Christ. Give your heart to the Lord Jesus Christ. If you have failed or sinned, bring it to Him. Isaiah 1:18b says, "Though your sins are like scarlet, they shall be as white as snow; though they are red like crimson, they shall be as wool." When you come to Him, He will forgive; He will not hold grudges. He will bury every stain, every blot, every blur, and every blemish in the grave of God's forgetfulness. Come to Jesus, and I promise you on the authority of the Word of God, He will cleanse you.

Now it's important to decide to live for Christ and depend on Christ. Let His life in you energize you and give you power. He doesn't merely forgive you and then say, "Now do better." He comes to live in you, to energize you, to give you power day by day. Finally, begin to pour out your love to Christ and your family. Love God and love your spouse with a supernatural love. Anyone who chooses to love can love. The Bible says, "Husbands, love your wives" (Ephesians 5:25a). That's not a suggestion; it's a command. Decide to love and then devote yourself to a love for God and a love for your family.

- How has dependence on God changed your relationship with others?
- How has Jesus given you life and energy when you needed it?

**PRACTICE THIS** Spend some time talking to God about the areas of life where you need to depend on Him more.

## 16

Or do you not know that your body is the temple of the Holy
Spirit who is in you, whom you have from God, and you are not
your own? For you were bought at a price; therefore glorify
God in your body and in your spirit, which are God's.

**1 CORINTHIANS 6:19-20**

**PONDER THIS** God's Word says, "You shall not steal" (Exodus 20:15). Do you know
the worst thievery is to steal from God? And so many are stealing from God. You
may ask, "How am I stealing from God?" Well, have you given Him your life? You
belong to Him. You are His creation. He made you. You are His by redemption.
He died for you. And when you live your life for yourself alone, as if Jesus Christ
never lived or died, you are a thief. You have taken from God that which belongs
to Him. You walk God's green Earth. You breathe God's air. You live the life that
God has given you, yet you don't pour your life back out to God.

Do you know why we tithe? The tithe is a symbol that everything belongs to God.
Don't get the idea that 10 percent of what you have belongs to God. All you have
belongs to God because the One who owns the sheep owns the wool. When we
steal—whether withholding tithe, doing a dishonest day's work, failing to give
love, or failing to honor God as we ought, we are ultimately robbing ourselves!
It pays to serve Jesus—it pays every day and every step of the way. You have
defrauded yourself. Ironically, in seeking to get, you're the one who loses.

- What does it look like to live daily like you belong to God?
- What are some ways you have learned to glorify God with
  your body and your spirit?

**PRACTICE THIS** Speak to another Christian about how you may be stealing from
God and from yourself. Encourage one another with practical ways you can live
like you belong to God.

But this I say: He who sows sparingly will also reap sparingly, and he who sows bountifully will also reap bountifully. So let each one give as he purposes in his heart, not grudgingly or of necessity; for God loves a cheerful giver.

**2 CORINTHIANS 9:6-7**

**PONDER THIS** If you were to clench your hand for a long time, eventually, you would feel pain. The relief comes when we let go. So many people go along in life with clenched fists, saying, "That's mine." Life is made up of takers and givers. Teach children, and there's so much they can give. Give them understanding, and they'll give you understanding. There are many people today who look for someone to understand and care. It's an amazing thing. Give acceptance. Give forgiveness to your children. Don't let bitterness poison you and them. Give love. Love means, "I'll do you good no matter what you do to me." Teach children to give this way.

John Wesley, founder of Methodism, a great man of God, said, "Make all you can, save all you can, and give all you can." Teach children integrity. Teach children industry. Teach children charity and generosity. Clean up a neighbor's yard. Help a widow carry groceries inside. Teach children to bring their own money to church. Give them their allowance. Teach them to take out of their allowance a gift. It may not be much, but let the children have the joy of bringing their offerings to the Lord. Exemplify a life of giving.

- What lessons have you learned from your parents?
- What are some valuable lessons you have received that you want to pass on to the next generation? How can you live as a model?

**PRACTICE THIS** Make a list of children and young people you know and pray for each of them.

"You shall not bear false witness against your neighbor."

**EXODUS 20:16**

**PONDER THIS** When I was younger, I was driving down to my little country church with one headlight, hoping I could make it back to school and get it fixed. The highway patrolman stopped me and said, "Son, do you know you only have one headlight." I responded, "I only have one headlight?" On the one hand, you could say I told him the absolute truth. I only had one headlight. But the way I said it insinuated that I didn't know that. When I got back in the car, the Holy Spirit tore me up and convicted me about my lie.

We can lie with the tone of our voice, and we also lie when we slander others. The Bible says in James 4:11a, "Do not speak evil of one another, brethren." It doesn't say whether or not it's true. We are not to slander. We're not to speak with an evil spirit. A.B. Simpson, the great Christian and Missionary Alliance pastor, once said, "I would rather play with forked lightning, or take in my hands living wires with their fiery current, than speak a reckless word against any servant of Christ, or idly repeat the slanderous darts which thousands of Christians are hurling on others, to the hurt of their own souls and bodies." When you listen to slander, you're as guilty as the person who spreads it.

- When have you felt convicted about how you spoke against someone or told a lie?
- How do you respond when you hear someone speak against a brother or sister in Christ?

**PRACTICE THIS** Consider your habits and practices regarding speaking negatively about others or telling lies. Repent and surrender those things to God.

## 19

> "You shall not covet your neighbor's house; you shall not covet
> your neighbor's wife, nor his male servant, nor his female servant,
> nor his ox, nor his donkey, nor anything that is your neighbor's."
>
> **EXODUS 20:17**

**PONDER THIS** One day, I was witnessing to a man, and I asked him to give his heart to Christ. He said, "I'm doing just fine. I've got a steady income. I have a good wife. My house and car are paid for. I'm doing fine. I really don't need what you're talking about." I looked him right in the eye and said, "Sir, would you be absolutely honest with me?" I asked him, "Sir, do you have peace in your heart?" I saw his eyes as they welled up with tears, and he said, "No! I don't have peace. How did you know?" I said, "Because the Bible says, 'There is no peace...for the wicked'" (Isaiah 57:21). If you don't have peace, you're poor! I don't care what else you have. If you have the peace of God that passes understanding, if you have a hope that is steadfast and sure, then you are abundantly rich.

What is the secret of satisfaction? Trust in the Lord; get to know Him. A covetous person is a person who has not put his or her eyes on the Lord. Only God can satisfy the deepest longing of your heart. God has engineered you so that this world will not satisfy the hole in your heart.

- How has your relationship with God given you peace?
- Who in your circle does not live at peace with God?

**PRACTICE THIS** Pray for those you know who do not have peace with God.

"But you shall receive power when the Holy Spirit has come
upon you; and you shall be witnesses to Me in Jerusalem, and
in all Judea and Samaria, and to the end of the earth."

**ACTS 1:8**

**PONDER THIS** When God says, "You shall not bear false witness against your neighbor" (Exodus 20:16), by implication God is saying you shall bear faithful witness. Jesus Christ is called "the faithful witness," (See Revelation 1:5.) and we're to be witnesses to Him. My home and your home ought to be witnesses to the saving power of the Lord and Savior, Jesus Christ.

When the Bible says the Early Church took the Gospel from house to house (Acts 5:42), that does not mean someone went door to door. It means the Gospel goes from the Jones' house to the Smith's house, and from the Smith's house to the Brown's house, and so forth. In other words, one family becomes a witness to another family. Our families are to bear witness of our Lord and Savior, Jesus Christ.

Has Jesus Christ saved you? Has He changed your home? Is He real to you? A witness tells what he or she has seen and heard. Jesus did not call you to be His lawyer. A lawyer argues a case. A witness simply shares what he's seen and heard. Just tell people what Jesus Christ has done for you and how you know He has done it. Don't give witness about things you don't know; witness about things you do know. If you fail, that's even a part of your witness. Tell how you failed and how God forgave you and gave you another chance. Your neighbor is waiting to hear the saving Gospel of Jesus Christ.

- Who has been a faithful witness of Christ to you?
- How do you interact with your neighbors? Does your life give evidence that you are a witness for Christ? Explain.

**PRACTICE THIS** Serve a neighbor today by witnessing about what Christ has done in your life.

Therefore, putting away lying, "Let each one of you speak truth
with his neighbor," for we are members of one another.

**EPHESIANS 4:25**

**PONDER THIS** Christians are called to lead by example. For parents, that means confessing and asking for forgiveness when you've done wrong. Let your children know you are a truth speaker.

You can fail in many ways and still come out fairly good with your children. But if you fail to keep your word, to keep your promises, or to tell the truth to your children, I promise you that your home is on the road to disaster. I cannot emphasize enough how important it is for parents to tell the truth.

Do your children know you tell the truth? Do you ever teach children to lie for you? If we teach them to lie for us, we should not punish them when they lie to us. I actually heard about a mother who told her son, "Johnny, if you don't stop lying, there's a green man that lives on the moon who's going to catch you and make you pick up sticks the rest of your life." Why would we expect our children to tell the truth based on the threat of a lie? Simply live the Word of God. Moms and dads, tell the truth and keep your word.

- How has a lie affected your perception of someone? How did it shape your relationship?
- How can you prioritize truth-telling in your life?

**PRACTICE THIS** Pray and ask God to help you value truth and keep your word to others. Consider anywhere you have lied and what you might do to rectify that.

But sanctify the Lord God in your hearts, and always be
ready to give a defense to everyone who asks you a reason
for the hope that is in you, with meekness and fear.

**1 PETER 3:15**

**PONDER THIS** Christians have faced bad times throughout history. Christians in the Roman Empire were perceived as enemies. The early Christians Peter wrote to were accused of insurrection because they would not proclaim Caesar as lord. Peter's letter was more or less of a handbook for survival for Christians in that time. Peter spoke to those Christians in distress, and in verse 15, he said, "Sanctify the Lord."

This is for us too. The very first thing we're to deal with is the principle of lordship. "Sanctify the Lord." You have to make up your mind that nothing will stand in the way of obedience to the Lord Jesus Christ. Have you enthroned Him as Lord? Or have you come down the aisle of the church and gotten baptized only because you want fire insurance and don't want to go to Hell? He must be Lord. Everything in your life must get in line behind the lordship of Jesus Christ, never ahead of it. Our job is not ultimately to save America. Our first responsibility is not to preserve our freedoms, as important as they are. Our prime responsibility is to stand up for Christ and witness to His grace and His power, telling and showing the world, "Jesus is Lord."

- What are some things that have come before, or threaten to come before, Jesus in your life?
- How do you need to take action to make Jesus Lord of your life?

**PRACTICE THIS** Talk with an accountability partner about how you can encourage one another to keep everything in line behind Jesus.

Remind them to be subject to rulers and authorities, to obey,
to be ready for every good work, to speak evil of no one, to
be peaceable, gentle, showing all humility to all men.

**TITUS 3:1-2**

**PONDER THIS** May I tell you that the Church is saturated with both ignorance and arrogance? The Bible teaches that you and I are to live a lifestyle of meekness. Meekness is not a weakness. Jesus said, "I am gentle and lowly." (See Matthew 11:29.) He was and is not weak. He's the One who spent 40 days and nights fasting in the wilderness. Jesus was the One who took a whip and drove the moneychangers out of the temple. But Jesus said, "I am gentle and lowly in heart." Meekness means strength under control.

The world calls the Church hate-mongers. They call us insensitive. The problem is that we often react to that with angry rhetoric, and it escalates on both sides. James 1:19 says, "So then, my beloved brethren, let every man be swift to hear, slow to speak, slow to wrath." And then verse 20 is key, "for the wrath of man does not produce the righteousness of God." There are many Christians you can find with their faces red, their fists in the air, or screaming and calling names. Do you think that's going to win anything for the Lord? It will not! The Bible says we are to have meekness and fear. We are to be slow to speak and quick to hear. The wrath of man does not produce the righteousness of God.

- Think about a recent time you lost your temper in a way that did not honor God? How did that affect the people around you?
- When have you witnessed meekness in someone else? How can you seek to live in meekness as Jesus did?

**PRACTICE THIS** Find a prayer or verse to recite when you feel ungodly anger welling up inside you.

**24**

Jesus said to him, "I am the way, the truth, and the life.
No one comes to the Father except through Me."

**JOHN 14:6**

**PONDER THIS** Did you know there is a difference between knowledge and truth? For example, knowledge will double and triple, but genuine truth does not. In school, there is a lot of study of the facts, but there's a difference between facts and truth. Facts are like a recipe; truth is like a meal. Digest a truth, and it will change your life. God wants us to have truth. Why did God give us the Bible? Jesus said in John 17:17b, "Your word is truth." Why did God send us the Holy Spirit? He's called in the Bible "the Spirit of truth." (See John 16:13.) Why did the Messiah come? He said, "I am...the truth" (John 14:6). Why do we have the Church? It is the pillar and the ground of truth. What is the greatest desire for every Christian parent? To echo the words of the Apostle John, "I have no greater joy than to hear that my children walk in truth" (3 John 1:4).

It's truth that we need today. Truth is to your spirit, what food is to your body, light is to your eyes, and sound is to your ears. You only have one short life to live, and in this life, you ought to make it your desire, your aim, your burning ambition to discover, to know, and to practice truth. To know truth is to know God and to know God is to know truth.

- What is the difference between having a lot of knowledge about God and being changed by the truth of God?

- Do you have a hunger to be changed by God's truth? Why or why not?

**PRACTICE THIS** Spend some time thinking about the things you know about God from His Word. Then consider how you have been changed by that truth.

**25**

All Scripture is given by inspiration of God, and is profitable
for doctrine, for reproof, for correction, for instruction in
righteousness, that the man of God may be complete,
thoroughly equipped for every good work.

**2 TIMOTHY 3:16-17**

**PONDER THIS** The days in life are short. We need to know who we are, what we believe, and why we believe it. There are good answers to the questions that come up from the Bible and life, and we are to be ready to give an answer to those who ask about these things. It is so important that we see the Bible as the Word of God—the incontestable and incorruptible Word of God. We need to see it as the indestructible Word of God. We need to see it as the indispensable Word of God. There is so much in the world that could change radically and quickly if we had a generation of preachers, church leaders, and church members—anointed with the Holy Spirit and a heart full of love from a pure life—who would teach, "This is what God says."

If this is going to happen, let it start in my heart. Let it start in your heart. Let it start in your church. Let's stand up and speak up while God gives us a voice. Search us, O God, and know our hearts today; try us, and see if there be some wicked way in us. (See Psalm 139:23-24) Cleanse us from every sin and set us free to live lives that show who You are and that Your Word is truth.

- How has God's Word changed your life?
- When was a time you recognized the value and beauty of God's Word? What helps you do this?

**PRACTICE THIS** Take some extra time to read God's Word today and see the beauty that is there.

Then God said, "Let Us make man in Our image, according to
Our likeness; let them have dominion over the fish of the sea,
over the birds of the air, and over the cattle, over all the earth
and over every creeping thing that creeps on the earth."

**GENESIS 1:26**

**PONDER THIS** Man is born and given a capacity and a craving for deity. Genesis
1:26 says, "And God said, 'Let Us make man in Our image.'" And God is Spirit.
Only man has a spirit. Man is made in the image of God, and the Bible says,
"God is Spirit, and those who worship Him must worship in spirit and truth"
(John 4:24). And the Bible says God "breathed into [our] nostrils the breath"—
the spirit—"of life." (See Genesis 2:7.) That makes man different from animals.
With our bodies, we know the world beneath us. With our souls, we know the
world around us. But with our spirits, we know the world above us. Only people
are created in the image of God.

In Colossians 3:10, Paul talks about what happens when we get saved. He says,
"You...have put on the new man who is renewed in knowledge according to
the image of Him who created him." This image makes us moral creatures and
makes us different from animals. Ephesians 4:24 says, "...you put on the new
man which was created according to God, in true righteousness and holiness."
Animals don't know righteousness. Animals don't know holiness. We're created
in righteousness, and our new creation brings us holiness.

- How does knowing that you are made in the image of God
  change the way you live?
- What are some things that come to mind when you think
  about who you are and who you are made to be?

**PRACTICE THIS** Take a walk in nature and thank God for how He designed all of
creation, including you.

## 27

Do all things without complaining and disputing, that you may become blameless and harmless, children of God without fault in the midst of a crooked and perverse generation, among whom you shine as lights in the world, holding fast the word of life, so that I may rejoice in the day of Christ that I have not run in vain or labored in vain.

**PHILIPPIANS 2:14-16**

**PONDER THIS** Has anyone ever asked what was different about you? I want to submit: if we're living under the lordship of Christ, if we're living as the Apostle Peter says we ought to be living, people will ask for an explanation of our lives. Paul and Silas were perfect examples of this. In Acts 16, they were in prison for preaching the Gospel of Jesus Christ. They were in the innermost prison, a disgusting place, and at midnight, they were praying and singing praise to God. The jailer had probably heard cursing from prisoners but not praising. He'd often heard moaning but not singing. He could not understand it. After an earthquake hit the jail, when Paul and Silas did not flee, the jailer came and asked, "Sirs, what must I do to be saved?" (v. 30). Why? He saw the difference in Paul and Silas. I hope people can see a difference in my life. I hope people who know me can say, "He is different." I hope people who know you can say, "He has hope! She has hope! This person stands out like a gardenia in a desert of mediocrity and filth."

- Who have you seen live differently because of their relationship with Jesus?
- What challenges are you facing that could be opportunities to stand out in faith and joy?

**PRACTICE THIS** Encourage a Christian you know who has stood out by living differently.

## 28

"A new commandment I give to you, that you love one another; as I have loved you, that you also love one another. By this all will know that you are My disciples, if you have love for one another."

**JOHN 13:34-35**

**PONDER THIS** We need to be people of love. If we're against abortion, and we are, we must ask ourselves, "What are we doing to help? How are we helping young, pregnant women?" Sometimes, our attitudes just simply push them away. If we believe in the permanency of marriage, and we do, how are we responding to those who have experienced the trauma of divorce and broken homes, some by their own choosing and others not by their choosing? These people are hurting! They don't need to be pushed further down. They need to be loved. Do we have open hearts and open arms to those different from us—to those who don't know Jesus? Only then can we tell them about Jesus and His power to radically, dramatically, and eternally transform people. But we must be very careful that we do not show such hostility and negativity that others would never come to us to learn about Jesus. We live in a society that is hurting, and we've got to bind the wounds up with salve, not with salt. They need the love of Jesus Christ, and people need to understand not only what we're against but also what we're for. The world is looking for answers. We need a Christian worldview that's backed up by a Christian lifestyle. If we have all the values but none of the lifestyle, we are in trouble.

- Why is it important to have a worldview backed up by a Christ-like life of love and service?
- Who is easy for you to love? Who is difficult to love?

**PRACTICE THIS** Love and serve someone you find difficult to love.

## 29

As the deer pants for the water brooks, so
pants my soul for You, O God.

**PSALM 42:1**

**PONDER THIS** There are many differences between man and animals. One main difference is man has a concern for destiny. No animal knows he's going to die. He doesn't think about dying. God gave animals instincts that He didn't give to human beings, but He gave human beings spiritual insight and revelation that He didn't give to animals.

A bee can build a six-sided cell in the honeycomb. Beavers can build dams. Spiders can build webs. But the spider cannot build a six-sided cell, and the bee cannot build a beaver's dam. They have instinct; they don't have knowledge. They don't have logic. A man may not have instincts like this, but he knows that he is here for more. Ecclesiastes 3:11 says God has set eternity in the hearts of humans. We are not mere animals. We don't believe in immortality because we prove it; we prove it because we believe in it. Immortality is instinctive in us.

Augustine, a church father, said our hearts are restless until they rest in God. You're made in the image of God. You are made to know Him and to rest in Him.

- How would your life change if you lived like you were made for God?
- What are some areas in life where you need to rest in God?

**PRACTICE THIS** Take some time to rest in God today by reading Scripture and meeting with Him in prayer.

## 30

Yet indeed I also count all things loss for the excellence of the
knowledge of Christ Jesus my Lord, for whom I have suffered the
loss of all things, and count them as rubbish, that I may gain Christ.

**PHILIPPIANS 3:8**

**PONDER THIS** After Joyce and I determined to get married, I bought an engagement ring. I was working my way through college, and I had many jobs to pay for school and living expenses, but I also wanted to buy an engagement ring.

I remember going into the jewelry store and finding the ring I wanted to give to Joyce. It's a very small ring with a very flawed diamond, and there have been so many times I have asked Joyce, "Would you let me buy you another diamond?" But I cannot even begin to get her to consider it. That ring is precious to her because, at that time, it cost me so very much. Though it may have been minimum to somebody else, it was maximum to me. I would go in each week and pay a little on that ring, and with great joy, I gave Joyce that ring.

Knowing the value of what you have been given is important. We need to understand what the Lord Jesus paid for us. He sought us. He bought us. He gave us the Holy Spirit, who dwells in us. When we know the value it costs Him, that changes us.

- What is something valuable to you? How do your actions show the value you place on that item?
- How valuable is Jesus to you? How is that evident in your life?

**PRACTICE THIS** Make a list of different reasons Jesus is valuable to you. Consider what changes you might need to make in your life to properly demonstrate that value.

"Let us be glad and rejoice and give Him glory, for the marriage
of the Lamb has come, and His wife has made herself ready."

**REVELATION 19:7**

**PONDER THIS** We are the bride of Christ, and like with every wedding, the bride must be ready. Every bride is beautiful. God wants a beautiful bride. Just as a woman spares no expense to be beautiful on her wedding day, the Church needs to make herself beautiful.

There will be no world order until the King is on the throne. Jesus is the King of kings and Lord of lords. Have you ever played checkers? In checkers, you move the checkers on the board, seeking to move your piece into the king's row. Then you say, "Crown me." The kingdoms of this world are being moved around like checkers, but soon God will move His Son into King's row and say, "Crown Him." And He'll be King in Zion. I cannot wait for the time until our Lord comes, and we are going to have a new world order. On that day, the Church, Israel, Satan, and Jesus will be in their rightful places.

- How do you invest in the bride of Christ, the Church?
- Is Jesus king of your life? Why or why not?

**PRACTICE THIS** Take time to consider how you are preparing for the day when Jesus will be fully recognized as King.

But I make known to you, brethren, that the gospel
which was preached by me is not according to man. For
I neither received it from man, nor was I taught it, but
it came through the revelation of Jesus Christ.

**GALATIANS 1:11-12**

**PONDER THIS** What is the origin of the Gospel? It came from Almighty God. The Gospel is not man's invention; it comes by divine revelation. Therefore, when it comes to the Gospel, you must put your intellect and your emotions to the side and pick up your Bible. So many times, we take the Word of God and parade it past the bar of human reasoning and judgment. Some say, "Well, it doesn't seem right that there's only one way to be saved, and all other ways are wrong." We try to bring human wit and wisdom against the Gospel.

Sometimes we measure the Gospel by our emotions. We say, "Well, that doesn't feel right to me. I just have a bad feeling about that." Again, I want to say respectfully that it doesn't matter what you think or what you feel. It's what God says that counts. I have heard from pilots that if a man doesn't know how to read the instruments on an airplane, he can't tell if he is absolutely flying level or if he's going down. If he says, "I think I'm alright, and I feel I'm alright," that does not change the altitude or the direction of the airplane. So many people are doing the same thing, making a tragic mistake in the realm of religion. They operate based on their feelings rather than on the instrument panel of God's Word.

- What are some things in the Bible that have been confusing to you?
- When have you trusted God even when it didn't make sense or "feel good" at the time?

**PRACTICE THIS** Talk to a pastor or leader in your church about some of the confusing parts of the Bible with which you have wrestled.

Grace to you and peace from God the Father and our Lord Jesus
Christ, who gave Himself for our sins, that He might deliver us from
this present evil age, according to the will of our God and Father.

**GALATIANS 1:3-4**

**PONDER THIS** God will not save apart from the Gospel of Jesus Christ because
He is a holy God, and sin must be atoned or paid for. But Jesus bought us with
His own precious blood. He obtained our salvation with His rich, red, royal blood!
It is the Gospel of the cross. It is the Gospel of the death, burial, and resurrection
of Jesus Christ. It's the Gospel that centers on Christ, not a gospel that simply
mentions Christ or alludes to Christ. It is the Gospel of Christ.

Do you know why so many churches today are filled with people who have never
been born again? They have never had a personal faith encounter with Jesus
Christ. They've met a creed, but not Christ; they've met a cause, but not Christ;
they've met a code, but not Christ; they've met a church, but not Christ.

Do you know Jesus Christ? I want to tell you today that Jesus Christ is real to me.
I put my faith in Him. This faith is more than something that brings Christ in; it
centers on Him. It doesn't simply mention Jesus Christ or give lip service to Him;
it is all about Him.

- When did Jesus become real to you?
- What are some ways your life is centered around Jesus?
  What needs to change?

**PRACTICE THIS** Speak to another follower of Jesus about how you can spur each
other on toward centering your lives on Jesus.

But when it pleased God, who separated me from my
mother's womb and called *me* through His grace, to reveal
His Son in me, that I might preach Him among the Gentiles,
I did not immediately confer with flesh and blood, nor did I
go up to Jerusalem to those *who were* apostles before me;
but I went to Arabia, and returned again to Damascus.

**GALATIANS 1:15-17**

**PONDER THIS** When Paul got saved, he wasn't seeking Jesus, but Jesus was seeking him. You say, "I'm just seeking the Lord." The only reason you are seeking the Lord is because He's first sought you. Don't get any idea that you just thought it up all by yourself. Romans 3:11 says, "There is none who understands; There is none who seeks after God." So then, why do we have this hunger? Why do we have this thirst for God? Because He gave it to us.

Let's think about a natural thirst. We all get thirsty for liquid. Why do we get thirsty? Because God created us where we would have a thirst. Had God not created us to have thirst, we would never get thirsty. We wouldn't just be walking down the street and say, "You know, I'd better get some liquid. I'm going to dehydrate." No. God made us that way. That thirst in us is a gift of God, and the thirst for God that is in you is a gift of God. It pleased God to do this. The grace that saved you is also from the God who loves you and is seeking after you. When God came into the Garden of Eden after Adam and Eve sinned, He asked, "Where are you?" (Genesis 3:9b). That wasn't the voice of a detective; that was the voice of a loving God. He is seeking you today.

- When have you felt God seeking you?
- How have you experienced a thirst for God in your life?

**PRACTICE THIS** Take a walk and recall the times when God worked in your life and sought you. Praise Him for those moments and for His pursuit of you!

**4**

For by grace you have been saved through faith, and that not of yourselves; it is the gift of God, not of works, lest anyone should boast.

**EPHESIANS 2:8-9**

**PONDER THIS** What is grace? Grace is the free gift of God. You are not saved by joining a church, getting baptized, singing in the choir, preaching a sermon, or leading a Bible study. You are saved by the grace of God.

Grace is not given because of works of any kind. Works don't save, and works don't help save. Romans 11:6 says, "And if by grace, then it is no longer of works; otherwise, grace is no longer grace. But if it is of works, it is no longer grace; otherwise, work is no longer work." You can't mix grace and works. If it's by grace, forget your good works. Baptism, whether a spoonful or a tankful, can't take away your sin. Your prayers, your pilgrimages—anything you do—cannot take away your sin.

This sufficient grace is all you'll ever need. You're not going to run out of the grace of God. According to 2 Corinthians 9:8, "And God is able to make all grace abound toward you, that you, always having all sufficiency in all things, may have an abundance for every good work." You've got all you need. I can testify to this. I've been on the trail a long time, and God's grace has never been insufficient. Do you think you're going to run out of grace? Is a minnow in the Atlantic Ocean going to run out of water? No. Thank God for His sufficient grace.

- What matters in life are you tempted to believe are too big or too small for God?

- When have you tried to work to earn God's favor? Why will this never work?

**PRACTICE THIS** Pray and tell God where you are struggling and ask for His grace in those areas.

**5**

Love suffers long and is kind; love does not envy;
love does not parade itself, is not puffed up.

**1 CORINTHIANS 13:4**

**PONDER THIS** True love enables us to be patient. If you're an impatient person, if you give up on people, if you quit loving, you become unlike the Lord Jesus. True love is long-suffering love. It is patient. It forgives "seventy times seven" and then keeps on. (See Matthew 18:22.)

True love is also serving love. The Bible says this love is kind. What is kindness? Kindness is serving one another. True love serves those who don't deserve to be served. If you love me, do you know what you'll do for me? You will not give me what I deserve; you will give me what I need. Jesus said in Luke 6:27-28, "But I say to you who hear: Love your enemies, do good to those who hate you, bless those who curse you, and pray for those who spitefully use you." What are you to do for your enemies or people you don't get along with? You're to do good, speak well, and pray hard. Show them kindness.

If there's someone that has done you wrong, find some way you can be kind to that person, lift the load for that person, mow a lawn for that person, carry some soup to that person, bless that person, pray for that person, or encourage that person. That's the way God loves you. That is agape love.

- Who have you been upset with recently? How have you treated that person?

- When has someone been patient with you though you didn't deserve it? How did that affect you?

**PRACTICE THIS** Serve someone you have been at odds with recently.

> But the fruit of the Spirit is love, joy, peace, longsuffering,
> kindness, goodness, faithfulness, gentleness, self-
> control. Against such there is no law.
> **GALATIANS 5:22-23**

**PONDER THIS** True love is self-denying love. It doesn't seek its own way. It doesn't say, "Me first." It doesn't say, "I know my rights." When you got saved, you lost all your rights. What right does a dead man have? You are crucified with Christ. You are not your own. You're bought with a price. You belong to the Lord Jesus Christ. Your rights have now become His rights. He is the One who has commanded you to love. You can no longer seek your own. You must seek the glory of Jesus and the welfare of others if you are to truly love.

True love is also sacrificing love. There can be no forgiveness without somebody paying a price. If you owe me ten dollars and I forgive it, it costs me ten dollars to forgive it. So many of us are bookkeepers. We keep a record of the things people do against us. We need to learn to forget those things and bury those things in the grave of God's forgetfulness. This requires that we pay the price. Take the hurt in. True love is sacrificial; it costs to forgive.

When we stop seeking our own way and start seeking to love and bless other people, even when it is costly, things will change in our world.

- When have you seen someone seek the welfare of others even when it was costly to him or her?
- What is your natural reaction when someone wrongs you? What would it cost you to respond differently?

**PRACTICE THIS** Think about a recent situation that frustrated you. Consider ways you might serve the person who offended you; take action toward this.

Rejoice in the Lord always. Again I will say, rejoice!

**PHILIPPIANS 4:4**

**PONDER THIS** What's the difference between happiness and joy? Happiness depends on what happens. If you put your trust in happiness, you're going to be a victim of circumstances because your circumstances will change. But God never changes. The Bible doesn't tell us to rejoice in circumstances; the Bible says to rejoice in the Lord. And since He never changes, the Bible means rejoice forever. Happiness is like cosmetics. Joy is like character; it comes from within. Happiness meets surface needs; joy meets your deepest needs. Happiness is like a thermometer; it registers conditions. Joy is like a thermostat; it regulates conditions. Happiness evaporates and disappears in times of suffering, but joy frequently intensifies in times of suffering and is often intertwined with suffering.

Happiness always functions best when rooted in joy. If you have joy, and then you overlay that joy with happiness, that's a wonderful thing. Joy, on the other hand, is not dependent on happiness and may function even better when happiness is taken away.

- When have you experienced joy in disappointing circumstances?
- How likely is your mood or demeanor to be dictated by your circumstances?

**PRACTICE THIS** Share with someone the reasons you have joy today, regardless of your circumstances.

## 8

Restore to me the joy of Your salvation, and
uphold me by Your generous Spirit.

**PSALM 51:12**

**PONDER THIS** Joy is important in winning people to Jesus Christ. Did you know we have nothing more winsome and attractive in bringing people to Jesus Christ than the joy of the Lord? A cold, dry faith has no appeal. David, the man who wrote the Psalms, lost his joy when he got out of fellowship with God. When he lost his joy, he stopped being a soul winner. And he prayed in Psalm 51:12-13, "Restore to me the joy of Your salvation and uphold me by Your generous Spirit. Then I will teach transgressors Your ways, and sinners shall be converted to You." David was saying, "When I get my joy back, I'll be a soul winner."

Joy is proof that what we have is real and that it satisfies. Joy is necessary in bringing unsaved people to Jesus Christ. Joy is necessary just to live as a follower of Jesus. The Bible says we are to serve the Lord with gladness. Nehemiah said, "The joy of the LORD is your strength." (See Nehemiah 8:10.) It is joy that lifts the burden. It is joy that takes the pain, the dreariness, and the weariness out of any work. There are times when I get weary in my body and weary in my mind. I begin to praise the Lord, and His joy floods my soul and my body, and it literally energizes my physical frame. The joy of the LORD gives us strength.

- Who has been an example to you of the joy of the Lord?
- When do you struggle to have joy? How can you submit this to the Lord?

**PRACTICE THIS** Talk to a trusted friend and ask him or her to honestly share how much you display the joy of the Lord. Pray about the things your friend shares and ask the Lord to cultivate His joy in you.

Now when they had left the multitude, they took Him along
in the boat as He was. And other little boats were also with
Him. And a great windstorm arose, and the waves beat into
the boat, so that it was already filling. But He was in the
stern, asleep on a pillow. And they awoke Him and said to
Him, "Teacher, do You not care that we are perishing?'"

**MARK 4:36-38**

**PONDER THIS** Don't get the idea that if you're in the will of God, you'll not have any storms. The disciples were in the will of God, and they went right into a storm. Jesus knew a storm was brewing. He was the One who could walk on the water. He was the One who could say to the waves, "Peace, be still" (See Mark 4:39.), and they would listen. The Bible says He knew all things. He knew there would be a storm, and knowing that, Jesus led them into a storm. There's a false teaching that says, "If we're just right with God, we won't have any problems, and we won't have any storms in our lives." There are two things wrong with that. Number one, it's not true. Number two, it's not biblical. You're going to have storms.

Regardless of the storm you face, God is overall. "Even the wind and sea obey Him." (See Mark 4:41.) In all things, God is in control. If you're in a storm right now, God is over it, beyond it, through it, above it, and in it. He is the providential God.

- What are some storms you have faced in life? How did they affect your relationship with God?
- What are some present storms you are facing? What are you learning through them?

**PRACTICE THIS** Take some time to praise and worship God for the way He is present in the storms of life.

Therefore, having been justified by faith, we have peace
with God through our Lord Jesus Christ, through whom
also we have access by faith into this grace in which we
stand, and rejoice in hope of the glory of God.

**ROMANS 5:1-2**

**PONDER THIS** The saddest word in the English language is *hopeless*. If you are a child of God, there is no situation for you that is hopeless. Hope is confidence. And we can always have confidence in God.

I know that no matter what happens to me, my God is greater. You ask, "What if they tell you you're going to die in five minutes?" Okay, I'm going to Heaven. I'm going to be made like the Lord Jesus Christ. Joy is steadfast in sorrow. Joy is triumphant in tribulation. The Apostle Paul said in 2 Corinthians 7:4b, "I am exceedingly joyful in all our tribulation." Joy is lasting in losses.

What if you found out your house had been broken into? Your jewelry is gone, your mementos are gone, your television is gone, and your microwave is gone. It's all gone. Would you still have joy? If you got joy from your house, you wouldn't still have joy. But if you got your joy from the Lord, you'd still have joy.

- When have you had joy in a difficult time?
- What are some matters in your life where you need to be reminded of God's hope?

**PRACTICE THIS** Spend some time with a fellow Christian and encourage one another to have joy in difficult moments.

**11**

"These things I have spoken to you, that My joy may
remain in you, and that your joy may be full."

**JOHN 15:11**

**PONDER THIS** When you commune with the Lord Jesus Christ, His joy comes into you. It's not an imitation of His joy. It's not your joy. It is His joy. You rejoice through the Lord because joy is the fruit of His Spirit. You don't produce this joy; it is produced by the Spirit in your life, and you just bear this joy.

I don't care how much you own, how handsome you are, how beautiful you are, how so-called happy you are, or what your family is like. If you don't have joy, life is meaningless.

To rejoice is a choice; it's not automatic. That's the reason the Bible tells us, "Rejoice in the Lord always" (Philippians 4:4a). And that choice begins with choosing Jesus and knowing Jesus. No Jesus—no joy. But know Jesus, and you'll know joy.

- How has knowing Jesus changed your joy?

- Recall a season in your life during which you communed with Jesus. How did that affect your joy? Are you experiencing joy today?

**PRACTICE THIS** Take time to commune with Jesus today.

Then He arose and rebuked the wind, and said to the sea, "Peace, be still!" And the wind ceased and there was a great calm. But He said to them, "Why are you so fearful? How is it that you have no faith?"

**MARK 4:39-40**

**PONDER THIS** Often, when we get in a storm, we put our eyes on the waves and not on the Lord. The difference between the amount you have your eyes on the storm and not on God, is called stress. Jesus said, "Don't be afraid. I am here. It is me. I have come to you in this storm."

You have the assurance of God. What is assurance? He has said, "I will never leave you nor forsake you." (See Hebrews 13:5.) Providence means His purpose brought me here. Entreaty means His prayers protect me here. Assurance means His presence comes to me here. If His presence comes to me here, I need to recognize Him. At first, the disciples didn't recognize Him, and they remained afraid.

Down in Florida, where I was raised, we had a lot of hurricanes that came through our city of West Palm Beach. Even as a child, I learned something about hurricanes. I learned that in the center of the very worst hurricane, the very worst storm, there's a calm spot—the eye of the storm. When the storm passes over—your storm, there is a center that is calm. It's the heart of God right in the middle of that storm.

- What storm is going on in your life?
- How have you been reminded to keep your eyes on Jesus during a storm?

**PRACTICE THIS** Encourage a friend who is going through a storm in his or her life.

**13**

...knowing that the testing of your faith produces
patience. But let patience have its perfect work, that you
may be perfect and complete, lacking nothing.

**JAMES 1:3-4**

**PONDER THIS** Suppose you're running a 100-yard dash, and you're 10 yards ahead of everybody else and three feet from the goal, but you quit. It doesn't matter how far ahead you were; you just lost the race. You're never a failure until you quit.

What does God want out of you? God wants you to be a full-grown Christian. He wants you to be mature. There is no maturity without patience and no patience without trials. But if you're not mature, you're not like the Lord Jesus Christ. The Bible says God wants to bring you to the fullness of Christ. And the way He does that is by allowing you to have trials and tribulations so that you might be mature. Are children patient? Of course not! Anybody who has children knows children don't know the difference between "no" and "not yet." If you just say, "Wait a while" to them, it might as well be "No!" They want it now! But God is interested in growing you up and making you mature. The only way you'll learn maturity is through tribulation that leads to patience.

- When have you needed endurance in a trial?
- What were some moments in your life that have helped you mature in your faith?

**PRACTICE THIS** Pray and ask God to show you the areas where you need to mature.

Wait on the LORD; be of good courage, and He shall
strengthen your heart; Wait, I say, on the LORD!

**PSALM 27:14**

**PONDER THIS** Patience is necessary for maturity, for victory, and for prosperity. You can't hurry the harvest. If you want prosperity, you need to have patience. Galatians 6:9b says, "In due season we shall reap if we do not lose heart." What is the law of the harvest? You reap what you sow. And you always reap later than you sow. The reason many of us don't reap is we don't wait. Patience and endurance are necessary.

When I was a little boy, sometimes we used to run up and ring somebody's doorbell and run away before anyone could answer. Did you ever do that? We do that sometimes with the Lord. And the Bible says over and over, "Wait on the Lord." Delays are not denials. If you want God to answer your prayer, you have to learn to wait on the Lord. You ask, "Why doesn't God answer right away?" Simple! He wants you to grow. It's His way of ripening you.

- When was a time you waited for a significant period on God?
- What are some things that cause you to grow impatient with waiting for God's timing?

**PRACTICE THIS** Write down the different things you are waiting on God for. Pray and give those things over to God.

Therefore, as we have opportunity, let us do good to all,
especially to those who are of the household of faith.

**GALATIANS 6:10**

**PONDER THIS** There are some of us who are afraid if we're too kind, people are going to take advantage of us. Have you ever felt that way? Aren't you glad that God keeps the score? Aren't you glad that God knows? It doesn't matter if somebody takes advantage of us if we're acting like the Lord Jesus. People took advantage of Jesus. But He was and is kind.

Has the Holy Spirit ever impressed you to do an act of kindness to someone, but you delayed, and you got too busy, and then it was just too late, and you would have been embarrassed to do it? What often happens is we have an opportunity to do good, but we just let it pass by. Do you remember the story of the Good Samaritan who saw a man bruised and bleeding? He was on his journey, he stopped, and he helped the man right away. He didn't make excuses. He didn't say, "I'm too busy," "It's too dangerous," or "It's none of my business." He stopped and did what he could. All around us, people are bruised and bleeding. Some are bleeding financially. Some are bleeding emotionally. Some are bleeding spiritually. And they need you to say, "This is an opportunity to help, and I'm going to take it right now."

- When has someone influenced your life with a simple act of kindness?
- What have been some of your excuses for not listening to the Holy Spirit about being kind to someone else?

**PRACTICE THIS** Look for any opportunity you have to be kind today. Act without delay.

## 16

Create in me a clean heart, O God, and
renew a steadfast spirit within me.

**PSALM 51:10**

**PONDER THIS** There are so many people who fall and stumble because of what they saw in someone else's life. When a giant oak falls in the woods, not only does that oak fall, but it also pulls down all kinds of saplings and other trees with it. What a tragedy. How terrible it is for these people to do this.

Others are looking on. Why be good? None of us live in isolation. You're the best Christian and the worst Christian that somebody knows. You're the only Bible that somebody is reading.

There are times when I grow cold in my faith. There are times when the things I do for the Lord Jesus seem to take the place of the Lord Jesus Christ. When that happens, I have to get down on my face before God and give God everything—give God my health, give God my family, give God my reputation, give God everything, and say, "Dear God, if there's something I haven't surrendered, I want you to show it to me." Sign a blank piece of paper and say, "It's yours, Lord. Fill it in. Whatever it is, O God, I give it all to you." And He will be faithful to fill you with His light.

- When have you been distant in your faith? How did things change?
- Who are some people who don't know Jesus that may be watching you to discover who He is?

**PRACTICE THIS** Ask God to fill in the blank page and show you what in your life needs to be surrendered to Him.

A wholesome tongue is a tree of life, but
perverseness in it breaks the spirit.

**PROVERBS 15:4**

**PONDER THIS** Are you a servant of the Lord? Then you can't be quarrelsome. You've got to be kind in times of conflict. We all have times of conflict, but you need to be very careful when you get into an argument with another human being. It doesn't matter whether that human being is saved or lost. There have been people who have opposed me, and I've tried to be kind to them. And I see God at work, not every time, but many times.

When I was a young pastor, I got a difficult letter from a member of the church. In the letter, he told me that he didn't like my mannerisms or the way I preached. I prayed, "Dear Lord, help me to write back the kindest letter I can write." I sent my response, and then one day, he came past the office and said, "You are the best friend I have." When I'm in a quarrelsome situation with anybody, I must remember that there are people watching all around.

One woman came to her pastor and said, I have become a Christian because of you. And he said, "What was it that I preached that brought you to Jesus?" She said, "It was nothing that you preached. I was watching when a woman criticized you to your face. Your kindness to that woman convicted my heart. I knew what you had was real, and I gave my heart to Jesus Christ."

- When has someone's kindness impacted your life?
- When is kindness most difficult for you?

**PRACTICE THIS** Seek to extend extraordinary kindness to someone today.

## 18

But the fruit of the Spirit is love, joy, peace,
longsuffering, kindness, goodness, faithfulness...

**GALATIANS 5:22**

**PONDER THIS** All around you, people are hurting. You may say, "I'm not good at helping people when they're suffering. I just don't know what to say." I can appreciate that. Sometimes though, it's not what you say; it's just that little act of kindness that means so much. Joyce and I lost our son Phillip to an unexpected crib death. It was such a difficult time, and members of our little church came by to see us to comfort us. I will never forget one deacon who visited us during that time. He didn't know what to say but just laid his hand on my shoulder, squeezed it, and looked into my face. A tear dropped from his eyes. He just looked at me and then turned his face away and went out. That touch, that squeeze, and that look meant more than a sermon would have. It was just an act of kindness. Oh, how we need to learn to be kind.

There are opportunities all around if we just look. Do you know where we need to be kind the most? In our homes. Why is it that we sometimes are the most unkind to those we love, making the most cutting remarks in our homes? The religion that doesn't begin at home doesn't begin. There are many marriages and families that could be saved by a little gentleness.

- Who are some people around you that are hurting?
- Who have you been unkind to? How do you need to seek reconciliation and make changes?

**PRACTICE THIS** Ask forgiveness from someone to whom you have been unkind.

## 19

There is therefore now no condemnation to those
who are in Christ Jesus, who do not walk according
to the flesh, but according to the Spirit.

**ROMANS 8:1**

**PONDER THIS** Have you ever been on an airplane? Those things are so heavy. The airplane sits there on the runway, and the law of gravity just holds it there. But the pilot gets behind the controls and eventually, that airplane goes up in the sky. All that weight, all that luggage, all those people, all that steel. When that happens, has the law of gravity been canceled? No, but there is the law of aerodynamics, which supersedes the effect of gravity. When you get saved and right with God, your old flesh is still there. But there's a new law—it's the law of life in Christ Jesus that makes you free from the law of sin and death.

Suppose when I was on that airplane, I decided to step outside for some fresh air. The law of gravity is still there. As long as you abide in the Lord Jesus Christ, the law of the Spirit of life in Christ Jesus makes you free from the law of sin and death. There are a lot of people today who would like to have an experience that would free them from sin and eradicate the old nature. God will never allow it. Do you know why? He wants you to abide in the Lord Jesus Christ.

- What does it look like for you to abide in Jesus?
- What has been your experience when you do not abide in Jesus?

**PRACTICE THIS** Put up a note in a place you see frequently to encourage you toward abiding in Christ.

Now may the God of peace Himself sanctify you
completely; and may your whole spirit, soul, and body
be preserved blameless at the coming of our Lord Jesus
Christ. He who calls you is faithful, who also will do it.

**1 THESSALONIANS 5:23-24**

**PONDER THIS** All my life, I wanted to go to Yellowstone National Park. One day some years ago, we went. Do you know the one thing I wanted to see more than anything else at Yellowstone? Old Faithful. There are many other geysers, and some of them are more spectacular. But let me tell you about Old Faithful: Every sixty-five minutes, there she goes. You can almost set your watch on it.

Faithfulness is a quality all of us admire. But God doesn't just admire it; He requires it. First Corinthians 4:2 says, "It is required in stewards that one be found faithful." No matter how much ability you have, how much personality you have, how much intelligence you have, or how hard you work if you can't be depended on, you are no good. What do we mean by faithfulness? Integrity, honesty, trustfulness, loyalty. Can you be counted on? Are you a faithful person?

The God who saved me is the God who keeps me. Isn't God faithful? His mercies are new every morning. (See Lamentations 3:22-23.) His compassions, they fail not. Thank God that "great is thy faithfulness." Now, if God has been so faithful to me, I need to return that faithfulness and be faithful to Him.

- How has God's faithfulness changed your life?

- What does faithfulness to God look like on a daily basis?

**PRACTICE THIS** Write down a list of ways God has shown His faithfulness to you.

Be kindly affectionate to one another with brotherly love,
in honor giving preference to one another; not lagging in
diligence, fervent in spirit, serving the Lord; rejoicing in hope,
patient in tribulation, continuing steadfastly in prayer...

**ROMANS 12:10-12**

**PONDER THIS** There was an English publication that had a contest to give the best definition of a friend. Here are some that won honorable mentions. One person said, "A friend is somebody who multiplies your joys and divides your griefs." Another said, "A friend is someone who understands your silence." But the one that won was this, "A friend is somebody who comes in when all the world has gone out."

Do you have a friend you can count on like that? A friend who loves at all times? It doesn't matter what you've done. Somebody wrote these words as a take on 1 Corinthians 13:

> Friendship is slow to lose patience. It looks for a way of being constructive. It is not possessive. It is neither anxious to impress others, nor does it cherish inflated ideas of its own importance. Friendship has good manners and does not pursue selfish advantage at the other's expense. It is not touchy. It does not keep account of slights or gloat over the mistakes of the other. On the contrary, it is glad when truth prevails. It knows no limit to its endurance, no end to its trust, no failing of its hope, and in this it can outlast anything. True friendship stands when all else has fallen.

Now, do you have a friend like that? Are you a friend like that? Be faithful in your friendships.

- When has a friend exemplified faithfulness to you?
- How have your friendships encouraged your relationship with Jesus?

**PRACTICE THIS** Meet with a friend and provide listening ears and support.

## 22

"Come to Me, all you who labor and are heavy laden, and I
will give you rest. Take My yoke upon you and learn from Me,
for I am gentle and lowly in heart, and you will find rest for
your souls. For My yoke is easy and My burden is light."

**MATTHEW 11:28-30**

**PONDER THIS** Meekness is not cowardliness. The Lord Jesus said, "I am meek [gentle] and lowly of heart." Was Jesus a coward? He was the strongest man that ever lived, and yet He said, "I'm meek and lowly of heart." His strength was under the control of God; He lived submitted to Him. A while back, I was driving in another state, and I saw a sign that said, "If you think that meekness is weakness, try spending a week being meek."

People say, "Oh, why doesn't God speak?" It is not that God is not speaking; we're not hearing. Do you want God to guide you? Do you want God to lead you? If you will get meek—if you will humble yourself with a repentant, receptive, and responsive spirit—God will guide you. You will not be like a ship at sail on a dark and stormy night without a compass, rudder, mast, or sail, being driven by the winds and the waves of this world. He will show you His way, and you will be able to hear because He can touch the bridle here, and you'll turn this way, and He'll touch the bridle there, and you'll turn that way because He has mastered you, and is guiding you.

- What wrong perception have you had of meekness in the past?
- Do you have a receptive, repentant, and responsive spirit toward God? How can you grow in this?

**PRACTICE THIS** Pray and ask God to show you where you need to grow in meekness.

For the word of God is living and powerful, and sharper
than any two-edged sword, piercing even to the division
of soul and spirit, and of joints and marrow, and is a
discerner of the thoughts and intents of the heart.

**HEBREWS 4:12**

**PONDER THIS** We are to receive the Word of God with meekness. Meekness is strength under control. To be controlled by the Lord, you have to know His will and His way, and to know His will and His way, you have to know His Word. You have to receive the Word with meekness. You need to be able to admit that you don't know enough to guide your own life.

You need guidance. God knows what you don't need. If God is going to guide your life, then you've got to receive the Word with meekness, which can save your soul. You have to come to a place where you say, "I set aside this wickedness; I turn from it." My friend, if you want God to speak to you—if you want to understand this Book and want the Bible to burst aflame in your heart and mind—then you've got to get the spiritual wax out of your ears. And the only way to do that is by repentance.

- How do you seek to grow in knowledge and love of the Word?
- Where do you struggle to look for guidance from God?

**PRACTICE THIS** Surrender to God a matter you have been trying to handle yourself. Ask for His guidance through His Word and His Spirit.

"He who is faithful in what is least is faithful also in much; and
he who is unjust in what is least is unjust also in much."

**LUKE 16:10**

**PONDER THIS** Be faithful in the small things. Big things are made up of smaller things. One example is the ocean which is made up of many drops of water. And all of those drops of water are molecules. And all those molecules are atoms. Think of all the ages and ages of time. Time is made up of ages, but ages are made up of millenniums, and millenniums are made up of centuries, and centuries are made up of years, and years are made up of months, and months are made up of weeks, and weeks of days, and days of hours, and hours of minutes, and minutes of seconds, and seconds of milliseconds. Everything big is made up of something small.

That's the way your life is. Your entire life is not just one or two big decisions; it is day by day. It is that honesty, smile, kindness, warmth; and integrity. When you're faithful in the little things, faithfulness in the big things follows.

- Who do you know that is faithful in the small things?
- Identify a moment or moments where you struggle to be faithful in something small.

**PRACTICE THIS** Write down the small responsibilities you have in a day and consider how you could be faithful in those things.

Therefore, whether you eat or drink, or whatever
you do, do all to the glory of God.

**1 CORINTHIANS 10:31**

**PONDER THIS** What you are in the dark when nobody else knows is what you really are. Let me give you a test of your character. What would you do if you knew that nobody else would ever know? I once read about when Michelangelo painted on the ceiling of the Sistine Chapel. He was painting that beautiful fresco in a niche where human eyes would not be able to see, and he spent so much time meticulously painting in this area. Someone said, "Michelangelo, why are you painting there? No one will ever see that." He said, "I see it, and God will see it." Whether anyone else ever knows or not, be faithful in the secret things.

Do you know why we admire people like the Apostle Paul? It is because he was faithful to the faith, faithful to the fight, and faithful to the finish. Do you know what I want for you? I want you to end well and to do well. It would be incredible what could happen in your church and community if each Christian would just be faithful.

- What are you like when no one is looking? How are you different when there are eyes on you?
- Where is God calling you to be diligent in the small things now?

**PRACTICE THIS** Take time for self-evaluation, considering how you may act differently when no one is watching. Pray and bring this before God.

> I say then: Walk in the Spirit, and you shall not fulfill the
> lust of the flesh. For the flesh lusts against the Spirit, and
> the Spirit against the flesh; and these are contrary to one
> another, so that you do not do the things that you wish. But
> if you are led by the Spirit, you are not under the law.
>
> **GALATIANS 5:16-18**

**PONDER THIS** To "walk in the Spirit" means the Spirit is to be the circumference of my walk. If I said to you, "Walk in this building." That means you are supposed to stay in this building. This building is the parameter, the circumference, the environment, and the element in which you walk. If you step outside this building, you're not walking in this building.

The Holy Spirit is to be the parameter in which you walk. Are you willing to do that? Our flesh often says, "Don't fence me in!" It tells us that outside of the Spirit, there are certain pleasures, ideas, and fulfillments you need to make you happy. A person with a Spirit-controlled life has come to this settled conclusion: there is nothing worth having outside of Jesus. If you don't come to that conclusion, you will never live a victorious life. All the things you do are to be within the context of the Holy Spirit of God leading and directing your life. When I step out of bounds, the Holy Spirit says, "You are out of bounds." And so, I repent, and I step back in. That is a Spirit-controlled life.

- Can you truly say you are seeking to live within the parameters set by the Holy Spirit?

- When has God shown you that you were out of bounds? How did you respond?

**PRACTICE THIS** Take some time in silence to consider where you have seen the Holy Spirit direct your life. Listen to where the Spirit is leading you now.

## 27

As you therefore have received Christ Jesus the Lord, so walk in Him.

**COLOSSIANS 2:6**

**PONDER THIS** What is a walk? It is one step at a time. It takes two feet to walk. Do you realize when you walk, you're off-balance? If you don't take another step, you'll fall after a while. You take one step, and then the other step is necessary, and then the other step is necessary. The way you walk is one step at a time, and it takes two feet to walk. What are the two feet of the Christian faith? Repentance and faith. How did you receive the Lord Jesus? By repentance and faith. What is repentance? Repentance is God's way of revealing myself to me, and faith is God's way of revealing Jesus to me. Repentance is where I see my bankruptcy; faith is where I see His glory.

When I became a Christian, I did not know much, but I had a hunger in my heart to know God. When I got saved, I gave all I knew of me to all I knew of Him. Frankly, I knew very little about myself or Him at that time. But I did know I was sinful, and I did know He was glorious. But since that time, I have learned a whole lot more about myself, and none of it is good. I've learned a whole lot more about Him, and it's better than I ever thought.

- What are some things you have learned about yourself since you became a Christian?

- How has your faith in God grown since you became a Christian?

**PRACTICE THIS** Share with someone your story of growing in your faith over time.

Now we know that whatever the law says, it says to those
who are under the law, that every mouth may be stopped,
and all the world may become guilty before God.

**ROMANS 3:19**

**PONDER THIS** What is guilt? Guilt is a reality; it's the result of the filthiness of our sin. And guilt can cause all kinds of emotional and physical baggage. Guilt brings anxiety and depression. The soul becomes a window covered with the dirt and grime of guilt, and, therefore, everything we look at is colored or discolored by the guilt in us. And guilt can make you sick. If you carry around a load of guilt, it can make you physically ill. David said in Psalm 32:3, "When I kept silent, my bones grew old through my groaning all the day long."

The man who is haunted by the ghost of guilt is not driven to God. You would think he would be. But the truth of the matter is that a person with unresolved guilt is driven further and further from God. So many people today, who are into things they ought not to be into, are there simply because of guilt. Satan is the accuser. He wants you to sin and then suffer the consequences. He wants to cripple you and then blames you for limping. He wants you to be doubly defeated. He is the accuser and also the enticer.

- When have you been overwhelmed with guilt?
- How do you typically respond when you are overwhelmed with guilt?

**PRACTICE THIS** Confess your sins, turn from the sinful practices that are promoting guilt, and walk surrendered and free.

For godly sorrow produces repentance leading to salvation, not
to be regretted; but the sorrow of the world produces death.

**2 CORINTHIANS 7:10**

**PONDER THIS** It is important to know the difference between accusation and conviction. The Holy Spirit is the convict-er; He will convict you of sin. The devil is the accuser; he will accuse you of sin. Accusation comes from Satan and causes you to feel hopeless and helpless. Judas was an example of this: he betrayed the Lord and was filled with remorse, which led him to suicide. His remorse did not draw him back to Jesus; it drove him from Jesus. True conviction draws you to the Lord. True conviction causes brokenness that leads you to be broken over your sin and to be broken from your sin. Simon Peter was convicted of his sin when he denied the Lord; he wept bitterly, and God restored him.

Satan accuses you not only before God, but he also accuses you to your face. He wants you to focus your attention on anything but Jesus. He wants you to live under the dark cloud of guilt and despair. When I teach about sin, I will not harp on guilt because that is not what brings true conviction and repentance. Guilt only brings remorse and beats people down; it becomes a tool of the devil.

- When have you experienced conviction? How did you respond?
- How have you seen the pain of guilt in your own life?

**PRACTICE THIS** Consider the last time you beat yourself up for something God has forgiven you of. Talk to God in prayer about that now.

...according to the working of His mighty power which He worked
in Christ when He raised Him from the dead and seated Him at
His right hand in the heavenly places, far above all principality
and power and might and dominion, and every name that is
named, not only in this age but also in that which is to come.

**EPHESIANS 1:17-21**

**PONDER THIS** We have something that Adam never had. Adam was innocent; we are righteous. Adam was there in the Garden of Eden, and he sinned. But you and I have the Lord Jesus Christ as part of us. Don't think of the Church as an organization with Christ as the president. The Church is an organism. It is a body with Christ as the head, and what is true about the Lord Jesus Christ is true about you. Jesus did not defeat Satan on His own behalf—He defeated Satan on our behalf. We have been co-executed, co-risen, and co-exalted with the Lord Jesus Christ. He became a son of man so that we might become sons and daughters of God. He took our sins so that we might be innocent. He became guilty so that we might be acquitted. He was filled with despair so that we might be filled with joy. He took our shame so that we might take His glory. He endured the pains of Hell so that we might have the blessings of heaven. The Lamb has triumphed. He has prevailed, and that's why He commissioned us in Matthew 28:18-20: "All authority has been given to Me in heaven and on earth. Go therefore and make disciples of all the nations, baptizing them in the name of the Father and of the Son and of the Holy Spirit, teaching them to observe all things that I have commanded you; and lo, I am with you always, even to the end of the age."

- How have you lived in defeat despite Jesus' victory on your behalf?

- If you are a follower of Jesus, how has your shared identity with Him changed your approach to life? If you are not, how do you need to respond to Him today?

**PRACTICE THIS** Make a list of ways you live in defeat daily. Make a corresponding list of ways Jesus has achieved victory in these areas.

**1**

Now Joshua was clothed with filthy garments,
and was standing before the Angel.

**ZECHARIAH 3:3**

**PONDER THIS** Joshua was the high priest; as such, he stood for the people. And we can view him as standing for us. Joshua, as the accused, must plead guilty. Satan has a good case against Joshua—no ifs, ands, or buts about it. Scripture doesn't say he might be in filthy clothes or that the clothes only appear to be filthy. He is dressed in filthiness. And that is a picture of all of us who are not dressed in the righteousness of our Lord and Savior Jesus Christ. Joshua has no defense. He's obviously guilty. That's what the Bible says concerning all of us. Romans 3:19 says, "Now we know that whatever the law says, it says to those who are under the law, that every mouth may be stopped, and all the world may become guilty before God." The very first thing you must do with your sin is admit your guilt. Without this, there can be no forgiveness and healing.

- Ironically, freedom from guilt is found in admitting our guilt before God. Where do you need to admit guilt before God today?
- Is there a friend to whom you might confess your sin for the sake of healing?

**PRACTICE THIS** Schedule time to talk with a trusted friend and confess your sin for the sake of freedom and healing.

Who can understand his errors? Cleanse me from secret faults.

**PSALM 19:12**

**PONDER THIS** Do you want forgiveness? Do you know what I do sometimes in my study? I sit down in my quiet time, and I lay myself open to the Lord and say, "Search me, O God, and try my heart."

And sometimes it's very painful. God will show me things, and I say, "No, Lord, that's really not true. You're wrong, Lord." No. He says, "You're wrong, Adrian. I'm right." I'll write it on a slip of paper, and sometimes that list will get pretty long. But then I'll take that list and go one at a time, and I'll deal with it. I'll name it. I will repent of it. Something on my list may seem like a harmless thing to you. It may not be wrong for you, but it is for me. Or something may be wrong for you that wouldn't be for me. But I deal with each item on the list, then take my pen and write 1 John 1:9 over the whole thing and tear it up into little pieces. By that act, I'm reminded that I've been set free.

- What is something God has told you is wrong for you, even if not for others?

- How have you experienced the freedom that comes through repentance?

**PRACTICE THIS** Take time this week to practice the exercise described in today's devotion. Read and write the truth of 1 John 1:9 over the list God brings to mind for confession.

Then I set my face toward the Lord God to make request by prayer and supplications, with fasting, sackcloth, and ashes.

**DANIEL 9:3**

**PONDER THIS** Have you ever "set your face" in prayer? Have you ever desperately sought the Lord? Many of us could not even remember what we prayed for this morning or last night. We rattle off our little prayers, like "Now I lay me down to sleep." But have you really set your face to prayer?

What's important is not the arithmetic of your prayers—how many prayers you pray. It's not the rhetoric of your prayer—how eloquent or beautiful it may be. It's not the geometry of your prayer—how long your prayer may be. It is not the emotion of your prayer—how sweet and juicy your prayer is. It's not the logic of your prayer—how argumentative your prayer is. It is the faith and fervency of your prayer that gets to God. We're too often guilty of playing church. We witness without tears. We pray without fasting. Is it any wonder that we sow without reaping and we have so little power in our lives? It's time for a change.

- When was the last time you prayed with the zeal described in today's devotion?
- What keeps you from this kind of prayer on a regular basis?

**PRACTICE THIS** Spend devoted time in prayer today. Don't spend your time seeking to drum up zeal for God. Instead, spend your time praying for the right heart and motivation in prayer. Ask God to give you His concerns as your own.

**4**

"Your kingdom come. Your will be done on earth as it is in heaven."

**MATTHEW 6:10**

**PONDER THIS** Why do you want revival? Do you want it for your own sake? Do you want it for your family's sake? Do you want it for your denomination's sake? Do you want it for your church's sake? Do you want it for your nation's sake, or do you want it for God's sake? Is our prayer the one Jesus taught us to pray, "Our Father in heaven, hallowed be Your name. Your kingdom come. Your will be done on earth..."? (See Matthew 6:9-13.)

It's not that God is not concerned about our personal needs. We can pray for our daily bread. We can pray about our trespasses. But first, we are to pray for the glory of God. When we begin to pray for the glory of God, God moves in. But God has said clearly that He will not share His glory with another. (See Isaiah 42:8.)

- What comes to mind when you hear the word *revival*?
- When you pray, are you most often seeking God's glory or something of your own?

**PRACTICE THIS** Make a list of things to pray that will be for God's glory. Use this list each morning to continually put your focus back on Him.

## 5

...when He comes, in that Day, to be glorified in His
saints and to be admired among all those who believe,
because our testimony among you was believed.

**2 THESSALONIANS 1:10**

**PONDER THIS** Notice the word *glorified* in this verse. In the Greek language, this word has the idea "of wonder, of awe." What are we going to wonder at when we see the Lord Jesus? Think about what we're going to see. We're going to wonder at His transforming love. We will see all the saints of the ages made like the Lord Jesus Christ in a moment. Some who've been stubborn or God-haters were conquered by His sovereign love. We're going to see some who were ignorant and blind and had their eyes opened to the glorious Gospel of our Lord and Savior Jesus Christ. We're going to see some who were demonized by sex, drugs, and alcohol and have been made pure. We're going to see all the saints of God rise in glorified bodies like His glorified body. Is He Prophet, Priest, and King? We will be prophet, priest, and king. Is He perfect? We will be perfect. Why will we wonder when we will see the Lord Jesus Christ? Not one vestige of sin will be left in me. I can hardly wait for the day when I am made in the likeness of my blessed Lord.

- How does today's description of the coming of Christ lead you to awe and wonder?
- What are those places in you that will be transformed in an instant?

**PRACTICE THIS** Make a list of your own "fatal flaws." Make a corresponding list of Jesus' perfection in respect to those things. Reflect on the fact that this is how you will be transformed at His return.

And now you know what is restraining, that he may be revealed in
his own time. For the mystery of lawlessness is already at work; only
He who now restrains will do so until He is taken out of the way.

**2 THESSALONIANS 2:6-7**

**PONDER THIS** The Apostle Paul made it clear that the spirit of the antichrist already exists in our world today. Reread today's verses: "And now you know what is restraining, that he may be revealed in his own time. For the mystery of lawlessness is already at work; only He who now restrains will do so until He is taken out of the way."

What is Paul saying in these verses? He is saying there is a spirit in the world today called "the mystery of lawlessness" or iniquity. Wickedness has been working. It was at work in Paul's time, and it has continued to work in the world today. We're up against spirit beings. We're up against organized, brilliant, invisible, tireless demon spirits that the Bible calls the mystery of lawlessness. It is a devilish conspiracy. And yet that conspiracy is going to come together in the Last Days under the Antichrist.

- Where do you see "the mystery of lawlessness" in the world today?
- How does it comfort and encourage you to be reminded that
  evil beings only work in the world according to the limits God
  has set?

**PRACTICE THIS** Spend some time praying against the spirit of antichrist that is already in the world today. Ask God to reveal any areas of your life that are in opposition to Him.

## 7

Write the things which you have seen, and the things which
are, and the things which will take place after this.

**REVELATION 1:19**

**PONDER THIS** I called the Book of Revelation the golden clasp that puts the whole sixty-six volumes of the Bible together. Wouldn't it be wonderful if we had a key that would unlock that golden clasp? We do. If you understand this one verse, you'll have the key that will unlock the whole book. The Apostle John, who wrote the Book of Revelation, was given a commission to write this book. This is the commission: "Write the things which you have seen, and the things which are, and the things which will take place after this." That's God's outline of the Book of Revelation. A lot of times, people come to God's Word and artificially divide it into different sections, categories, and divisions. But if you find God's outline, the picture will come together very clearly.

- What does this verse tell you about the purpose of the Book of Revelation?
- How do John's words help you better understand the rest of the book?

**PRACTICE THIS** Read at least one full chapter of Revelation today (more if you are able), keeping God's purpose statement in mind as you do.

> The coming of the lawless one is according to the working of
> Satan, with all power, signs, and lying wonders, and with all
> unrighteous deception among those who perish, because they
> did not receive the love of the truth, that they might be saved.
>
> **2 THESSALONIANS 2:9-10**

**PONDER THIS** What is the Church? The Church is salt and light. What does salt do? Salt purifies. Salt preserves. Salt decontaminates. It also stings and irritates. We are the salt of the earth, and when that salt is taken out, decay will begin. We are the light of the world. When that light is taken out, darkness will engulf the globe. And when the Holy Spirit stands aside, Hell will have a holiday.

The people of this world don't like Bible-believing Christians. They think we're an impediment. They think we're odd. They think we're weird. They think we're stubborn. They think we're standing in the way of progress. One of these days, we'll be gone. And then the Restrainer will no longer be here, and at that time, you might as well try to dam up Niagara Falls with toothpicks to hold back the flood of wickedness and evil that will come upon this world. That time is known in the Bible as the Great Tribulation.

- How do passages like the one we read today give you urgency to share the Gospel with others?
- How does thinking of God's coming judgment give you compassion for others who are far from God today?

**PRACTICE THIS** Take time to share the Gospel with someone today.

And while they looked steadfastly toward heaven as He went
up, behold, two men stood by them in white apparel, who also
said, "Men of Galilee, why do you stand gazing up into heaven?
This same Jesus, who was taken up from you into heaven, will
so come in like manner as you saw Him go into heaven."

**ACTS 1:10-11**

**PONDER THIS** If I did not know the Bible, if I did not know Bible prophecy, if I did not understand who Jesus is and what God has planned, I would be a world-class pessimist. This world is like a Shakespearean tragedy. When you read a Shakespearean tragedy, you know it's coming to an untimely end, and nothing can stop it. The same is true for this world apart from Jesus. Without the Lord Jesus Christ, I would be an industrial-strength pessimist, but I'm a glowing optimist. We need not be disturbed! We must not be deceived because, friend, we will not be disappointed. You can be sure that Jesus Christ, who came the first time, is coming again. "This same Jesus," that angel said, "who was taken up from you into heaven, will so come in like manner as you saw Him go into heaven."

- How does remembering Jesus' promised return give you hope even in the most difficult times?
- Who do you know that needs to hear of this hope today?

**PRACTICE THIS** Make a list of world events or personal events that trouble your heart. Make a corresponding list of how Jesus gives you hope in those matters.

"I know your works, that you are neither cold nor hot. I could
wish you were cold or hot. So then, because you are lukewarm,
and neither cold nor hot, I will vomit you out of My mouth."

**REVELATION 3:15-16**

**PONDER THIS** Do you know the greatest obstacle the Church has to overcome?
It is lukewarm Christians—people who have their names on church roles, people
who claim to love the Lord Jesus Christ, but they just are not excited about the
Lord Jesus Christ. Often, we can't reach the goal because we stumble over our
own players. If there were fewer self-proclaimed Christians and all were on fire
for the Lord Jesus Christ, we'd do more than we do with an army of lukewarm
people. Jesus said He would rather have you cold than lukewarm. He then said,
"You make me sick to my stomach."

Why would lukewarmness make the Lord Jesus sick to His stomach? A great
Bible teacher named G. Campbell Morgan said, "Lukewarmness is the worst form
of blasphemy." Think about it—a man who's on fire for the Lord Jesus says, "I don't
want to ever lose my first love." The man who's cold says, "I don't believe in You;
I hate You; You're a false prophet. You're an imposter; I have nothing to do with
You." But the lukewarm person says, "I believe in You, but You just don't excite me.
I believe in You, but You died on the cross. What's new?" Do you see what I mean?
Jesus would rather you say, "I don't even love You; I don't know you; I don't desire
you; or I hate you," than say, "I believe in You, but You don't impress me, and You're
not worthy of my love or devotion."

- These are some of the most sobering words in the Bible.
  Where are you unimpressed with Jesus?

- How is God calling you to repent and turn back to Him today.

**PRACTICE THIS** Take time to sit in silence, asking God to reveal the places
you've been lukewarm toward Him. Repent of this posture and revisit passages
that remind you of God's amazing love. (For example, read Ephesians 2 and
Colossians 2.)

## 11

And I saw one of his heads as if it had been mortally
wounded, and his deadly wound was healed. And all
the world marveled and followed the beast.

**REVELATION 13:3**

**PONDER THIS** The Antichrist will be an appealing man in the eyes of the world. When we call him a beast, don't think of him as being hideous in appearance. The beast speaks of his nature. Remember that the devil himself appears as an angel of light. Doubtless, this beast will be handsome; he will be charming; he will be clever; he will be greatly intelligent; he will be a persuasive speaker; and he will be a global charmer. One of the reasons the entire world will wonder after him is that he will have a deadly wound in his head that will be healed. This will be Satan's counterfeit resurrection. Of course, it will be a resuscitation because the devil does not have the power to give life, but this one who appears to be dead will be brought back to life, and at that time the world will greatly admire him.

- How does the devil make ungodly temptations attractive today?
- How does regularly denying yourself better prepare you to face the schemes of the devil?

**PRACTICE THIS** Where do you need to deny yourself to reject the attractive schemes of the devil today? Take action in obedience to God.

Go therefore and make disciples of all the nations, baptizing them
in the name of the Father and of the Son and of the Holy Spirit.

**MATTHEW 28:19**

**PONDER THIS** Three is the divine number. We worship one God, but that one God has revealed Himself in three Persons. Matthew 28:19 says, "Go therefore and make disciples of all the nations, baptizing them in the name of the Father and of the Son and of the Holy Spirit" because our God is a triune God. When heavenly creatures praised the Lord in Isaiah 6:3, how did they do so? One cried unto another and said, "Holy, holy, holy is the LORD of Hosts." Holy is the Father, holy is the Son, holy is the Spirit. And since man is made in the image of God, man is triune in his nature. First Thessalonians 5:23b says, "May your whole spirit, soul, and body be preserved blameless at the coming of our Lord Jesus Christ."

There are also reflections of God's triunity all around us. Space is height, width, and depth. Each is distinguishable from the other, but each is inseparable from the other. You cannot have height without width; you cannot have width without depth; you cannot have depth without height. All are part of the same, and all are inseparable, but all are distinguishable. And everything is not only made of space, but it also exists in time. Time is past, present, and future. Now, you can distinguish the past from the present and the present from the future, but you cannot separate them because they are all part of one seamless garment, and you cannot have one without the other. They all reflect the triunity of the Creator because three is the divine number.

- Where else have you seen the number three in the Bible?
- Why is it worth our time to try and learn the meaning of various signs and symbols throughout the Bible?

**PRACTICE THIS** Take time today to thank God for His three-in-one nature as Father, Son, and Spirit.

And I looked, and behold, in the midst of the throne and of the
four living creatures, and in the midst of the elders, stood a Lamb
as though it had been slain, having seven horns and seven eyes,
which are the seven Spirits of God sent out into all the earth.

**REVELATION 5:6**

**PONDER THIS** Seven is a perfect or complete number. Seven is used to reference the Lord Jesus Christ many times. It is used also to reference the Holy Spirit. The Bible speaks of the seven spirits of God, but that doesn't mean there are literally seven spirits of God; it means the Holy Spirit is the perfect Spirit of God.

Six stands for perfect imperfection, and that's what Man is. So, you'll find six being used in the Bible to symbolize Satan and evil. For example, Goliath of Gath, that great giant that David killed—remember how David killed Goliath? His height was six cubits and a span; his spearhead weighed 600 shekels of iron; Goliath had six pieces of armor. There is Goliath, and he represents 666. Little David represents David's greater Son; he killed Goliath. One man won the battle for all the rest. What a picture and prophecy of the Lord Jesus, who has defeated Satan for all of us.

- How did David's defeat of Goliath point to the promised defeat of sin, death, and Satan by Jesus?
- What similarities do you find in this account with the work of Jesus on behalf of sinners? (See 1 Samuel 17.)

**PRACTICE THIS** Note the ways David acted in this limited moment that is similar to the way in which Jesus has acted on behalf of all sinners for eternity.

## 14

Then they will deliver you up to tribulation and kill you, and
you will be hated by all nations for My name's sake."

**MATTHEW 24:9**

**PONDER THIS** Did you know this world has room for almost every religion except that of our Lord and Savior, Jesus Christ? Our persecution is going to center in the name of Jesus. The world does not mind religion, but it resents Jesus. Jesus said, "I am the way, the truth, and the life. No one comes to the Father except through Me" (John 14:6). It is estimated that 360 million Christians live in countries where persecution is significant. Every year, tens of thousands are kidnapped, detained, or imprisoned. Every year, thousands of Christians are murdered, and thousands of churches are destroyed. And if you are paying attention at all, you know that Christian bashing is a favorite sport now for many forms of media.

- How does it make you feel to be reminded that Jesus has promised His people would be persecuted for following Him faithfully?
- Why is it worth facing this harsh reality?

**PRACTICE THIS** Spend time today reading about a few well-known Christian martyrs. Pray for Christians facing significant persecution and for your own faithfulness to Christ, no matter what you face.

**15**

"For the great day of His wrath has come, and who is able to stand?"

**REVELATION 6:17**

**PONDER THIS** God is not going to pour His wrath out upon His children. That doesn't mean we're not going to have tribulation because coming events cast shadows ahead of time, and Jesus said, "in the world you will have tribulation" (John 16:33b). We'll find that it's going to be open season on Bible-believing Christians until Jesus comes, but He's going to come and take us out, and then He's going to pour out His wrath on this Earth.

The Bible calls it the great day of His wrath. The flood did not come until Noah was in the ark. (See Genesis 7.) Fire and brimstone did not fall upon Sodom and Gomorrah until Lot was taken out (See Genesis 19.), and the wrath of Jehovah will not be poured out on the Earth until the Church is taken out. It's going to be dark for Israel; it's going to look like the end. The kingdoms of this world will be gathered there at Armageddon to obliterate Israel. And just when 666 thinks he has it all made, 777 is coming from Heaven. Jesus is coming again. 666 represents the Antichrist; 777 represents perfection in Jesus Christ.

- What feelings arise in you as you read today's passage and consider the coming wrath of God on those who don't know Him?

- How does this make you urgently want to align your heart with God and tell others about Him?

**PRACTICE THIS** This week, have a Gospel conversation with one person who doesn't know Jesus.

Here is wisdom. Let him who has understanding calculate the
number of the beast, for it is the number of a man: His number is 666.

**REVELATION 13:18**

**PONDER THIS** God is a God of order and design, and you see that in all of creation. Numerical law is written into the Universe. In astronomy, we can chart the heavens past and future by mathematics. The same is true in chemistry, which is primarily a study of mathematics and numbers. Study biology: just as flowers have a certain number of petals, there is a mathematical arrangement to everything that is biological. For example, there are 46 chromosomes in the cell of a man; there are trillions of cells, but all of them have one number of chromosomes, 46. God does nothing by accident.

God has also provided the symbolism of numbers in the Bible. The study of the spiritual significance of numbers is called Gematria. The use and consistency of numerical symbolism in God's Word is one of the many supports for the Bible's divine inspiration.

- How does the order observable in creation increase our desire to praise our Creator?

- How does understanding the spiritual significance of numbers help us better understand God's message in His Word?

**PRACTICE THIS** Use a Bible commentary or other trusted resource to research numerical symbolism in the Bible.

## 17

And to wait for His Son from heaven, whom He raised from the dead, even Jesus who delivers us from the wrath to come.

**1 THESSALONIANS 1:10**

**PONDER THIS** We are on a collision course with destiny, and we cannot afford to be ignorant. The signs of Jesus' coming are everywhere. I've stopped looking for the signs; I'm listening for the shout. I believe Jesus is at the door. One of the most wonderful, blessed, and biblical truths is this: His coming is imminent. That means He may come at any moment. We're not looking for some event in history; we're looking for Jesus Christ Himself. Do you know what the last prayer in the Bible is? "Even so, come, Lord Jesus" (Revelation 22:20b). And that ought to be our prayer today and every waking day: "Even so, come, Lord Jesus." For that's exactly what Jesus taught us to pray: "Your kingdom come. Your will be done on earth as *it is* in heaven" (Matthew 6:10).

- How often do you think about Jesus' promised return?
- How does remembering Jesus' return is imminent lead us to live differently?

**PRACTICE THIS** Spend time this week reading Bible passages that refer to Jesus' return (for example, Matthew 24:27-31 and 1 Thessalonians 4:13-18).

## 18

> "Blessed are you when they revile and persecute you, and
> say all kinds of evil against you falsely for My sake."
>
> **MATTHEW 5:11**

**PONDER THIS** When I was in college, I had a job as a construction worker—I was a carpenter's helper. The people I worked with asked me, "What are you going to do, son?" And I said, "God's called me to preach." Well, I got it in the neck from that time on—all the preacher jokes, all the dirty language, and so forth. And then one man called me aside, and he looked at me seriously. He said, "Young man, if you're going to be a preacher, let me tell you how to be a good one. I know a preacher. Everybody loves him. He never talks about politics or religion. If you'll just be a preacher that never talks about politics and religion, you can be loved."

Now if you're a Christian, there is a way you can escape persecution—just fail to be salt and light, just compromise. Rub shoulders with this old world. You won't get any persecution. Let me tell you something: in the Christian life, joy is the thermostat. You can set the thermostat and decide that you're going to live with joy because joy is internal, and it doesn't depend upon circumstances. But if joy is the thermostat, persecution is the thermometer. It shows whether you are living for the Lord Jesus Christ.

- How have you seen the truth that joy is the thermostat and persecution is the thermometer of Christian living?

- Where have you faced opposition as you've lived for Jesus? If you've never faced this, what might this imply about the way you are living?

**PRACTICE THIS** Ask a trusted friend this week for an honest assessment of how much your life points to Jesus regularly.

Looking for the blessed hope and glorious appearing
of our great God and Savior Jesus Christ.

**TITUS 2:13**

**PONDER THIS** Some years ago, a submarine sank off the coast of Massachusetts that went by the title S-4. It sank in deep waters. Many ships sped to the rescue to see if they could raise the ship and rescue the crew. They sent a diver many feet beneath the surface, and that diver put his gear up to the shell of that submarine, and he heard a message in Morse code. The message was a question: "Is there any hope?" And that's what this world wants to know.

For some people, there is no hope. As one person said, it looks like we're looking into the muzzle of a loaded cannon. Somebody said that hopelessness is the saddest word in the human language. Other people have hope, but it is a false hope. Somebody said there is no greater false hope than the first four hours of a diet. For many people, there is hope, but it is a false hope. Other people have hope, but it is an uncertain hope. But this passage of Scripture speaks of the Second Coming of Jesus. It calls the Second Coming "the glorious appearing of our great God and Savior Jesus Christ." And the Bible calls it a certain hope, a "blessed hope."

- Where would you say you look for hope?
- How do your daily actions support or contradict this claim?

**PRACTICE THIS** Spend some time in prayer, asking God to reveal the places you've put your hope outside of Jesus. Ask Him to lead you toward the certain hope of Jesus.

For the Lord Himself will descend from heaven with a shout,
with the voice of an archangel, and with the trumpet of God.
And the dead in Christ will rise first. Then we who are alive and
remain shall be caught up together with them in the clouds
to meet the Lord in the air. And thus we shall always be with
the Lord. Therefore comfort one another with these words.

**1 THESSALONIANS 4:16-18**

**PONDER THIS** Imagine you walk into a home where a father, a mother, and several children are red in the face. They're calling each other names, kicking shins, and pulling hair. They're having a family feud! And you ask, "Why are you, members of the same family, at one another's throats?" They say, "Our beloved elder brother William has been away for many years. We received a telegram that said he was coming home, and we met to make plans for his homecoming. But we don't agree on how he's coming. Susie says he's coming by car, Jim says he's coming by train, and Dad says he's coming by airplane. Mother says he's bringing some friends with him, and others say he's coming by himself. We don't agree on the details, so we're fighting about it." About that time, the door opens, and there stands William.

Does that remind you of anything? There are details about prophecy no one understands, but we know that our elder brother, the Lord Jesus, is coming, right? And when we have this hope in Him, we are to encourage one another and love one another. The closer we get to the Second Coming of Jesus Christ, the closer we ought to be to one another, and the more we ought to love one another. Our primary focus should not be *how* He's coming but *that* He's coming.

- What are some ways you are prone to be distracted by details about Jesus' return and lose focus on the promise of His return?

- How should the promise of Jesus' return lead us to greater unity?

**PRACTICE THIS** Take time today to reflect on Matthew 24:27-31 and 1 Thessalonians 4:13-18 and thank Jesus for the certainty of His return.

Unless the LORD builds the house, they labor in vain who build it;
unless the LORD guards the city, the watchman stays awake in vain.

**PSALM 127:1**

**PONDER THIS** A home must be built, but the Bible says here that human ingenuity, human wit, and human wisdom cannot build your home. There are many people who think they know exactly how to build a home. Some of them are preachers, and some of us have ideas we have gotten from ourselves and not from the Word of God. You need a divine plan. You need a blueprint. And you need a builder to build your home. And that builder and that plan is Christ and His Word, the Bible.

You can break all the laws in the Bible but one, and you'll never break that one. It is the law of sowing and reaping. Whatever you sow, you will reap. (See Galatians 6:7.) So, think with me about the construction of the home. Jesus built the first home in the Garden of Eden. The Lord Jesus Christ is away now building your heavenly home, for He says, "I go and prepare a place for you" (John 14:3a). And Jesus Christ alone can properly build your family home. Jesus is the greatest home builder, and the devil is the greatest home wrecker because the devil knows if he can hurt you at home, he has really hurt you. It doesn't matter how pious you look and act around the Lord's Table if you've just been arguing around the breakfast table. We need Christ, who is the great home builder.

- How can you properly assess whether you have built your life on Jesus?
- What needs to change in the way you are building your family?

**PRACTICE THIS** Make a list of principles that are important in your home. Next to each of these, honestly assess if this is a principle that honors God and is of Him or one you have built by your own wisdom. Ask Jesus to lead you to build your home on Him.

## 22

It is vain for you to rise up early, to sit up late, to eat the
bread of sorrows; for so He gives His beloved sleep.

**PSALM 127:2**

**PONDER THIS** Do you know what is wrong with so many American families today? We have succumbed to the myth, "They lived happily ever after." Nobody's supposed to live happily ever after. Nobody's supposed to be happy all the time. You wouldn't even want to be happy all the time. You'd get sick of being happy all the time. It would be like having ice cream for every meal. All of us have three basic needs. We have a need for security, for significance, and for satisfaction or sustenance. So many times, we get married and expect our spouses to meet those needs.

But sufficiency, security, and significance are something no man or woman can give you. If you don't find those things in Jesus, you won't find them. You're looking in the wrong place. Some people look at marriage like a tick looks at a dog. That tick is on that dog for what he can get out of that dog. But in marriage, there are two ticks and no dog. People come to marriage trying to get some level of satisfaction that God never really intended. I'm not saying that marriage doesn't meet needs, but I'm saying there are the deepest needs that only God can meet. You're not going to have real contentment unless you find it in Jesus.

- Where have you sought contentment outside of Jesus?

- How can you seek contentment in Him today?

**PRACTICE THIS** List the current things you are pursuing in life. Consider where you focus your time and resources. Evaluate whether you are seeking contentment in Jesus or in something or someone else.

## 23

Behold, children are a heritage from the LORD,
the fruit of the womb is a reward.

**PSALM 127:3**

**PONDER THIS** Children are not a penalty or a burden. Children are meant to be a blessing. Some people today believe, "If you have children, they will cramp your style. And if you do have them, don't have very many. And don't let that keep you from fulfillment. Don't let them keep you from your career and from being 'somebody.'" Others have very selfish ideas about children. They say, "Well, you know, children are so expensive. If I have children, or if I have more than one or two, I might not be able to drive the kind of car I want to drive. It costs to educate them. I might not be able to live in the kind of house I want to live in. I'd be tied down. We wouldn't be able to go to Hawaii on our vacation. Maybe it would be better not to have those children. They might be a burden. After all, children make a rich man poor."

But this is backward. Children make a poor man rich. A rich man can't take his money to Heaven. I'm taking all my children to Heaven with me. Children are the heritage of the Lord. They're a gift of God. My heart goes out to people who want children and cannot have them. But for those who are able, you want to be blessed? Oh, children are a heartache. They're a pain. They're problems. Sure, they are—but they're worth it. Children are the heritage of the Lord.

- Where might you have had wrong views about children?
- How can you encourage your children by telling them the ways in which they've blessed you? If you don't have children of your own, who are some children you might encourage in this way?

**PRACTICE THIS** This week, take time to encourage a child by telling him or her how he or she has blessed you.

Train up a child in the way he should go, and
when he is old he will not depart from it.

**PROVERBS 22:6**

**PONDER THIS** Do you know the word *train* comes from a Hebrew root related to what the midwives used to do when the little Hebrew babies were born? They would take an index finger, dip it in olive oil, and then dip it in crushed dates. Then they would take the little newborn baby and touch the pallet of that baby. That would begin the nursing instinct. It was to create a desire in the heart of that child to take nourishment. As a matter of fact, if you take your finger and rub it right back over the roof of your mouth, you'll find instinctively you want to swallow. And that was the root of this word, which means to train up. It literally means to create a desire.

Oh, if parents today could create a desire for God in the hearts of their children. That's the idea—create a desire in the heart of your child for God, and when he's old, he will not depart from it. That's what many have done throughout the generations of God's people. And that is what God is calling us to do.

- What are some ways to train children with a desire for God?
- How can you actively be involved in this work with your own children or those close to you?

**PRACTICE THIS** This week, take one action toward training children to have a desire for God.

## 25

> "And these words which I command you today shall be in your
> heart. You shall teach them diligently to your children, and
> shall talk of them when you sit in your house, when you walk
> by the way, when you lie down, and when you rise up."
>
> **DEUTERONOMY 6:6-7**

**PONDER THIS** I believe in family worship, but sometimes family worship can be painful. It's almost like you just try to cram something down the throats of the kids. "You sit still while I instill." It's "a dose a day keeps the devil away." But according to today's passage, that's not the real way to teach the Bible. There is a time and place when a family comes together and shares. But you begin to verbalize it when you rise up, when you lie down, when you're in the way, when you go out, when you come in, and when you speak the things of God normally and naturally, consistently every day. Then you're really teaching. You see, you need to vitalize it. It needs to be in your heart. Then, you need to verbalize it.

- Which form of teaching discussed today are you more prone to?
- Why is it important to teach consistently with our lives and not only with our words?

**PRACTICE THIS** Consider one way you can teach with your life and not only with your words. Put this into practice today.

So God created man in His own image; in the image of God
He created him; male and female He created them.

**GENESIS 1:27**

**PONDER THIS** A man is never to lose his masculinity. A woman is never to give up her femininity. God gave the male the maleness. And God gave you that femaleness. A female might object, "Well, I'm not inferior to a man." That's right! You're not inferior to a man. As a matter of fact, you're superior to a man...at being a woman. And a man is superior to a woman at being a man. God made them different so that He might make them one. Any society that blurs the distinction between male and female is headed for disintegration and disaster. And in America today, we are reaping the results of disregarding these God-given differences. God made them in the beginning male and female. We honor Him by honoring the way He made us.

- What are some unique ways God has made you according to your gender?
- What are some ways you honor God by living as a male or female?

**PRACTICE THIS** Choose one action today to honor God through the gender He has given you.

Children, obey your parents in all things, for
this is well pleasing to the Lord.
**COLOSSIANS 3:20**

**PONDER THIS** I can honor my parents with the life that I live. My life will either honor or dishonor my parents. When we're children, we are to obey our parents. Even when we're grown, we learn to take their advice. But children are to obey. Today's verse makes this clear: "Children, obey your parents in all things, for this is well pleasing unto the Lord." Do you want to please God? You cannot please God by displeasing your parents. Obey your parents in all things. There's a blessing in obedience. And not only is there a blessing in obedience, but there's also great danger in disobedience.

- What are some practical ways young children honor their parents?

- How can you honor your parents as an adult? How can you do this even if you have a strained relationship with your parents or if they are no longer living?

**PRACTICE THIS** Practice one way of honoring your parents today as a means of worship to the Lord.

## 28

Wives, submit to your own husbands, as to the Lord.

**EPHESIANS 5:22**

**PONDER THIS** Submission to authority does not mean inferiority. Think of some different examples. Is a church member inferior to me because I'm the pastor? Of course not. Do you think I'm inferior to a policeman because I stop when he says stop and go when he says go? Of course not. Do you think a child is inferior to his parents because that child obeys his parents? Of course not. Here's the capstone. Do you think God the Son is inferior to God the Father? No, of course not. If you know anything about Christian theology, you know the basic prime tenant of our faith is the full deity of Jesus Christ, co-equal and co-eternal with God the Father. And yet the Bible says the head of Christ is God the Father. Jesus was submissive. He "humbled Himself and became obedient to the point of death, even the death of the cross" (Philippians 2:8b). Submission does not mean inferiority.

- How does today's devotion challenge your thinking about submission?

- Who has God put in authority over you? How are you called to submit to them?

**PRACTICE THIS** Make a list of ways you might honor God by submitting to those He has put in authority in your life.

## 29

Therefore a man shall leave his father and mother and be joined to his wife, and they shall become one flesh.

**GENESIS 2:24**

**PONDER THIS** There are three verbs here that I want to underscore—*leave, cleave* (or be joined), and *become one flesh*. There you have an outline for preparing any child for marriage. This is the marriage relationship summed up in a verse and one of the key verses in all the Bible. I've been a pastor for many years, and I've done a lot of marriage counseling. But I have not done any marriage counseling, nor shall I ever do any, in which the problem was not caused by people not understanding the meaning of this one verse. Not understanding what it means to leave. Not understanding what it means to cleave. Not understanding what it means to be one flesh. In those three verbs, you have the priority of marriage, the permanence of marriage, and the purpose of marriage.

- How is your understanding of marriage tied to the three verbs in today's verse?
- How does this understanding of marriage lead us to the deep commitment God intends?

**PRACTICE THIS** Take some time to study this verse today. If you don't know much about its meaning, look at some commentaries to learn more about its intention.

"Therefore what God has joined together, let not man separate."

**MARK 10:9**

**PONDER THIS** The word *cleave* means "to weld, to glue, to fasten together in an unbreakable bond." Marriage is to be God's superglue. Divorce is a transgression of the will, the law, and the purpose of God. Parents need to teach children that divorce is never an option. Show me two people who begin their marriage with the idea that, if it doesn't work out, they'll get a divorce, and I'll show you two people who are highly likely to get a divorce. Show me two people who begin a marriage with a total commitment of "no matter what," and I'll show you two kids who are likely to make it. When you get on the airplane of marriage, you throw away your parachute. If somebody mentions divorce, you give a blank look and say, "What does that word mean? I don't understand that word. What language is that? We don't even discuss that. That is not even an option. We don't even talk about it. It is not God's will. It is not God's way. No to divorce." For this cause shall a man leave his father and his mother, and he shall cleave unto his wife.

- Who do you know that has the type of marriage described in today's passage?

- Though divorce is not God's desire, many in the Church have experienced this painful reality. How can you encourage those who have gone through the pain of divorce?

**PRACTICE THIS** If you are married and have a printed dictionary, cross through the entry on divorce and show that to your spouse. Married or not, take one practical step today to bless someone who has experienced the pain of divorce.

"Now therefore, I pray, if I have found grace in Your sight, show
me now Your way, that I may know You and that I may find grace
in Your sight. And consider that this nation is Your people. And
He said, 'My Presence will go with you, and I will give you rest.'"

**EXODUS 33:13-14**

**PONDER THIS** Moses said, "Lord, I want to know your ways." In reply, God promised to give Moses rest. When you know God's ways, it is the difference between rest and relapse. You can know God's works without knowing God's ways. The land of Canaan represents the believer's rest. They were to have rest, but they never found rest. Those of us who know God's ways will live in a perpetual Sabbath, not a seventh-day Sabbath, a 365-day-a-year Sabbath. Every day can be a day of rest if you know the ways of God.

Now, why don't we know this? Why don't we have this blessing? There is no blessing without obedience. And there is no obedience because there is no trust. There is no trust because there is no love. And there is no love because there is no knowledge. You can't trust someone you do not know. And you cannot know someone if all you see is their works and you don't know their ways. You have to know an individual. You have to know their ways to love them. You have to love them in order to trust them. And you have to trust them in order to obey them. Israel saw the works of God. They saw the miracles of God. They saw the plagues on Egypt. They saw the Red Sea open. They saw all these things, but they never understood the ways of God, and they never found rest. The difference between knowing the works of God and the ways of God is the difference between rest and relapse.

- How would you describe the difference between knowing God's works and knowing His ways?
- How can you seek to learn more of God's ways this week?

**PRACTICE THIS** Spend time with God in His Word and in prayer, seeking to learn His ways and not just His works. Make a list that compares God's works and His ways.

**1**

> For the husband is head of the wife, as also Christ is head
> of the church; and He is the Savior of the body. "

**EPHESIANS 5:23**

**PONDER THIS** One man confessed, "I lied on my income tax. In the place where it said head of the house, I signed my name." This verse doesn't say he is the dictator of the house. He is the head of the house. And he is to be a loving leader. So many husbands think the Bible says he is the dictator of the house. Being the head means he is to love his wife as Christ loved the Church.

The husband is the head of the wife, as Christ is the head of the Church. This wonderful little word *as* means that the husband is not a top sergeant beating his wife over the head with a Bible club and saying, "Submit, submit, submit." Why does the Church submit to Jesus? Does He force us to submit? If He did, we'd be a lot different, wouldn't we? We'd all tithe. We'd all say amen. If He forced us to submit, we'd all be here every Sunday evening, even if it rained. But He doesn't force us. He loves us. Do you know why I love Him? Because He first loved me.

- How does it change your perspective on submission to realize Jesus doesn't force us to submit to Him, but leads us through love?
- Who has God called you to lead in this way?

**PRACTICE THIS** Take time this week to practically love someone God has given you influence or leadership over.

Husbands, love your wives, just as Christ also loved
the church and gave Himself for her.

**EPHESIANS 5:25**

**PONDER THIS** Christ gave Himself to the Church by dying for the Church. Now you don't have to die physically to die to your ambitions. You don't have to die physically to die to your pride. You know, I had to die before I got saved. I had to die to self to receive Christ as my Savior. He had to die on the cross before He could save me. Do you know what most marriages need? What most homes need? It's two funerals and a wedding where the husband and wife die to themselves and are married to one another. Then they begin to live sacrificially, giving themselves one to another. Some people think when the Bible says the wife is to submit to the husband that means the wife is to wait on him.

That's not what the Bible teaches. That's not the way Christ loves the Church. He gave Himself as a sacrifice for us. A husband who loves his wife as Christ loved the Church is going to love her selflessly and he is going to love her sacrificially.

- How is God calling you to sacrifice for another today (whether a spouse, family member, friend, or someone else)?
- How will you respond as Christ loved the Church?

**PRACTICE THIS** Make a sacrifice in love for another person today.

**3**

"And you shall know the truth, and the truth shall make you free."

**JOHN 8:32**

**PONDER THIS** When you believe the Word, when you believe in Jesus, when you continue in the Word, and when you become a disciple, you know the truth, and you become liberated. There are a lot of people who claim belief in the Lord Jesus Christ but are not liberated people because they have never really absorbed truth. They've never aligned their lives with the truth. People don't like discipline because we have a generation that wants to be free. Many see truth and discipline as restricting.

I read a quote somewhere. I don't know who said it, but it stuck with me: "He who is a slave to the compass is the master of the oceans; the rest have to sail close to the shore." Is that not great? "He who is a slave to the compass." The compass is what the ancient mariners used to guide their ships with. Submitting to the compass actually gives freedom. This is also the case with truth. Truth liberates you. Truth makes you free.

- How have you experienced the reality that the truth of Jesus sets you free?
- What are some ways rejecting the truth leads to bondage?

**PRACTICE THIS** Spend time in prayer thanking God for the truth about Jesus that sets people free.

> Then Jesus said to those Jews who believed Him, "If you
> abide in My word, you are My disciples indeed."
>
> **JOHN 8:31**

**PONDER THIS** Discipleship is costly, but ignorance is far more costly. How do you buy the truth? How do you purchase the truth? First, it's going to cost you precious time. That's one of the costs you're going to have to pay. You're not going to get it by osmosis. Time is precious, but it is not as precious as truth. Hurry is the death knell of prayer and Bible study. You want to buy the truth? It's going to cost you time.

Many won't pay that price. This is evidenced by the reality that prayer and Bible study are one of the lowest things on our priority lists in the morning. We wake up a little late, hurry through the morning, check the day's news, drink a scalding cup of coffee, rush out the door, and say, "Lord, bless this mess." But discipleship is going to cost you time. Take time to be holy.

- How willing are you to pay the cost of time for the sake of discipleship to Jesus?
- How does your schedule and routine support or contradict this claim?

**PRACTICE THIS** Pay the cost of time today to spend time with God in prayer and Bible study.

...who also made us sufficient as ministers of the new covenant, not of the letter but of the Spirit; for the letter kills, but the Spirit gives life.

**2 CORINTHIANS 3:6**

**PONDER THIS** Truth without power is deadening and depressing. If all you have is the letter of the law, you don't have the Spirit. You have the words, but you don't have the music. That's a deadening truth. You see, knowledge without transformation avails nothing. All it does is increase your judgment. The Bible says it'd be better for you not to have known the way of righteousness than to know it and then not live by it. (See 2 Peter 2:21.) Maybe we ought to put a sign over the Church doors: "Warning: Attendance may be dangerous to your spiritual health." It may be. It would be better for you not to hear truth than to hear truth, learn truth, and not act on truth.

- What are some ways we might learn the truth but not act on it?
- If we do this, have we really received the truth? Why or why not?

**PRACTICE THIS** Take one step of action today regarding the truth of God's Word.

"For in Him we live and move and have our being, as also some
of your own poets have said, 'For we are also His offspring.'"
**ACTS 17:28**

**PONDER THIS** Dr. Warren Wiersbe said if you were to spend thirty minutes a day on any subject—nutrition, history, or something else—in ten years you would have the equivalency of a PhD in that subject. As a Bible student, you are to measure and test everything that you read by the Word of God. You have a grid that it all has to pass through. You have a radar. You see, all truth intersects, and one of the tests of any good book is this: When you put that book down, do you begin to think? Because it will relate to everything else you know.

All genuine truth intersects because all truth is of God. But God did not make you just to be a reservoir of truth, He means for you to be a channel of truth. If you're growing in knowledge but not growing in grace, you're going to be dangerous. I've met those people. They can split a theological hair into nine separate sections, but they're not growing in the grace of our Lord and Savior, Jesus Christ.

- What are some ways you might be in danger of being a reservoir of truth instead of a channel of truth?
- How can you focus on the grace of Jesus and not just on the facts of Jesus?

**PRACTICE THIS** Take time today to reflect on the grace of Jesus and not only the facts of Jesus. Ask the Lord to lead you to live out His grace and not only take it in.

**7**

> "But the word of the LORD endures forever." Now this is
> the word which by the gospel was preached to you.
>
> **1 PETER 1:25**

**PONDER THIS** There was a Scottish missionary named Alexander Duff who set sail for Holland in 1829. He had all his belongings on board, and the ship was wrecked. Alexander Duff and the others got to shore safely, but everything on board the ship went down. After they made it to shore, they were standing and watching to see if there was something that might wash ashore from the ship, something they might save. Duff, being a missionary, wanted his books, and he had taken eight hundred selected books.

After a while, they saw something bobbing along the shore and moving closer and closer. The only thing that survived out of the entire shipwreck was Duff's Bible. All the other volumes had gone to the bottom, but there was the Word of God still afloat. What a parable. Books come and books go, but you can't drown God's holy Word. "The Word of the LORD endures forever."

- How have you seen the reality that God's Word outlasts the knowledge and wisdom of people?
- How can you prioritize the Word of God over other sources of knowledge in daily life?

**PRACTICE THIS** Spend time today taking in the wisdom of God revealed through His Word.

And we heard this voice which came from heaven when we were with Him on the holy mountain. And so we have the prophetic word confirmed, which you do well to heed as a light that shines in a dark place, until the day dawns and the morning star rises in your hearts.

**2 PETER 1:18-19**

**PONDER THIS** Peter was not saying that the things he saw did not happen. Peter was not saying the things he felt, he did not feel. He's simply saying, the Word of God that survives human teachers is the Word of God that surmounts human testimonies. He was saying, "I saw it. I know it is true. I was an eyewitness. I saw Him. But we've got a more sure word of prophecy—the Word of God."

When he says a confirmed prophecy, he wasn't talking about prophecy that foretells the future; he was talking about the revealed body of God's truth, the Bible. The Bible survives human teachers. And the Bible surmounts human testimonies. Many of us say, "Oh, if I could only have been there when Jesus was on Earth. If I could only have been on the mount of transfiguration. If I could only have seen that." But I want to tell you, you've got something better right now. You have a more sure Word of prophecy.

- What are some ways you have prized experience over the revealed Word of God?
- How can we be sure that we are prioritizing the Word of God above any other means of encounter with God?

**PRACTICE THIS** Make a list of some of the ways you have experienced God. Make a corresponding list to reference ways these experiences align with (or don't align with) the Word of God.

## 9

And many will follow their destructive ways, because
of whom the way of truth will be blasphemed.

**2 PETER 2:2**

**PONDER THIS** Heresies always cause division. When someone comes along and teaches something contrary to the Word of God, we can't just open our arms and say, "Oh well, that's all right. We're un-American if we don't admit that what you believe is just as authentic as what we believe." No, there is the Word of God. And so, a heretic is someone who causes division in the Church. You may say, "Pastor Rogers, rather than letting them cause division, why don't we just welcome them in?" No, my dear friend, a little leaven leavens the whole lump. And listen to me, division is painful and terrible, but it is better to be divided by truth than united by error. There are certain things God calls us to stand firm on and one of those is the truth of His Word.

- How does regular time spent in the Word help you know what is worth dividing with others over for the sake of truth?

- What is the cost if we fail to divide over the things God has made clear in His Word?

**PRACTICE THIS** Spend time today reflecting on the cost of failing to stand on God's Word as ultimate truth.

> But there were also false prophets among the people, even
> as there will be false teachers among you, who will secretly
> bring in destructive heresies, even denying the Lord who
> bought them, and bring on themselves swift destruction.

**2 PETER 2:1**

**PONDER THIS** Look at the word *secretly*. In this case, the word has the idea of laying something alongside something else. Laying something good alongside something that is bad. Very few false teachers and false prophets will directly deny the whole scope of Christianity. In fact, some of them will affirm what you and I believe. They might say, "Yes, we believe Jesus Christ is the Son of God." Or they may say, "Yes, we believe that the Bible is the Word of God." Or they might say, "Yes, we ought to live good, godly, Christ-filled lives and so forth."

But then they will secretly lay their false doctrine alongside that. The devil is very clever. The Bible says he's "more cunning than any beast of the field" (Genesis 3:1a). We are called to be on guard so that we won't be deceived by partial truths and half gospels.

- What examples have you seen of false teaching being brought in alongside truthful teaching?
- How are we to be on guard to ensure we are not deceived in this way?

**PRACTICE THIS** Spend some time in prayer, asking God to give you discernment and wisdom to recognize false teachings, even when they are brought in next to the truth.

**11**

They have forsaken the right way and gone astray, following the way of Balaam the son of Beor, who loved the wages of unrighteousness.

**2 PETER 2:15**

**PONDER THIS** What do you do when you learn of counterfeit money? Do you throw away all your money? What do you do when you learn that some doctor is an impostor? Do you refuse to go to any doctor? What do you do when you learn that some lawyers are dishonest? Do you refuse ever to use a lawyer? Of course not. It is the counterfeit that proves the worth and the validity of the genuine item.

Why do people counterfeit Christianity? Counterfeit Christians prove the worth, the validity, and the reality of that which they are counterfeiting. Never let a hypocrite keep you away from the true riches of the Lord Jesus Christ. Don't be so foolish. You may say, "Well, I'm not going to church. There are hypocrites there." May I give you some advice? It would be far better for you to spend a few days with some hypocrites than to spend eternity with all hypocrites in Hell. Don't let a hypocrite keep you from the true riches of the Lord Jesus Christ.

- How have you found it true that counterfeits prove the worth of the genuine item?
- What are we missing about ourselves if we say we will avoid the Church because hypocrites attend?

**PRACTICE THIS** End your time in prayer, thanking God for the worthiness of Jesus and the beauty of the true Gospel that redeems the worst of sinners and hypocrites.

By covetousness they will exploit you with deceptive
words; for a long time their judgment has not been
idle, and their destruction does not slumber.

**2 PETER 2:3**

**PONDER THIS** What is the predominant thing about most ads? Joy, fun, beauty, and youth. The advertisement is appealing because the product is presented alongside something else so that by association, you think the product is good and will bring you those things. The devil is very clever—he deceives people exactly the same way in the realm of religion as he does with deception in other areas of life. This verse says he uses deceptive words. In Greek, that word is *plastos*. It's the word we get plastic from. False prophets use plastic words. Now, what is plastic? Plastic is something you can mold to fit almost any situation. It is also something that can be made to look like the real thing. You can have plastic leather that looks like real leather. It looks valuable, but over time, you can clearly see it is not the real thing. That's the kind of deceptive words these people used. They are words that sound appealing but are not the truth of God. They are words that sound enticing but will ultimately lead you to destruction. The lies of the enemy are disguised with plastic words. Oh, how we need to know the Word of God to combat these wicked schemes!

- When have you needed to use discernment when something sounded enticing?
- How does knowing God's Word help you guard against deceptive words?

**PRACTICE THIS** Spend time in God's Word today to help you discern truth.

## 13

For the time will come when they will not endure sound
doctrine, but according to their own desires, because they
have itching ears, they will heap up for themselves teachers;
and they will turn their ears away from the truth, and be
turned aside to fables. But you be watchful in all things, endure
afflictions, do the work of an evangelist, fulfill your ministry.

**2 TIMOTHY 4:3-5**

**PONDER THIS** There are a lot of people who don't want sound doctrine. Paul warned Timothy about those with "itching ears." What does that mean? It means these people turn away from the truth; they don't want sound doctrine. Do you know what the word *sound* means? *Sound* is the word we get the word *hygiene* from. They don't want spiritual hygiene. They don't want sound doctrine. They want to hear a more convenient message, one that is customized to their desires and wishes. They want a preacher to tickle their ears, scratch their ears, and tell them what they want to hear.

There's a whole movement of church growth in America today that says, "Don't stand up on Sunday morning and tell people they're sinners. They won't come back. Scratch and tickle their ears and say smooth things to them, and you'll build a crowd." So what? Jesus won't be your best friend until He becomes your Savior and you're born again. No, it's not fun to stand up and tell people they're lost. It's not fun to preach the Word of God, but it is the truth that will set you free. (See John 8:32.)

- Do you listen to others, even when it isn't what you want to hear? Why or why not?
- When was the last time someone spoke a word of wisdom you needed to hear but didn't like? How did you respond?

**PRACTICE THIS** Talk to a trusted friend and ask if there is any area in which you have itching ears to hear only what you want.

## 14

They have forsaken the right way and gone astray, following the way of Balaam the son of Beor, who loved the wages of unrighteousness.

**2 PETER 2:15**

**PONDER THIS** False prophets never get enough. They are greedy. We all make mistakes. I've made plenty of them, and I'll make plenty more, but false prophets are people who have rotten characters. They are not merely mistaken. They are willfully wicked, and every one of them once knew the truth. Peter said in this passage, "They have forsaken the right way." It's not that they've never known. It is that they have willfully, deliberately forsaken the right way. Peter went on to say in 2 Peter 2:21, "For it would have been better for them not to have known the way of righteousness, than having known it, to turn from the holy commandment delivered to them." They know what's right, and they refuse it. They willfully prostitute the Gospel of Jesus Christ for gain.

- When is it important to spend personal time in the Word to discern God's truth?

- When have you been tricked into buying something that was not worth what you paid? How did you guard yourself from making the same mistake another time? How can this apply to being wise about those to whom you listen?

**PRACTICE THIS** Pray and ask God to help you practice discernment with the voices and teachers to whom you listen.

**15**

> While they promise them liberty, they themselves are slaves
> of corruption; for by whom a person is overcome, by him also
> he is brought into bondage. For if, after they have escaped the
> pollutions of the world through the knowledge of the Lord
> and Savior Jesus Christ, they are again entangled in them and
> overcome, the latter end is worse for them than the beginning.
>
> **2 PETER 2:19-20**

**PONDER THIS** Sin always promises freedom, but it brings bondage. And the deceitfulness of sin is such that those who are in the deepest bondage think they are free. As a matter of fact, the Lord Jesus said in John 8:36, "...If the Son makes you free, you shall be free indeed." Do you know the difference between the freedom Jesus gives and the freedom that liar the devil promises?

When the devil says he's going to give you freedom, it's freedom to do what you want. The freedom that Jesus gives is not freedom to do as you want; it is freedom to do as you ought. Those who do as they want are not free at all. They are actually servants of corruption. You may say, "I'm not going to be a Christian. I'm just going to be free to do my thing. I'm free to choose." You are free to choose, but you are not free to choose the consequences of your choice. But Jesus said if the Son makes you free, you will be free indeed.

- Why does the freedom to do what we want sound so appealing?
- How have you experienced true freedom in Jesus?

**PRACTICE THIS** Pray for those you know who are living in bondage to sin but do not know it.

## 16

Nevertheless we, according to His promise, look for new
heavens and a new earth in which righteousness dwells.

**2 PETER 3:13**

**PONDER THIS** Some people think that as we discover the physical, material Universe, there is no reason to believe Jesus Christ is going to come again or that there will be a new birth for planet Earth. They think nothing cataclysmic has ever happened, so there's no reason to think anything cataclysmic will happen.

I can imagine a little boy in Noah's time coming back to his dad and saying, "Dad, listen. I want to tell you something. There's a man named Noah who says God is going to destroy the world with a flood and so he is building a great big boat; he calls it an ark. Noah says that if we want, we can get on board that ark. Dad, listen, I don't want to die in any flood, whatever that may be. Could we go over there and talk to Mr. Noah about it?" Imagine the response of the father saying something like, "Son, forget about the flood. Nobody's ever seen a flood, and there's no such thing as a flood. All things will continue as they are." That argument may be compelling, but depending only on our natural mind will never give us the full picture.

- What are some ways you are prone to depend on your natural mind? What is positive about that? What is negative about that?

- Why do we tend to be skeptical about cataclysmic things?

**PRACTICE THIS** Pray and ask God to prepare your heart to see Him move in a mighty way.

For by Him all things were created that are in heaven and that are
on earth, visible and invisible, whether thrones or dominions or
principalities or powers. All things were created through Him and
for Him. And He is before all things, and in Him all things consist.

**COLOSSIANS 1:16-17**

**PONDER THIS** Whether it be the planets in orbit or the electrons whirling around
the nucleus of an atom, Jesus Christ is the glue of the galaxies. The Bible says He
upholds "all things by the word of His power" (Hebrews 1:3b). "He spoke," the Bible
says, "and it was done" (Psalm 33:9). If you were to look at my pulpit, the atoms
are raised in such a way that you can see and touch and feel them, or you seem
to feel them. But actually, the pulpit stand is primarily energy. It is made out of
invisible entities. In Hebrews 11:3b, the Bible says, "...the things which are seen
were not made of things which are visible." Isn't it incredible how the Bible said
all this long before Einstein?

The things that are seen are made out of things that do not appear. We see how
that relates to the atoms that make up the things we see, but here is the bottom
line—what holds it all together is Jesus. He spoke, and it was done! By Him, all
things exist.

- How does it encourage you to know Jesus is the One who holds
  all things together?

- Who do you know who feels like things are falling apart? How
  can you encourage them with today's truth?

**PRACTICE THIS** Consider any areas of your life in which you don't include Jesus.
Ask God to help you remember that He holds all things together.

**18**

Therefore, since all these things will be dissolved, what manner of persons ought you to be in holy conduct and godliness, looking for and hastening the coming of the day of God, because of which the heavens will be dissolved, being on fire, and the elements will melt with fervent heat? Nevertheless we, according to His promise, look for new heavens and a new earth in which righteousness dwells. Therefore, beloved, looking forward to these things, be diligent to be found by Him in peace, without spot and blameless.

**2 PETER 3:11-14**

**PONDER THIS** In this passage, it sounds like Peter is asking a question. He's not asking a question; he's making a statement. He is speaking about what manner of person you ought to be. He is saying, for emphasis, if this is going to happen, what kind of people should we be? What manner of persons? The word *manner* means "from another world."

It has the idea of being a stranger, an alien. He's saying what "out of this world" kind of behavior ought you have? The idea speaks of exotic behavior, something that is not normal. He is saying that when we know what we know, we can't be like everybody else. Our behavior is not of this world. We are to be different because Peter has already told us we are strangers and pilgrims. A stranger is not at home, and a pilgrim is on his way home. This world is not my home, I'm just passing through. We are not citizens of Earth trying to get to Heaven. We are already citizens of Heaven sojourning here on Earth. Therefore, we are to be different.

- What are some ways you act like the world? What are some ways you act differently?
- How does knowing who Jesus is change how we live?

**PRACTICE THIS** Ask an accountability partner how you act in a way that reflects the world instead of your heavenly home. Pray and repent of these things, asking God to help you live in line with His character and will.

But, beloved, do not forget this one thing, that with the Lord
one day is as a thousand years, and a thousand years as one
day. The Lord is not slack concerning His promise, as some
count slackness, but is longsuffering toward us, not willing that
any should perish but that all should come to repentance.

**2 PETER 3:8-9**

**PONDER THIS** The Lord has kept the door of mercy open for you. God is a God of mercy. And Peter answers the apostates with three things. He says, "There's a memorable promise." He says, "There's God's mighty power." But there is also God's merciful patience, "The Lord is...not willing that any should perish but that all should come to repentance" (2 Peter 3:9). God is waiting for you to be saved. You say, "If God is so full of mercy, I don't have to worry." But in verse 10, Peter says the Day of the Lord will come. The wrath of God and the mercy of God are both attributes of God. If you see God as all wrath and no mercy, that's only part of the truth. If you see God as all mercy and no wrath, that's only part of the truth. When you make part of the truth all the truth, that becomes an untruth. God is not willing that any should perish, but the Day of the Lord will come.

- What do you tend to focus on more: God's mercy or God's wrath?
- Why is it important to understand both sides of God's character?

**PRACTICE THIS** Write down the distinct characteristics that come to mind when you think about God. Assess where you see those things in Scripture.

## 20

"Repent therefore and be converted, that your sins
may be blotted out, so that times of refreshing
may come from the presence of the Lord."

**ACTS 3:19**

**PONDER THIS** How do you avoid perishing? Come to repentance. What is repentance? It is a change of mind. The Greek word *metanoia* means "I changed my mind." I have been trusting myself, living in sin, and going this way—and I have a radical, dramatic change of mind. I repent; I turn from sin to Jesus. It means you shift from placing faith in yourself to placing faith in Him. Have you said, "Lord, once and for all, now and forever, I trust you; I receive you to be my Lord and my Savior"? That is repentance. Jesus said, in Luke 13:3b, "...unless you repent, you will all likewise perish." Second Peter 3:9b reminds us, "The Lord is not willing that any should perish, but that all should come to repentance." Repentance is not just turning over a new leaf; it's receiving a new life. It's trusting Christ as your personal Savior.

This is not only a decision you make once but an act of trust every day, turning to Him as your Savior and putting faith in Him instead of in yourself.

- What are some ways you have trusted in yourself instead of God?
- What has changed in your life since you began following Jesus?

**PRACTICE THIS** Consider if there is anything you need to repent of today. Pray and ask God for forgiveness and receive His new way of life.

...but as He who called you is holy, you also be holy in all your
conduct, because it is written, "Be holy, for I am holy."

**1 PETER 1:15-16**

**PONDER THIS** What does the word *holy* mean? It means "to be separated, different, set aside for a purpose." In the Church, we observe and celebrate various holidays. Holidays are holy days, days set aside for special purposes. So, a holy person is a person set aside for a special purpose. I don't belong to me; I'm not my own. I belong to the Lord.

Holiness is not a prideful attitude; it's just being different. Holiness is not withdrawing. It's not going off to a monastery or convent somewhere. To be holy means simply to be different from this world. It means to be like God. God is holy, so to be holy is to be like God. Second Peter 3:11 says, "Therefore, since all these things will be dissolved, what manner of persons ought you to be in holy conduct and godliness?" What is godliness? It simply means to be devoted to and pleasing to God. If you please God, it doesn't matter whom you displease. And if you displease God, it doesn't matter whom you please. We are meant to be pleasing to God.

- Who in your circle exemplifies this type of set-apart life?
- What are some things that please the Lord according to Scripture?

**PRACTICE THIS** Look in the Word and make a list of things that are pleasing to the Lord. Consider how this list is different from the things you would naturally value and prioritize.

For if these things are yours and abound, you will be neither
barren nor unfruitful in the knowledge of our Lord Jesus Christ.

**2 PETER 1:8**

**PONDER THIS** Do you know God, or do you know about God? If you only know about God, you study and learn facts about God, but that is not enough. The way to have a life where you will not fall is to have an intimate, personal knowledge of God.

For years, I used to carry a card in my wallet about my wife. It told all the vital statistics. It told about her size, her shoe size, her height, and various other things. You know it is extremely hard to buy a dress for a woman if you don't know the size she wears. On that card, I even noted her birthday, anniversaries, and other special occasions so I would remember them. This card gave me information about my wife. Imagine you have never met Joyce, and you said, "Tell me about your wife." So, I pulled out that card and handed it to you. You would know about her, but you would not know her. You can sit in a church and get all the facts about God. That is knowledge. But we need an intimate relationship with the Lord.

- What are some things you know about God?
- What does it look like to have a close relationship with God?

**PRACTICE THIS** Pray and ask God to show you where you are settling for knowledge *about* Him; ask Him to help you grow your relationship *with* Him.

As His divine power has given to us all things that
pertain to life and godliness, through the knowledge
of Him who called us by glory and virtue.

**2 PETER 1:3**

**PONDER THIS** Have you ever seen an elephant at the circus? That elephant will generally have an iron ring around one of its rear legs. That iron ring will have a chain that is fastened to a stake. That stake will be driven into the ground. That elephant will be there, rocking back and forth. Now, here is the interesting thing. That stake is shallowly put in the ground. That elephant could pull it out at any time. But he never tries because he thinks he cannot. When he was a baby elephant, they trained him by putting a stake in the ground very deep and putting that chain around his leg, and he pulled and could not get free. And now as a grown elephant, he has been convinced that he cannot pull that stake from the ground, and he never tries.

There are some who have been trained by the devil in the same way. You don't understand the power you have. And Satan's got you chained by some little insignificant thing when God wants to set you free and make you what you ought to be. Freedom comes through the knowledge of Jesus. Jesus died for you, and grace comes through the knowledge of Jesus. The peace all of us need—the peace *of* God, peace with God, and peace *with one another*—comes through the knowledge of Jesus Christ.

- What does it look like to live in bondage to something?
- What has Jesus set you free from? Where are you still living in bondage unnecessarily?

**PRACTICE THIS** Share with another person what you have been set free from through Jesus.

But you must continue in the things which you have
learned and been assured of, knowing from whom you
have learned them, and that from childhood you have
known the Holy Scriptures, which are able to make you
wise for salvation through faith which is in Christ Jesus.

**2 TIMOTHY 3:14-15**

**PONDER THIS** Faith goes beyond evidence. God does not need to prove anything to you. God gives you evidence, but there comes a time when you must go beyond evidence to faith. In John 7:16-17, Jesus was talking to the doubters of His day and said, "My doctrine is not Mine, but His who sent Me. If anyone wills to do His will, he shall know concerning the doctrine, whether it is from God or whether I speak on My own authority." Now what that means in plain English is if you surrender your will, God will reveal Himself to you. Faith is not an intellectual response to God.

Jesus said, "My sheep hear my voice..." (John 10:27a). If you want to know the truth, God will speak to you out of the Scriptures, and you will gain faith. The Bible says, "Beware, brethren, lest there be in any of you an evil heart of unbelief..." (Hebrews 3:12a). Note the problem is not an empty head but an evil heart. You may think you only have intellectual problems. No, you have an evil heart. God will reveal Himself to the one who wants to understand. When my eye is right, it responds to light. When my ear is right, it responds to sound. When my heart is right, it responds to God.

- How have you heard the Good Shepherd's voice through Scripture and through other believers?

- How has God given you faith as you have surrendered to Him?

**PRACTICE THIS** Ask God to speak to you through His Word today. Share what you learn with someone.

All Scripture is given by inspiration of God, and is profitable
for doctrine, for reproof, for correction, for instruction in
righteousness, that the man of God may be complete,
thoroughly equipped for every good work.
**2 TIMOTHY 3:16-17**

**PONDER THIS** All Scripture is the breath of God. When I speak, you're hearing my breath. I've taken breath into my lungs. My diaphragm is pushing against my lungs and pushing that breath up out of my throat, over my larynx, and over my tongue. My lips and teeth are taking that breath, and my vocal cords are making noise. My lips, my teeth, and my tongue are forming sounds you hear. What you hear when I speak is actually my breath. The Bible is the breath of God.

God saved me in my middle teens. I had a passing interest in the Word of God. I was in high school, just goofing off, playing ball, not studying. But then I got serious about studying. I made better grades in college than I did in high school. I made better grades in seminary than I did in college. As the work got harder, the grades got better. The reason is I began to be interested in this book, the Bible. I have grown more convinced that the Bible is the Word of God than when I started as a young preacher many years ago. I'm not finding hidden flaws. I'm finding hidden beauties. There's no way you can explain the Bible apart from divine inspiration. Faith is rooted in evidence. Faith goes beyond evidence. Faith then becomes its own best evidence.

- How has the Bible changed your life? How have you grown in your belief of the Bible?
- Why is it important to trust and believe Scripture is God-breathed?

**PRACTICE THIS** Spend some extra time in the Word today, thanking God that He has chosen to communicate with us.

## 26

But also for this very reason, giving all diligence, add to your
faith virtue, to virtue knowledge, to knowledge self-control,
to self-control perseverance, to perseverance godliness.

**2 PETER 1:5-6**

**PONDER THIS** When you observe babies, you can see they are often out of control. They often struggle with tantrums. If you have young children, you know that is true. Paul taught the importance of self-control. Are you under control? How about your sexual desires? How about your appetite for food? How about your sleep? How about your recreation? How about your quiet time?

Paul also mentioned patience or perseverance. That means steadfastness. Are you a patient person? Traffic jams, losing your keys, long lines, late airplanes, flat tires, interruptions, why do these things happen? I spilled something the other day. It went all over my stuff on my desk, ran all over into my papers that I had stacked up neatly and everything. I asked, "Why God? What is the purpose of all of that? Why would that happen?" Then I thought, "Thank You, Lord, for that—if for no other reason than just to help develop my patience." Things happen to us that we can't explain. If we can just praise God for the unexplainable, we know and understand what real patience is.

- What is more difficult for you: self-control or patience? Why?
- How can small, frustrating moments become opportunities to practice patience and self-control?

**PRACTICE THIS** The next time you feel tested in your patience or self-control, turn to the Lord in prayer and use the moment as an opportunity to grow in your faith in Him.

...to godliness brotherly kindness, and to brotherly kindness love.
For if these things are yours and abound, you will be neither
barren nor unfruitful in the knowledge of our Lord Jesus Christ.

**2 PETER 1:7-8**

**PONDER THIS** When people see you, they should be reminded of Jesus. They should also see brotherly kindness. This passage is interesting because Simon Peter, by nature, was not given to brotherly kindness. He was a debater and an arguer. One of the great pieces of evidence of the new birth is that you are kind. A little girl once said, "God, make all the bad people good and all the good people nice."

You can't imitate kindness and love, and you can't manufacture them. These are the fruit of the Spirit. Throughout your walk in faith, you can use these things as a checklist to say, "Am I growing in the grace and knowledge of our Lord and Savior Jesus Christ?"

We need a faith that knows intimately. Then we need a faith that grows: Add to your faith virtue, and add to your faith knowledge, and add to your faith these things. Don't be satisfied. Are you a growing Christian? Remember, to cease to be better is to cease to be good. We all need to grow in the grace and knowledge of our Lord and Savior at all stages of our lives.

- When was the last time you grew significantly in your faith? How can you measure this?

- How has God worked in your life to show familial love and kindness to others?

**PRACTICE THIS** Ask another believer to honestly assess how you are growing in your faith.

**28**

As you therefore have received Christ Jesus the Lord, so walk in
Him, rooted and built up in Him and established in the faith, as
you have been taught, abounding in it with thanksgiving..

**COLOSSIANS 2:6-7**

**PONDER THIS** If I said to you, "Walk in this building," where are you to walk? In this
building. The parameters of this building are to contain your walk. This building
would be the boundaries, the circumference, of your walk. Now, in this passage,
you're told to walk in the Spirit.

Now, the natural person says, "I don't like that. I don't want to be hemmed in. Are
you telling me that's all I can do, just walk in the Spirit? I want more." You are to
walk in the Lord Jesus Christ. What I'm trying to say is that nothing outside of
Jesus is worth having. You say, "Well, what about my car?" No, you can have a
house, you can have a car, you can have your clothes, and you can have all these
things, but all these things are a subset of knowing the Lord Jesus. That is, if
Jesus allows you to have them, they're gifts He gives to you. But if you must go
outside of Jesus to get any of these things, if you must transgress the law of God
to have something else, then you don't need it. He will supply everything you
need "according to His riches in glory by Christ Jesus" (Philippians 4:19b). Jesus is
the circumference of your walk.

- When have you been dissatisfied to walk in the Spirit?
- Where do you struggle to trust that God will supply all you
  need?

**PRACTICE THIS** Spend some time in prayer asking God to help you walk in His
Spirit.

"But I say to you, love your enemies, bless those who curse you, do good to those who hate you, and pray for those who spitefully use you and persecute you, that you may be sons of your Father in heaven; for He makes His sun rise on the evil and on the good, and sends rain on the just and on the unjust. For if you love those who love you, what reward have you? Do not even the tax collectors do the same?"

**MATTHEW 5:44-46**

**PONDER THIS** We are a peculiar people. As Christians, we are children of light. But the world is full of children of darkness. We live by the Spirit; they live in sin. We live by faith; they live by sight. We understand them; they do not understand us. So, what should you do when you're persecuted? Surprisingly, Jesus said to release love to those who persecute us.

And this love is not mere sympathy; it means doing good. Notice Jesus said God makes it "rain on the just and the unjust." Don't say, "Well, I'm going to treat some people nicely because they're good people and other people wrongly because they persecute me." Be like God and love them! Aren't you glad God loves sinners? Where would we be if He didn't love us? These people are blind. They don't have life. They don't understand. As a matter of fact, the Bible says in the Last Days that those who kill us will think they are doing "God's service." (See John 16:2.) They are blind and need love; we need to treat them as God has treated us.

- How do you stand out from the culture around you?
- How do you typically treat people when they hurt you?

**PRACTICE THIS** Ask a friend to tell you honestly how you react when people hurt you. Consider what it would look like to release love instead.

"So he went to him and bandaged his wounds, pouring on oil and wine; and he set him on his own animal, brought him to an inn, and took care of him. On the next day, when he departed, he took out two denarii, gave them to the innkeeper, and said to him, 'Take care of him; and whatever more you spend, when I come again, I will repay you.' So which of these three do you think was neighbor to him who fell among the thieves?" And he said, "He who showed mercy on him." Then Jesus said to him, "Go and do likewise."

**LUKE 10:34-37**

**PONDER THIS** The English word *compassion* comes from two words, *com*, meaning "with," and *passion*, which means "to feel deeply." A person who has compassion sees people through the eyes of Christ. *Compassion* means "with suffering, with feeling." The problem with so many of us is we that just don't see. We just don't look! We're so busy. We pay no attention. Suffering people are all around us. Thank God that Jesus, the Good Samaritan, saw him.

A long time ago, back when they allowed smoking in airports, I was waiting for a flight. I needed to study, so I spread out all my papers. After a while, I felt the effect of people smoking around me, so I went to another gate to get a smoke-free space. After I got settled in, a man followed me, took out a pack of cigarettes, and lit up. The old Adrian wanted to rise up, but Jesus said, "Down, boy." As I was considering moving somewhere else, he said, "Don't move, don't move. I'll put it out." The man said, "Aren't you Adrian Rogers? I need to talk to somebody. I need help. I'm hurting." And I thought to myself, *Adrian, how blind you could've been that day. How obnoxious you could've been if you would have let your old nature take over.* I'm glad God overruled the old Adrian for a moment and let the new man come through because suffering people are all around us; they're hurting, and they need help.

- Who do you know that is hurting and needs help?
- Have you ever felt God's nudging toward compassion for someone else? What was that like?

**PRACTICE THIS** Think about a time when someone had compassion for you. Thank that person for being an example of Christ to you.

Jesus answered and said to her, "Whoever drinks of this water will thirst again, but whoever drinks of the water that I shall give him will never thirst. But the water that I shall give him will become in him a fountain of water springing up into everlasting life."

**JOHN 4:13-14**

**PONDER THIS** Most people in America don't need religion. We've got enough religion. What we need is a personal, vital relationship with Jesus Christ, the Son of God, and true salvation with joy. Will you draw water from the well of salvation? What a wonderful lesson there is for us here today.

Is that your experience? Is there in you a river bubbling up? Is there in you a satisfaction because you have drunk deeply of Jesus? But more than satisfaction, are you being a blessing? Is your life overflowing with blessing? It's amazing to me how many people today are trying to find the answer. Some people think the answer is intellectual. They think if they can just learn more facts if they can just learn more theology if they can just learn more history, or if they can just learn more of this or that, then they will be satisfied. So, they go from class to class and church to church with their heads getting fuller and their hearts getting emptier.

The Pharisees thought the answer to life was the way they lived, primarily noted by what they did or didn't do. Does that sound familiar? I don't do this. I don't do that. They had religion, but they didn't have reality. It's time to stop enduring religion and start enjoying salvation. It is time that you come to understand what the great heart of Jesus longed for.

- How would you describe the difference between religion and having a relationship with God?
- What are some ways you have tried to find satisfaction with life?

**PRACTICE THIS** Consider where you may be deferring more to religion than investing in a personal relationship with Jesus. Pray and repent about these things.

And we know that all things work together for good to those who
love God, to those who are the called according to His purpose.

**ROMANS 8:28**

**PONDER THIS** Here is the faulty logic many people follow: "God is the author of all things. Evil, pain, and suffering is 'something,' so God is the author of evil, suffering, and pain." That's not the right argument. Here's the argument: God made everything, and He made it perfect. When God finished, God rested. God said, "It is good." He made man. He made man perfect, but He made man perfectly free. That is, He gave man a choice.

Why did God give man a choice? Because God wanted something from man that is unique, special, wonderful, and glorious. He wanted man's love. He wants you to love Him. That's the highest good—to love God and to love one another, for God is love. Now, why didn't God just force us to love Him? Well, forced love is a contradiction in terms. There's no such thing as forced love. Love must choose. For lovers to choose to love, they must be able to choose not to love, or else it's forced love, and it's not love at all. So, God has given us a choice.

- How do you express your love for God?
- Have you ever blamed a hard situation on God? Reflect on that situation and how you might view it differently.

**PRACTICE THIS** Spend some time thanking God for the freedom He gives us to love Him.

On the last day, that great day of the feast, Jesus stood
and cried out, saying, "If anyone thirsts, let him come to
Me and drink. He who believes in Me, as the Scripture has
said, out of his heart will flow rivers of living water."

**JOHN 7:37-38**

**PONDER THIS** Jesus stood and cried out, "If anyone thirsts." Are you thirsty? "Well," you say, "God knows I'm empty." I didn't ask if you were empty. I asked, "Are you thirsty?" My car has been empty many times, but never once has it been thirsty. Are you thirsty, or are you satisfied?

Not many people today are thirsty. Some people come to church on Sunday morning like they've done God a wild favor, but they don't come seeking God. They don't come with a burning, blistering thirst. Some might have a shallow thirst. Those who have a shallow thirst will get shallow satisfaction. Many are not thirsty at all because they're filled with the stagnant waters of self-love and worldliness.

I don't know how much of God you have, but you have all you want. It's not your job to persuade God to fill you. He wants to fill you. If you don't have any more, it's because you don't want any more. It's not because God somehow has neglected you. You've neglected God. And if you're not thirsty, I would suggest the very first thing you do is analyze your life and pray that God would help you see things and that God would give you a burning, blistering thirst so you will say, "I'm done with religion. I want reality. I am thirsty today for what's real."

- When have you been thirsty for God? What was that like?
- Do you crave to grow in your relationship with God? Why or why not? How do you need to respond to God today?

**PRACTICE THIS** Analyze your life and pray that God would help you get things in order, with Him as the One you are thirsty for.

"...but whoever drinks of the water that I shall give him will never thirst. But the water that I shall give him will become in him a fountain of water springing up into everlasting life."

**JOHN 4:14**

**PONDER THIS** Holiness is not the way to Christ; Christ is the way to holiness. You don't work your way to the way. He is the way. Don't get the idea that if you could live right, God would fill you with the Holy Spirit. You can't live right until you are filled with the Holy Spirit. If you could be holy and live right in order to be filled, why do you need to be filled anyway?

God is not like a banker. Do you know how to get a banker to loan you money? Prove to him you don't need any. Then he'll loan you some. Well, God's not that way. Come to Jesus. Don't wait 'till you're better. Don't wait 'till you're stronger. Bring your weakness. Bring your fears. Bring your failures. Bring your heartaches. Bring it all to Jesus. Jesus throws open His arms to you today and says, "Are you thirsty? Come to Me." If we could only learn that! I'm not saying you come clinging to your sin. I'm not saying you come to Him with your fingers crossed behind your back. I'm not saying you come to Him while intending to cling to Satan and this world. Oh, no. Let go of everything but come to Jesus.

- When have you tried to get your life together to "be better" for Jesus? Why does this always fail?
- What happens when we depend on our own works instead of on Jesus to be close to God?

**PRACTICE THIS** Talk to God and confess the broken parts of your life right now.

Likewise the Spirit also helps in our weaknesses. For we do not
know what we should pray for as we ought, but the Spirit Himself
makes intercession for us with groanings which cannot be uttered.

**ROMANS 8:26**

**PONDER THIS** I've been to the hospital so many times. I've seen precious saints of God writhing in pain, groaning. They're not there because of their personal sin or some clenched fist in the face of God. Some of God's choicest saints have suffered. We've all known them, have we not? And yet they groan.

Christians may groan because of their suffering, but we aren't alone—the Comforter groans because of our suffering, too. Thank God there's One in glory who groans. We serve a God with tears in His eyes. We serve a God who loves us, who cares, who said, "Cast all your care upon Me, for I care for you." (See 1 Peter 5:7.) There's the groaning of creation, the groaning of the Christian, and the groaning of the Comforter, the Spirit. Why did I say Comforter? He's called the *paraclete*. That means "One who's called alongside us." You don't have to bear the pain alone.

- When have you felt alone in your faith?
- How does it make you feel to know God has given you a Comforter for every situation and trial in your life?

**PRACTICE THIS** Look up some verses that remind you God is with you during difficult times. Write them down on sticky notes and place them around your home as reminders that God is with you.

O my God, my soul is cast down within me; therefore I will remember You from the land of the Jordan, and from the heights of Hermon, from the Hill Mizar. Deep calls unto deep at the noise of Your waterfalls; all Your waves and billows have gone over me.

**PSALM 42:6-7**

**PONDER THIS** The River Jordan is called the river of death. *Jordan* means "descent and judgment." It starts up on Mount Hermon. Mount Hermon towers 9,000 feet above sea level. It takes a torturous path down to the Dead Sea. The Dead Sea is 1,300 feet below sea level. And the River Jordan just flows down to the Dead Sea never to emerge again. In Bible typology, Jordan has been a picture of death and despair. I've been up the headwaters of the Jordan where the waterfalls are. David felt like he was just being washed over by circumstances. God's waterspouts were coming over him. He was deluged with problems, and he didn't know where to turn. His circumstances seemed overwhelming. Maybe you feel that way today.

Don't let Satan blow out the candle of hope. You need to look inward and analyze your heart. You need to look upward and realize your help. You need to look onward and realize your hope. God's going to turn your Calvary to an Easter. God is going to turn every tear into a pearl. God is going to arch the rainbow of His grace over your sorrows. God will never be satisfied until he meets the deepest needs of your heart, and you will never be satisfied until your greatest desire is for Him alone.

- Have you ever felt overwhelmed by circumstances like David? How do you respond in those moments?
- What are some of the deepest needs of our hearts that God meets?

**PRACTICE THIS** Tell a friend about the circumstances in life that are overwhelming you and bring them to the Lord together.

**6**

"Look at the birds of the air, for they neither sow nor reap
nor gather into barns; yet your heavenly Father feeds
them. Are you not of more value than they? Which of
you by worrying can add one cubit to his stature?"

**MATTHEW 6:26-27**

**PONDER THIS** When I was young, someone told me something I've never forgotten: "Adrian, there are two categories of things you should never worry about. Number one: things that you can do something about. If you can do something about it, don't worry about it, do it. The second category that you should never worry about are things you can't do anything about. If you can't do anything about it, worry's not going to change it." Now that may seem simplistic, but there's a lot of wisdom there. At best, worry is useless; at worst, worry is absolutely harmful.

Worry is harmful to you physically. It'll do the same thing to you physiologically that sand will do to machinery. Someone said that little ants can pick the carcass of a dead animal cleaner than lions can. It seems like it's those little nagging things that ultimately pull us down. Not only is worry harmful to you, but it's also harmful to others. Do you like to be around people who worry all the time? I know individuals, when they walk into a room it seems like somebody just turned the lights off, and they brighten up the room when they leave it. Worry is harmful to you and it's harmful to other people.

- What do you tend to worry about the most?
- How have you seen the harm and damage of worry in your life?

**PRACTICE THIS** Talk with a trusted friend about the things that worry you most.

"So why do you worry about clothing? Consider the lilies of
the field, how they grow: they neither toil nor spin; and yet I
say to you that even Solomon in all his glory was not arrayed
like one of these. Now if God so clothes the grass of the field,
which today is, and tomorrow is thrown into the oven, will
He not much more clothe you, O you of little faith?"

**MATTHEW 6:28-30**

**PONDER THIS** I had a couple come to see me who were in their early twenties, and they had a little baby with them. The woman was in tears. The man was near tears. I said, "Well, tell me what your difficulty is." And without telling you the whole story, they said their difficulty was they didn't have anything. They didn't have a house or a car. They had meager jobs, and they saw everybody else had all these things. I said, "I want to tell you kids something. You don't know how wealthy you are." I said, "Would you sell this baby?" They said, "No! We wouldn't sell our baby for anything." I continued, "Let's look at your health. Suppose a millionaire were to come to you and say, 'Let's do a head exchange. Take your head and put it on my body; take my head and put it on your body, and we'll just exchange, and I'll have your body.'" I said, "If such an operation were possible, would you exchange your body for an old man's body who is about to die, for millions of dollars?" I concluded, "Look at that baby. Look at your health. Look at your marriage. You are wealthy!" After that their tune changed. The problem had been they were focusing on what they felt was an uncertain future, rather than thanking God for the blessings they had right there. Worry buries blessings.

- How have you seen the reality that worry buries blessings?
- What are some things you can thank God for today?

**PRACTICE THIS** Write a list of the blessings you have today and thank God for them.

Let all bitterness, wrath, anger, clamor, and evil speaking be put away from you, with all malice. And be kind to one another, tenderhearted, forgiving one another, even as God in Christ forgave you.

**EPHESIANS 4:31-32**

**PONDER THIS** Don't forgive after you have collected your revenge. Sometimes people hurt us, and we say, "They don't know how much they hurt me. I'm going to teach them how much I've been hurt. I'm going to blame them; I'm going to castigate them; and I'm going to make them suffer. And after they've suffered, after they've wept, after they've pleaded, after they've bled, after I've gotten my pound of flesh—then perhaps I'll forgive." Has anybody ever treated you that way and then finally said, "OK, I'll forgive you"? What do you feel like saying? You don't need to be forgiven. You've already paid. Followers of Jesus are called to forgive freely. You should be so anxious to forgive people that you chase them and catch them to forgive them.

Isn't that what God has done for us? Why do we love Him? Because He first loved us. When Adam and Eve sinned against God in the Garden of Eden, God did not sit up in Heaven and say, "Well, I'm going to wait, and if they come to me, I might be persuaded to forgive them." God came to the garden and God said, "Adam, where are you?" That wasn't the voice of a detective. That was the voice of a brokenhearted God who was seeking someone who had sinned against Him to forgive him freely.

- Who do you need to forgive today?
- What does it look like to be eager to forgive? How can you forgive even when full reconciliation is not possible?

**PRACTICE THIS** Consider if there is anyone you are holding a grudge against. Ask the Lord to help you forgive that person freely today.

Why are you cast down, O my soul? And why
are you disquieted within me?
Hope in God; for I shall yet praise Him, the help
of my countenance and my God.

**PSALM 42:11**

**PONDER THIS** If you're down, you can get up with the help of God. God has a way for you. Not by some cheap pop psychology. Not by somebody slapping you on the back and saying, "Atta boy or girl." We are called to hope in God. God Himself will see you through.

Somebody once said, "God is too good to be unkind, too wise to make a mistake, and when we cannot trace His hand, we can trust His heart." Look inward and analyze your heart. "Why am I cast down?" Look upward and recognize your hope and your help.

You also can look onward and realize your hope. Look again at today's verse, "Why are you cast down, O my soul? And why are you disquieted within me? Hope in God; for I shall yet praise Him." No matter how bleak your circumstances, God is with you. Don't lose hope. God has a future for you filled with hope. "I shall yet praise Him." The psalmist took his soul and said, "Hope in God." Hope does not mean a vain wish. It means "a definite assurance based on anticipation."

- How do you seek hope in God on a regular basis?
- How would hoping in God affect what you're walking through right now?

**PRACTICE THIS** Talk to a friend to find out where he or she is struggling. Remind that friend of the hope of God in every circumstance.

Why are you cast down, O my soul? And why are you
disquieted within me? Hope in God, for I shall yet
praise Him for the help of His countenance.

**PSALM 42:5**

**PONDER THIS** The psalmist said to his soul, "Why are you cast down, O my soul?" Now this is where you have to take control. You have to look your soul straight in the eye and say, "Soul, why are you feeling this way?" You have to look within and analyze your heart. Why are you depressed?

Maybe you've lost a loved one to death. Maybe it's a child. Maybe it's a spouse. If you've lost a loved one, pour out your grief to God. Ask your friends to help share your grief and realize that life is not over for you. Whatever it is, refuse to brood and rehearse it over and over again. It does no good. If you've had a heartbreak, see what you've learned from that heartbreak and then go out and begin to develop some new relationships. Perhaps you have sinned or done some grievous thing, and you're being haunted by the ghost of guilt. What do you do? Confess it to God. If you need to confess it to someone else and ask for forgiveness, do it. If you can make restitution, do it. Do what you do and then close the door behind it. Analyze. Look at your heart. Ask yourself, "Why am I cast down?"

- What are some things that have caused you to be cast down?
- Where do you typically turn when you are downcast?

**PRACTICE THIS** Share with someone how God has worked in your life in a moment when you were downcast.

Bearing with one another, and forgiving one another,
if anyone has a complaint against another; even
as Christ forgave you, so you also must do.

**COLOSSIANS 3:13**

**PONDER THIS** Make sure you forgive. I had somebody come to me yesterday and say, "I want you to forgive me." My first inclination was to say, "Don't worry about it. That's okay." But I realized that would have been wrong of me because that was not forgiveness. What that individual needed and deserved was forgiveness. So, I didn't just say, "Don't worry about it. Forget it." I said, "I forgive you." That's very important. You see, sometimes when we do wrong, we don't go to another individual and say, "Forgive me." We say, "If I have hurt your feelings, I'm sorry. I want to apologize." Essentially what we are saying with that is, "I want to apologize and explain to you why I did what I did."

The word *apologize* comes from the Greek word, *apologia*, which means "to make a defense." In apologetics, we're defending the faith. So many of us want to apologize and what we're doing is defending ourselves. If you've wronged somebody, don't apologize, instead say, "Would you forgive me? I was wrong." And if somebody's wronged you, don't just say, "Oh, forget it. Never mind." Say, "I forgive you." Do it fully. Then it's buried in the grave of God's forgetfulness. Forgive fully.

- What is the difference between an apology and asking for forgiveness?

- When have you felt tempted to defend your actions in an apology?

**PRACTICE THIS** Take a moment and consider who you have offended or hurt and ask that person to forgive you.

Then Jesus said to them, "Most assuredly, I say to
you, unless you eat the flesh of the Son of Man and
drink His blood, you have no life in you."

**JOHN 6:53**

**PONDER THIS** So many people have never understood what it means to eat Jesus' flesh and drink His blood. You want me to tell you why we're failing? We can be going to Heaven, and we can thank God for the shed blood, which is saving blood, but He gave Himself for us so that we might take Him in and receive what we need. He said we are to do this so that His life might be in us.

In Romans 5:10, Paul said, "If when we were enemies we were reconciled to God through the death of His Son, much more, having been reconciled, we shall be saved by His life." We are saved by His life! God didn't just forgive you and say, "All right. Now gut it out. Live it as best you can." No. Just as in my human body, everything that I need to exist is delivered by red blood cells—those little boats coursing through all these channels in my physiological makeup—so everything I need to live the Christian life is in Jesus. But I must take Him in to receive it.

- What have you learned from Jesus about the Christian life?
- How has your relationship with Jesus changed the way you live your life?

**PRACTICE THIS** Pray and thank God for giving you everything you need for life with Him.

But if we walk in the light as He is in the light, we
have fellowship with one another, and the blood of
Jesus Christ His Son cleanses us from all sin.

**1 JOHN 1:7**

**PONDER THIS** Did you know your blood cells are not only bringing the things you need, but those cells are also hauling away the garbage? Those red cells give you all the stuff you need. Then they pick up all the uric acid, carbon dioxide, and so many other poisons and toxins and carry them away. They're carrying them to the lungs to be expelled or to the kidneys to be pushed out. It would be amazing if you could get the delivery truck to be the garbage truck at the same time, wouldn't it? That's what God has done. No wonder the Psalmist said, "I am fearfully and wonderfully made" (Psalm 139:14a).

The blood not only supplies every need, but it also cleanses constantly. Jesus cleanses us from our sins. Not "it cleansed," past tense; it is continually cleansing us. I know a lot of people who live painfully because they've let toxins build up in their lives: worry, envy, jealousy, fear, pride, bitterness, and doubt! Those things build up. And if you don't allow the shared blood to constantly cleanse you, you're going to live a life of pain.

- When was the last time you asked Jesus to cleanse you?
- When have you been overwhelmed with toxins like worry or bitterness? How does Jesus give freedom from these things?

**PRACTICE THIS** Consider what toxins may be building up in your life. Ask Jesus to cleanse you from your sin.

The sting of death is sin, and the strength of sin is the law.
But thanks be to God, who gives us the victory through
our Lord Jesus Christ. Therefore, my beloved brethren, be
steadfast, immovable, always abounding in the work of the
Lord, knowing that your labor is not in vain in the Lord.

**1 CORINTHIANS 15:56-58**

**PONDER THIS** What's the difference between a diamond and a lump of coal? Both are made of carbon. The coal is carbon in humiliation; the diamond is carbon in glory. They are the same substance, only improved and changed. Likewise, one day, we're going to go from corruption to incorruption. We're going to go from dishonor to glory.

None of us has ever even seen a man as man was intended to be. You don't realize what God made when He made you. Centuries of sin have marred and scarred and debilitated mankind.

Suppose you had never seen a railroad train. There's a train wreck nearby, and I take you out to see it and say, "There's a train." Have you seen a train? It's debatable. I guess you could say you've seen a train, but what you've really seen is a train wreck. One of these days, all the limitations of this world will fall away, and there will be no more weakness, no more sighing, no more crying, no more dying, and no more trying. We will have that perfection God wants us to have.

- How should victory in Jesus change your perspective on life today?

- How does it encourage you to remember the hope of glory?

**PRACTICE THIS** Pray and ask God to help you live for your hope in eternity rather than for the temporary pleasures of today.

For we walk by faith, not by sight. We are confident, yes,
well pleased rather to be absent from the body and to
be present with the Lord. Therefore we make it our aim,
whether present or absent, to be well pleasing to Him.

**2 CORINTHIANS 5:7-9**

**PONDER THIS** A little boy and his sister were with their mother in the garden and a big bumblebee stung the little boy. He cried and jumped up into his mother's arms. The bee continued to buzz around, and the little girl was frightened to death. The little boy, by this time, had his tears dried, and the mother said, "Sweetheart, you don't have to be afraid of that bee." She said, "But he stung brother." She said, "Yes, but come over here and look." And there on brother's hand was the stinger, still in that flesh, and she pulled it out and said, "See there? He left his stinger in brother. You can't be stung because that bee has lost his stinger."

I want to tell you: the Lord Jesus took the sting of sin for me and for you. Death may buzz and frighten you, but friend, the sting is gone because of the Lord Jesus Christ. "Oh, Death, where is your sting? Oh, Hades, where is your victory" (1 Corinthians 15:55)? Jesus has taken the pain out of parting, the dread out of dying, and the gloom out of the grave. Because of Him, we have steadfast and sure hope.

- How afraid are you of the sting of death? Does this change with your circumstances? Why or why not?

- How does Jesus' victory over death and sin change the way you live today?

**PRACTICE THIS** Spend some time praising God for how He has taken away the sting of death.

"I have been crucified with Christ; it is no longer I who live, but Christ lives in me; and the life which I now live in the flesh I live by faith in the Son of God, who loved me and gave Himself for me."

**GALATIANS 2:20**

**PONDER THIS** I start my day by lifting my hands to God and saying, "God, I thank You for Jesus. Jesus, thank You that You gave Yourself *for* me." That is saving blood. Then I lift my hands, and I say, "Thank You, Jesus, that You gave Yourself *to* me!" That is the shared blood. Then I lift my hands in surrender, and I say, "Now, Lord, live Your life through me. I am Yours today." He didn't just forgive me and say, "Okay, Adrian, it's up to you." He gave Himself for us so that He might give Himself to us so that He might live His life through us.

Just as you survive by the blood flowing in your body right now, the blood of Jesus Christ, the life of God, flows through His Church. It is the blood that cleanses. It hasn't just cleansed; it continually cleanses us each day.

- When have you tried to live life on your own terms? What was that like?
- How do you remind yourself to daily surrender to Christ?

**PRACTICE THIS** Find a way like the one described today to remind yourself of God's purpose through you every morning.

"These things I have spoken to you, that in Me you may
have peace. In the world you will have tribulation; but
be of good cheer, I have overcome the world."

**JOHN 16:33**

**PONDER THIS** Smallpox used to be a devastating disease. When Cortez, the explorer, came and visited the Aztec Indians, he left behind one of his soldiers who had smallpox. In two years, four million of the Aztecs died because they didn't have any antibodies. Then, one day, scientists learned how to immunize by taking a weakened form of a disease and putting it in a human body so that the weakened form of that disease could then mobilize and get the name, rank, and serial number of these invaders and call the army to war. Do you know what they call blood that has had this disease and overcome this disease? They call it wise blood.

The blood of Jesus is wise blood. Anything Jesus has overcome, we can overcome. Satan has no power against the blood of Jesus Christ that flows through His body, the Church. This is the shared blood. Jesus said in John 6:53-54, "Most assuredly, I say to you, unless you eat the flesh of the Son of Man and drink His blood, you have no life in you. Whoever eats My flesh and drinks My blood has eternal life, and I will raise him up at the last day."

- When was a time you felt powerless against the influence of the world?

- How can you remind yourself of the wise blood of Christ when you feel powerless?

**PRACTICE THIS** Spend some time in prayer about the things in life that threaten to overwhelm you. Ask Jesus to help you overcome through His wise blood.

For if anyone thinks himself to be something, when he is nothing,
he deceives himself. But let each one examine his own work, and
then he will have rejoicing in himself alone, and not in another.

**GALATIANS 6:3-4**

**PONDER THIS** Do you know Jesus raised three people from the dead? He raised a little girl who had just died (See Mark 5:21-43.), a young man on the way to his funeral (See Luke 7:11-17.), and He raised Lazarus. (See John 11:38-44.) How did He raise that little girl? She had just died. Jesus went into her bedroom and said, "All the rest of you just stay out. You don't believe." But Jesus took that little girl and said, "Darling, get up!" She woke up. Her body was still warm. And then Jesus raised a man. He was on the way to the funeral. He was being transported. Now he was dead also, but his body was cold. Rigor mortis had set in. And Jesus raised him. Then Jesus raised Lazarus. Lazarus had been in the grave for four days. Corruption had already begun. The stench of death was there. And God raised Lazarus.

I want to ask you a question: Which one was the deadest? Dead is dead. It doesn't matter whether you were like that little girl, like that young man, or like Lazarus. Dead is dead. There may be degrees of corruption but not degrees of death. Dead is dead. We must stop comparing ourselves to others and saying, "I'm better than him. I'm better than her." That's like dead people saying, "You're more dead than I am." Dead is dead; we all need God's power at work in us.

- When have you compared yourself to someone else in matters of faith?
- How does pride inhibit intimacy with Christ?

**PRACTICE THIS** Take time and consider where you have pridefully compared yourself with others. Repent and ask God to show His power in you.

Therefore lay aside all filthiness and overflow of
wickedness, and receive with meekness the implanted
word, which is able to save your souls.

**JAMES 1:21**

**PONDER THIS** You've got to grow in the grace and knowledge of our Lord and Savior, Jesus Christ. When we get saved, we receive life through the Lord Jesus Christ, but all of us have the graveclothes of the old life. Maybe you are saved, but you hit your thumb with a hammer, and those old words come out. Or you're in a grocery store, and there are some questionable magazines, and your eyes want to go there. And you wonder, "Lord, have I been saved at all?" Yes, if you've trusted Jesus, if you have exercised faith in Jesus, then you're saved. But what you need to do now is initiate freedom in Jesus.

Do you know what the job of the Church is? For one thing, it's to unwrap the saints. There are a lot of people who need to be unwrapped. There are a lot of people who do not have freedom. I want to tell you about Jesus. The One who gives us life also gives us liberty.

If you're still in the graveclothes, you need to be unwrapped. Jesus is not a probation officer; Jesus is our Savior. He will see you through all the way. You might have some hangover sins for a while. But He will save you; the One who gives you life will give you liberty.

- What "graveclothes" are you still wearing?
- How have you experienced freedom in Christ?

**PRACTICE THIS** Talk to another Christian about the grave clothes you may still be wearing. Ask your friend to pray alongside you as you ask the Lord to free you from those things.

...and they commanded the people, saying, "When you see the ark
of the covenant of the LORD your God, and the priests, the Levites,
bearing it, then you shall set out from your place and go after it."

**JOSHUA 3:3**

**PONDER THIS** A while ago we got our family together to go look at the Christmas lights. I have a neighbor whose house is so beautifully decorated, and they were telling us about another beautiful house, and he said, "Now you need to go here." He began to explain it to me, and it got kind of convoluted. So, the neighbor said, "Wait a minute, Pastor, just let me get in my car, and I'll lead you there." I didn't have to worry about a street name or a direction; the only thing concerning me was his taillights as I followed where he went. When he moved, I moved, and he took me right where I needed to go. This is similar to what we see in this passage, which says, in effect, "When the ark moves, you go after it. Let God guide you with His presence."

Have you ever wanted God to explain things to you? Have you ever argued with God and said, "Lord, tell me why?" The reality is you couldn't understand if He told you, and if He did, you would likely try to bend God's will to fit yours. In my life, the only way I've known the plan of God is not to look into the future but to call to God and say, "Lord, lead me."

- When has God guided you, even if you didn't know where you were going?
- What do you do to discern how to best follow God?

**PRACTICE THIS** Ask a fellow Christian to share a testimony about how God has led him or her.

Wait on the LORD; be of good courage, and He shall
strengthen your heart; wait, I say, on the LORD!

**PSALM 27:14**

**PONDER THIS** Have you ever become impatient with the Lord, wondering why God doesn't move sooner? Did you know you can do the right thing at the wrong time? Moses sought to deliver the children of Israel, but he didn't wait on God, so he ended up killing an Egyptian and spent forty years on the back side of the desert, going around in circles. (See Exodus 2:11-22.) He moved before God moved.

Jesus was never in a hurry; Jesus was never late, and Jesus accomplished everything God gave Him to do. Now, I'm sure many people were impatient with Jesus; they wanted to know, "Jesus, why aren't you in a bigger rush?" Jesus spent thirty years in a carpenter's shop. We might think *Hey if you're the Messiah, why are you wasting thirty years*? Do you know what He said repeatedly? "My hour has not yet come" (John 2:4b). He was waiting on God.

Mary and Martha came to Jesus saying, "Come, help, Lazarus is sick" (John 11:3, author's paraphrase). Jesus delayed and waited until Lazarus was dead, and then He came and raised him. At first, the people were pouting and then they were praising. Trust God's timing.

- When have you tried to do something in your time instead of God's? How did that work out?
- What makes it difficult to trust God's timing?

**PRACTICE THIS** Make a list of the things you are impatient with God about. Ask Him to guide you to patience in those areas.

"Nevertheless I tell you the truth. It is to your advantage
that I go away; for if I do not go away, the Helper will not
come to you; but if I depart, I will send Him to you."

**JOHN 16:7**

**PONDER THIS** There is a problem when we ask the question, "What would Jesus do if He were here?" Here's the problem: He is here. He's not far away beyond the blue, peering down through the clouds, saying, "You work it out." He says, "I will come to you. I will abide in you now." The Christian life is not lived by you; it's lived by Jesus in you. If it's lived where you live, it will be Jesus Christ living that life in you. That's the secret.

It is better that Jesus went back to Heaven and sent the Holy Spirit. Most of us think, "Wouldn't it be wonderful if we could just have lived back in the time when Jesus was here in the flesh, walking the shores of Galilee?" But the truth is, we have the advantage over those who walked bodily with Jesus. They experienced Jesus on the outside; we have His presence inside to guide us.

- What intimidates you about serving God? How does it encourage you to know God's power is in you?
- How can you remind yourself that the Holy Spirit lives in you and will guide you each day?

**PRACTICE THIS** Write out Galatians 2:20 on an index card and put it somewhere you will see it every morning to remind yourself of your identity in Jesus.

Behold, I stand at the door and knock. If anyone
hears My voice and opens the door, I will come in
to him and dine with him, and he with Me.

**REVELATION 3:20**

**PONDER THIS** Being saved is not about a penalty you pay to get to Heaven. When I invite you to come to Jesus, I'm not inviting you to a funeral; I'm inviting you to a feast. Jesus is saying, "Come and dine. Come and dine." He says, "I'll come in as the guest, and then I'll become the host." Jesus bids you to come and have fellowship with Him.

First, you put faith in Jesus. Then you have freedom through Jesus and fellowship with Jesus. Are you having that fellowship? I can tell you Jesus is as real to me as a person sitting in the same room with me. I don't see Him, but Jesus is a friend. And I feast with Him and fellowship with Him. The devil wants to get you thinking negatively about God. God is good all the time, and He's saying to you, "Come and dine."

- When have you thought negatively about God or had a hard time experiencing fellowship with Him?
- How does it change your perspective to remember Jesus is inviting you to His feast?

**PRACTICE THIS** Have a meal with other Christians and praise God for all He has done.

Therefore, if anyone is in Christ, he is a new creation; old things
have passed away; behold, all things have become new.

**2 CORINTHIANS 5:17**

**PONDER THIS** When a man is no longer afraid to die, he's ready to live for the first time. Lazarus knew Jesus was the resurrection and the life. Lazarus' testimony, loyalty, and faithfulness to Jesus caused many other people to believe. (See John 12:9-11.) He exercised faithfulness to Jesus. The chief priests and others came to intimidate him. But that didn't slow Lazarus down at all. Are you exercising faithfulness to Jesus? Are you afraid of what people think? You don't want to carry your Bible to work? You don't want to bow your head in a restaurant and pray and thank God because you're afraid somebody might be watching? Let me tell you something: the best argument for Jesus and the best argument against Jesus is the life of a Christian. They came to see Lazarus, whom Jesus raised from the dead, and there were people being saved because they could see in Lazarus' supernatural life.

What about you is different than the rest of the people who live on your street? What about you cannot be explained apart from a miracle? The only right we have to ask anybody else to believe in our Savior is something they cannot explain in our lives. We are the evidence, as well as the witnesses. We are the changed lives. Is that true of you?

- What is different about your life relative to the lives of those around you?
- Who is an example to you of living a changed life? What can you learn from that person?

**PRACTICE THIS** Ask another Christian to share with you about how Jesus changed his or her life.

"And I will pray the Father, and He will give you another Helper,
that He may abide with you forever—the Spirit of truth, whom
the world cannot receive, because it neither sees Him nor
knows Him; but you know Him, for He dwells with you and will
be in you. I will not leave you orphans; I will come to you."

**JOHN 14:16-18**

**PONDER THIS** You can go deeper into Jesus, but you'll never go beyond Jesus. A Spirit-filled person, a Spirit-filled church, will make much of Jesus Christ. That's what it's all about. You'll never go beyond the Lord Jesus Christ. The Spirit has come to promote the worship of Jesus. And, by the way, this is the key to being filled and staying filled. Some of you pray, "Dear God, fill me with the Holy Spirit." Why do you want to be filled with the Holy Spirit? Well, I want to be a great preacher. God says, "I'm not interested." You may pray, "God, fill me with the Holy Spirit. I want to understand the Bible," or "I want to be a soul winner," or "I want to live a holy life." Again, God says, "I'm not interested." Even though all those things sound noble and important to God, there is still something wrong. The prayer needs to be, "Lord, I want Jesus Christ to be glorified in my life." He says, "Is that what you want? That's what I want, too. Let's get together." God will fill you with the Holy Spirit. And, by the way, He may make you a great preacher, help you understand the Bible, help you to be a soul winner, and guide you to live a holy life. But all of those are subsets of the main thing, and that is the glory of Jesus Christ. That's why the Holy Spirit has come. He will not speak on His own authority. He will take of what is Mine and declare *it* to you. (See John 16:13-14.)

- What does it look like to glorify Jesus with your life?
- What reasons have you asked God to fill you with the Holy Spirit?

**PRACTICE THIS** Share with another Christian the reasons why you want to be filled with the Holy Spirit. Pray together to ask God to fill you with the Holy Spirit to glorify Jesus.

"These things I have spoken to you, that My joy may
remain in you, and that your joy may be full."

**JOHN 15:11**

**PONDER THIS** In the Book of Hebrews, the Bible says God the Father has anointed the Lord Jesus with the oil of gladness above His companions. (See Hebrews 1:9.) The word *gladness* there is another word for joy. What it literally means is "joy that leaps and dances." Can you imagine Jesus leaping and dancing? That's the kind of joy He has. It is an abounding joy—not half-hearted, not maybe-so joy—but supernatural, abundant joy.

If you don't see Jesus as joyful, you've not seen Jesus. Don't think of Jesus as some pale, sanctimonious, religious recluse with ice water for blood. Jesus had a life of abounding joy. Happiness depends on what happens, and that's why we call it happiness. If that's what you're waiting for and that's what you depend on, then I can tell you clearly and plainly you're going to be a prisoner of circumstances. That's the time you're going to need joy. Happiness depends on what happens; joy depends on what? The Lord. "Rejoice in the Lord always" (Philippians 4:4a). The only way you can rejoice always is to rejoice in the Lord because He never changes. Joy is not the subtraction of problems from life; joy is the addition of power to meet those problems. You're going to have problems, but the joy we have in the Lord Jesus Christ is abundant.

- How have you experienced Christ's joy? When is it most difficult for you to rejoice in the Lord?

- Are you more likely to be driven by your circumstances or by hope in Jesus?

**PRACTICE THIS** Spend some time rejoicing, praising God for who He is by singing, writing, or dancing.

"Abide in Me, and I in you. As the branch cannot bear fruit of itself, unless it abides in the vine, neither can you, unless you abide in Me. I am the vine, you are the branches. He who abides in Me, and I in him, bears much fruit; for without Me you can do nothing."

**JOHN 15:4-5**

**PONDER THIS** A branch exists for one reason: the vine. It makes a full surrender to the vine. You say, "But, Pastor, I've got a family; I've got a job; I've got this; and I've got that. How can I just have one issue?" Well, you must totally, completely abide in the vine. If you don't do that, you're not going to have joy. And how do you abide? Full surrender. Have you ever made a full surrender?

Imagine a human being could have a conversation with a branch. The branch would say to the human being, "Now, you human beings think you're so intelligent, but you always seem frustrated to me, rushing around, knocking things over; no rest, no peace." And the man says to the branch, "Well, you seem to have peace. How do you do it?" He says, "I've reduced all my concerns to one, and that is to abide in the vine. And once I do that, worry has to go. When summertime comes and I need a drink of water, I don't worry about where it comes from. That's the vine's business. I abide in the vine, and the vine puts its roots down into the soil and brings up that moisture for my wilted leaves. And then, in springtime, when I need buds, I don't worry about where those buds are going to come from. I abide in the vine. And when the time of vintage and harvest comes, I don't worry about the grapes: how big, how few, how sweet. It's none of my business. I don't produce the fruit." You will have joy when you abide in the vine.

- What does it look like to abide in Jesus?
- How has abiding in Jesus impacted your life?

**PRACTICE THIS** Through prayer, surrender anything you have been wrestling with to God and abide in Him.

I will lift up my eyes to the hills—from whence comes my help?
My help comes from the LORD, who made heaven and earth.

**PSALM 121:1-2**

**PONDER THIS** The psalmist's first thought was not his last resort. He didn't turn to the Lord after he'd tried everything else like so many of us do. The very first thing he did when trouble came was seek the Lord. That's what Jesus told us to do. "Seek first the kingdom of God and His righteousness" (Matthew 6:33a).

Let me tell you something that seems backward. You might be getting in the way by trying to solve someone's problem. The problem may be God's way to bring that individual to Himself. Rather than trying to solve the problem, the best thing might be simply to encourage that individual to seek the Lord. A problem is an opportunity to seek God in times of trouble. At the very least, we seek the Lord as we seek to solve problems. Hebrews 4:16 says, "Let us therefore come boldly to the throne of grace, that we may obtain mercy and find grace to help in time of need." We have times of need. We can come boldly to the Lord and establish our purpose to seek Him.

- Have you ever tried to solve someone's problems without pointing that person to God? Why might that lead to further trouble?
- When has someone counseled you to seek God? How has He met you in these moments?

**PRACTICE THIS** When you speak to a friend today, remind him or her to seek God.

"The queen of the South will rise up in the judgment
with this generation and condemn it, for she came from
the ends of the earth to hear the wisdom of Solomon;
and indeed a greater than Solomon is here."

**MATTHEW 12:42**

**PONDER THIS** I'm so happy in Jesus. It may sound corny, but I love Him with all my heart, and I want to love Him more. I am His worker. You're His worker. Solomon's workers were happy, but Jesus gives more. Jesus gives joy unspeakable and full of glory. Jesus gives joy that is conspicuous, continuous, and contagious. Solomon's workers eventually had to give up all the things that brought them happiness. The palace was gone. The tables were gone. The robes were gone. Solomon was gone.

But the source of my joy does not diminish because my joy does not depend on what happens; it depends on the Lord Jesus Christ. I thank God for the joy of serving Jesus. I am incredibly blessed that God has let me serve Him these years and be a pastor. You are not living for a temporary purpose; your joy is lasting because of Jesus. First Corinthians 15:58 says, "Therefore, my beloved brethren, be steadfast, immovable, always abounding in the work of the Lord, knowing that your labor is not in vain in the Lord." That is because the work of the Lord has an eternal purpose. Jesus pleases His workers; Jesus rewards His workers, and Jesus is far greater than Solomon.

- How does serving Jesus bring you joy?
- How does it encourage you to know that when you live for Jesus, you live for an eternal purpose with eternal joy?

**PRACTICE THIS** Serve your church in some way today with joy, whether by volunteering to help somewhere or by sending an encouraging note to your pastor.

Make a joyful shout to the LORD, all you lands! Serve the LORD
with gladness; come before His presence with singing. Know
that the LORD, He is God; it is He who has made us, and not we
ourselves; we are His people and the sheep of His pasture.

**PSALM 100:1-3**

**PONDER THIS** In 2 Chronicles 20:18, as Jehoshaphat prepared for battle, the
Bible says, "And Jehoshaphat bowed his head with his face to the ground, and
all Judah and the inhabitants of Jerusalem bowed before the LORD, worshiping
the LORD." He fell on his face in worship; then he was ready for battle. Nothing
will prepare you for battle like worship. The person who can kneel before God
can stand before any problem. It will be a great day when we learn that worship
comes before either work or warfare. So many times, we just want to get at it
without worshiping God.

It reminds me of the little boys who were playing ball. They only had one ball, and
they lost it, so they were out in the weeds looking for it. And after a while, one of
them said, "Forget the ball. Let's get on with the game." I think sometimes that's
what we do as believers. We forget to worship and think we can just go on about
our business. Worship reminds us of what we are made for; it reminds us of the
point of the game.

- Why is it important that worship comes before all we do? Why
  do we often forget this?

- We all worship something. How are our days and priorities
  shaped by what we worship?

**PRACTICE THIS** Look up Psalms about worshiping God. Pray these back to God
in worship.

Continue earnestly in prayer, being vigilant in it with thanksgiving...

**COLOSSIANS 4:2**

**PONDER THIS** The battle is the Lord's, but God says you're going to have a part. What was Jehoshaphat's part in 2 Chronicles 20? Praise. God says, "The battle is mine, but I'm not going to do one thing until you praise." What if they said, "Well, Lord, as soon as You give us the victory, we're going to sing"? God says, "No, I'm not going to give you any victory until you start singing." Are you willing to praise God during your problems? Can you praise in the face of your enemy when you don't have anything but the promise of God? He says, "I will not leave you or forsake you. The battle is not yours; it's Mine." (See 1 Chronicles 28:20.) Now get out there and praise the Lord!

You see, a lack of praise is really unbelief. The Bible teaches that when we praise the Lord, we're really expressing faith in God. Prayer and praise go together. Prayer and praise are the two wings of spiritual power. Prayer infuses us with the energy of God, and praise confuses the enemies of God. The devil is allergic to praise. When we praise God, He sends confusion into the camp of our enemies.

- When have you praised God before going into something difficult? How does this impact you and your perspective?
- Why is God worthy of praise, no matter our circumstances?

**PRACTICE THIS** What are some things you have been wrestling with lately? Praise God for who He is and pray through these matters.

Let this mind be in you which was also in Christ Jesus, who,
being in the form of God, did not consider it robbery to be equal
with God, but made Himself of no reputation, taking the form
of a bondservant, and coming in the likeness of men. And being
found in appearance as a man, He humbled Himself and became
obedient to the point of death, even the death of the cross.

**PHILIPPIANS 2:5-8**

**PONDER THIS** Jesus Christ came in human form. It's as much a heresy to deny the humanity of Jesus as it is to deny the deity of Jesus. He wasn't all God and no man; He wasn't all man and no God; He was the God-Man. There has never been another like the Lord Jesus Christ. So, remember the humanity of the Lord Jesus Christ. If you deny the humanity of Jesus, you're denying Christianity. He is an eternal fact, and He is a physical fact. Thank God for Jesus' humanity. Apart from His humanity, we couldn't be saved. He became a man to die on the cross, and apart from "the shedding of blood, there is no remission" of sins (Hebrews 9:22b). Apart from His humanity, we have no example. We can't follow as an example the God of glory because we're human, but we can walk as Jesus walked. When Jesus Christ was on this Earth, He did not pull rank on us. Every miracle He did, He did not as God but as man filled with the Holy Spirit. He lived as a man and depended on the same power that we can depend on, day by day and moment by moment.

- What are some things you have learned from Jesus' example as a human?
- How does it feel to know Jesus depended on the same Holy Spirit you have inside of you as His follower?

**PRACTICE THIS** Read multiple passages in the Gospels and write down what you learn from the example of Jesus.

That which was from the beginning, which we have heard, which
we have seen with our eyes, which we have looked upon, and our
hands have handled, concerning the Word of life—the life was
manifested, and we have seen, and bear witness, and declare to you
that eternal life which was with the Father and was manifested to us.

**1 JOHN 1:1-2**

**PONDER THIS** There was a college professor who was an atheist, and he loved to ridicule his students. He asked his students, "Have any of you ever heard God?" Nobody answered. "Any of you ever seen God?" Nobody answered. "Have any of you ever touched God?" Nobody answered. He said, "So, there is no God." All the students were amazed until one student lifted his hand and said, "Professor, may I ask a question to the class?" He said, "All right." He said, "Have any of you heard the professor's brain?" Nobody answered. "Have any of you touched the professor's brain?" Nobody answered. "Have any of you seen the professor's brain?" Nobody answered. He said, "Then we can conclude the professor has no brain, according to his logic."

John said what we've seen and what we've heard, we declare to you. The Bible says if we receive the witness of men, the witness of God is greater. I don't depend on speech, illustration, or logic to convince you. Thank God the Holy Spirit of God is here to say what is true. That is the witness of God. Jesus is an eternal fact; Jesus is a physical fact; Jesus is a spiritual fact; and the Holy Spirit of God testifies to the Lord Jesus Christ.

- How does God's work in your life provide evidence of Him?
- What do the Gospels teach you about what the disciples saw and learned about Jesus?

**PRACTICE THIS** Make a list of things you can learn about Jesus from the Gospel accounts.

Now by this we know that we know Him, if we keep His
commandments. He who says, "I know Him," and does not
keep His commandments, is a liar, and the truth is not in him.
But whoever keeps His word, truly the love of God is perfected
in him. By this we know that we are in Him. He who says he
abides in Him ought himself also to walk just as He walked.

**1 JOHN 2:3-6**

**PONDER THIS** We have two vital relationships as Christians. One is as a child when we're born into the family of God. Sonship or daughtership is established and will never change. In a parallel way, I was born into the Rogers family. When the sun, the moon, and the stars have grown cold, my birth and my identity as a Rogers can never be undone. That's the way it is when you're born again.

But there's another relationship that can change, and that is called fellowship. I am my father's son, and when I was growing up, I always had a relationship with him, but I didn't always have fellowship. Sometimes, when my dad would tell me to do something, and I would not listen, that would cause a rupture in fellowship, and my dad would carry out discipline. He was not abusive, and he did not just discipline out of spite; he did it because he loved me. Likewise, the Bible says, "For whom the Lord loves He chastens, and scourges every son whom He receives" (Hebrews 12:6). Sonship or daughtership is established by birth, and fellowship is established by conduct.

- What is your fellowship with God like right now? How could it grow?
- Why is it important to remember your unchanging status as God's son or daughter when you are saved?

**PRACTICE THIS** Write down an area you would like to grow in your fellowship with God and ask a fellow Christian to keep you accountable in that area.

If we say that we have no sin, we deceive ourselves, and the truth is
not in us. If we confess our sins, He is faithful and just to forgive us
our sins and to cleanse us from all unrighteousness. If we say that
we have not sinned, we make Him a liar, and His word is not in us.

**1 JOHN 1:8-10**

**PONDER THIS** Sometimes we hide sin in our hearts. It may be big or it may be
small, but it is there. We come to church, go to Sunday school, teach the class,
sing in the choir, and do other things, but there's a secret fault.

What happens when a person does that? He or she gets to believe his or her
own lie. When you set out to deceive somebody else, do you know who you're
going to deceive most of all? You are going to deceive yourself. Many of you have
convinced yourselves that, after you've stonewalled God for a while and moved
in and out of fellowship, nothing seems to happen. You still sing in the choir,
you still teach the Sunday School class, you are still in the congregation, you still
shake hands, and you are still friends with all the people. But you say, "Maybe
God doesn't call that sin, and maybe I am a pretty good person." So, you begin to
smooth over your sin.

How does God bring us back? God will not bring us back unless we expose
ourselves to the light. If you stay in the darkness, there'll never be any conviction.
But if you, as a child of God, will step back into the light, God will shine the light of
His holiness on your life. And God will bring you under conviction.

- When have you deceived yourself about your sin? How might
  you be doing that now?

- Why is it important to be honest about our sin struggles with
  ourselves, God, and others?

**PRACTICE THIS** Take some time in prayer and talk to God about the sin you have
kept in the dark.

"As the Father loved Me, I also have loved you; abide in My love. If you keep My commandments, you will abide in My love, just as I have kept My Father's commandments and abide in His love."

**JOHN 15:9-10**

**PONDER THIS** The word *keep* was used by sailors in ancient times when they didn't have GPS like we have. A sailor at nighttime would look up and steer by the stars. They called that "keeping the stars." He would set his course by keeping the stars.

Christians set our course in life by keeping the commandments. You treasure those commandments, and you steer by those commandments. That doesn't mean you never get blown off course. That doesn't mean in a time of carelessness, you may not take your eyes off the stars. But if you have no desire to live by the Word of God, or you can sin carelessly, flippantly, without any conviction, then you need to get saved.

Are you steering by God's stars? Do you treasure God's Word? Are you keeping God's commandments? We are not saved by keeping the commandments; we are saved by Jesus, and the Holy Spirit equips us to follow God's commandments as we follow Him.

- What does it look like to be guided by God's Word?
- Who has shown you a good example of treasuring God's Word?

**PRACTICE THIS** Ask a trusted Christian brother or sister to share insights he or she has about treasuring God's Word each day.

...as His divine power has given to us all things that pertain
to life and godliness, through the knowledge of Him who
called us by glory and virtue, by which have been given to
us exceedingly great and precious promises, that through
these you may be partakers of the divine nature, having
escaped the corruption that is in the world through lust.

**2 PETER 1:3-4**

**PONDER THIS** What is fellowship? Fellowship is not coffee and donuts. Fellowship is not, as some people cutely say, "two fellows in the same ship." This is a very technical word. It is the Greek word *koinonia*, which means "to hold things in common." Because of Jesus, we experience fellowship with God, and we have fellowship with one another. What do I have in common with the Father? Nothing. He's holy, and I'm unholy; He is almighty, and I am a worm. So how can Adrian have fellowship with God? This is how: God, who knows the chasm between us, sent the Lord Jesus Christ to take on human flesh. Jesus became a man. He never discarded His deity but took on humanity. Because of His work, we begin to have likeness together. Jesus took the very nature of man so that we might take the nature of God. So, I have fellowship with God through the Lord Jesus Christ. Because of this, I can walk and talk and have fellowship with Him.

- How have you experienced fellowship with God?
- Why is having fellowship with God so valuable?

**PRACTICE THIS** Take a walk and talk to God about your life and struggles. Thank Him for the work He did so that you might have fellowship with Him and others.

...that which we have seen and heard we declare to you,
that you also may have fellowship with us; and truly our
fellowship is with the Father and with His Son Jesus Christ.
And these things we write to you that your joy may be full.

**1 JOHN 1:3-4**

**PONDER THIS** What is fellowship? Fellowship is not coffee and donuts. Fellowship is not, as some people cutely say, "two fellows in the same ship." This is a very technical word. It is the Greek word *koinonia*, which means "to hold things in common." Because of Jesus, we experience fellowship with God, and we have fellowship with one another. What do I have in common with the Father? Nothing. He's holy, and I'm unholy; He is almighty, and I am a worm. So how can Adrian have fellowship with God? This is how: God, who knows the chasm between us, sent the Lord Jesus Christ to take on human flesh. Jesus became a man. He never discarded His deity but took on humanity. Because of His work, we begin to have likeness together. Jesus took the very nature of man so that we might take the nature of God. So, I have fellowship with God through the Lord Jesus Christ. Because of this, I can walk and talk and have fellowship with Him.

- Have you experienced full joy in Jesus?
- How does John's message of the true fellowship you have with God give you hope today?

**PRACTICE THIS** Listen to a friend's testimony about how he or she has experienced the joy of the Lord.

...till we all come to the unity of the faith and of the knowledge of the Son of God, to a perfect man, to the measure of the stature of the fullness of Christ; that we should no longer be children, tossed to and fro and carried about with every wind of doctrine, by the trickery of men, in the cunning craftiness of deceitful plotting, but, speaking the truth in love, may grow up in all things into Him who is the head—Christ...

**EPHESIANS 4:13-15**

**PONDER THIS** What is maturity? Maturity is Christlikeness. Are you becoming more like Jesus? That was the goal of Paul's ministry. In Colossians 1:28, Paul said, "Him we preach," that is Jesus, "warning every man and teaching every man in all wisdom, that we may present every man perfect in Christ Jesus." The word *perfect* means "mature."

Now, maturity is a lifelong process. It's not a hundred-yard dash; it's a marathon. Nobody is instantly mature. A wise man said if you want to grow a squash, you can do that in forty days. If you want to grow an oak, you can do that in forty years. You can be instantly spiritual, you can be gifted, you can be healthy, but you cannot be mature. This is why it is so important to know how to move into maturity and to grow spiritually from childhood to adolescence to fatherhood. We need to grow in our faith daily—it will bring us to maturity in Christ, closer fellowship with each other, and a more intimate relationship with God.

- Who in your life is mature in his or her faith?
- How can you pursue maturity in your faith?

**PRACTICE THIS** Consider one step you could take to grow in maturity in your faith, whether it's sharing your faith, praying, or reading your Bible.

I write to you, little children, because your sins are forgiven you for His name's sake. I write to you, fathers, because you have known Him who is from the beginning. I write to you, young men, because you have overcome the wicked one.

**1 JOHN 2:12-14**

**PONDER THIS** Have you ever heard anybody say, "If that's a Christian, I don't want to be one"? They're usually looking at a little baby Christian. Thank God for little baby Christians, but little baby Christians must grow up. When you get saved, nobody is saved full grown. Believers must grow up. I used to think that a great church was one in which everybody was a mature Christian. That's not a great church; that's a failing church. That would be like saying a great home is a home where there are all adults and there are no children or grandchildren. That's not a great home.

Thank God for the spilled milk, thank God for the dirty diapers, thank God for the Cheerios on the floor. We need to make these baby Christians who come to Jesus feel at home and loved. The Church, in one sense, is a maternity ward. The problem is some stay in the maternity ward nursery far too long. You can choose to be different, but when you are still on the bottle, still sucking your thumb, not growing, not serving, not working, having to be served, still selfish, still rude, still crude, still lazy, and still unthoughtful, there is a problem. You're to grow. There is a time for spiritual childhood, but all are called to maturity.

- What are the areas of your faith where you need to grow?
- Who is a new Christian that you know? How can you pour into that believer?

**PRACTICE THIS** Ask a fellow believer to keep you accountable for growth in Christian maturity.

Do not love the world or the things in the world. If anyone loves the world, the love of the Father is not in him. For all that is in the world— the lust of the flesh, the lust of the eyes, and the pride of life—is not of the Father but is of the world. And the world is passing away, and the lust of it; but he who does the will of God abides forever.

**1 JOHN 2:15-17**

**PONDER THIS** The word *cosmos* means "a system or an order of things." It is a way of doing things. For example, we talk about the "world" of finance, sports, or fashion. That's the way the word *world* is being used here. The Bible says: "Do not love the world," or *cosmos*. There is a system that we are not to love. John was not talking about planet Earth; he was not talking about the people, either. He was talking about an ungodly system set against our Lord and His Christ. You're not to love that world. Although it may act very friendly toward you or cozy up to you, it is a friendly enemy.

It is important to see what the Bible has to say and understand why we're not to love the ungodly world system. When we feel tempted to join the worldly system, we need to think about where it is headed and the consequences of following and loving the world.

- What are some things in the world's system that are tempting to you?
- What are some things of the world you've held onto in the past?

**PRACTICE THIS** Make a list comparing the system of the world and the system of God's kingdom. Consider how they are different.

"For after all these things the Gentiles seek. For your
heavenly Father knows that you need all these things.
But seek first the kingdom of God and His righteousness,
and all these things shall be added to you."

**MATTHEW 6:32-33**

**PONDER THIS** What really motivates you? What are your personal goals? Is the first thing in your life to be a godly person? To seek the kingdom of God? Or are you trying to be a successful person? Are you more consumed with material things than spiritual things? Have you tried to put God in second place when the Bible says: "Seek first the kingdom of God?" Your eyes look around, and you say, "I need this, and I want that." That's the lust of the eyes. Are you more concerned about the schools your children graduate from and their degrees and successes or about their holy, godly character? Are there any material possessions you would not depart with for the glory of God? Are you more interested in the lives of the rich and famous than the lives of the righteous and faithful?

The lust of the flesh deals with doing. The lust of the eyes deals with having. And the pride of life deals with being. This world says, "Be somebody." It says, "Be recognized; get a name for yourself." So many young couples are in difficulty today because of the pride of life. Do you think you have to be noticed? May I encourage you? In Christ, you have all you need. He will keep supplying your needs. He should be your top priority; He should be your motivation.

- What things motivate you in a worldly way? Why can these things never truly fulfill you?
- What does it look like practically to seek first the kingdom of God?

**PRACTICE THIS** Talk to a close friend and ask him or her what motivations he or she sees in you. Pray and consider how you need to surrender your motivations to God.

Little children, it is the last hour; and as you have heard that the
Antichrist is coming, even now many antichrists have come,
by which we know that it is the last hour. They went out from
us, but they were not of us; for if they had been of us, they
would have continued with us; but they went out that they
might be made manifest, that none of them were of us.

**1 JOHN 2:18-19**

**PONDER THIS** Joyce and I once went to see the Grand Canyon. Now, I was not at the edge of the Grand Canyon when we drove toward it a hundred miles away. While we were at the rim, we were not headed toward it—we were right on the very edge. We could've walked miles around it, but we would have continued to be on the edge.

Similarly, we're not moving toward the Last Days; we're living on the edge of the Last Days. The Second Coming of Jesus Christ is imminent. There is no sign we're waiting for. There is no event in history we're waiting for. Jesus Christ could have come back three weeks after He ascended into Heaven. And He may come back today. The Bible teaches that we're on the very edge, on the very brink, and therefore, we should be yearning and not yawning. We should be ready for the Second Coming of the Lord Jesus Christ.

- What are some things you would change in your life if you knew Jesus was coming back next month?
- Why is it important to know Jesus' return is imminent?

**PRACTICE THIS** Consider things you would change if you knew the exact time of Jesus' return. Ask God for help to change those things in your life now.

Finally, my brethren, be strong in the Lord and in the power of His might. Put on the whole armor of God, that you may be able to stand against the wiles of the devil. For we do not wrestle against flesh and blood, but against principalities, against powers, against the rulers of the darkness of this age, against spiritual hosts of wickedness in the heavenly places. Therefore take up the whole armor of God, that you may be able to withstand in the evil day, and having done all, to stand.

**EPHESIANS 6:10-13**

**PONDER THIS** The Apostle John said in 1 John 2:12, "I write to you, little children, because your sins are forgiven you for His name's sake." That's the blessing of getting saved. Thank God my sins are forgiven, and I'm on my way to Heaven. That's the main thing a little child is concerned about—getting to Heaven. When a little child gives his testimony, he'll go all the way back to the only testimony he has about how he got saved and how his sins are forgiven, and that is wonderful.

But there are more stages than just childhood in the faith. There is also the triumphant warfare of manhood. That means you are no longer on milk bottles but in mighty battles. So many people can say they're saved, but they're not workers, not warriors, not in the battle. They have simply gotten saved and said, "Hallelujah, thank God, my sins are forgiven," and there they've stopped.

It is time to move on to the next stage in your faith. Dive in deep, serve God, and get into the battle. John says the Word of God has made you strong, and you've overcome the wicked one. Well, you say, "I'm not afraid of the devil." That's not even the question. The question is, "Is the devil afraid of you?" Are you any threat to Satan's kingdom? Are you living for the Lord with your life?

- How would you assess your level of spiritual maturity? Are you a baby Christian? Are you mighty in battle? Are you mature in your faith?

- In what specific ways have you experienced growth in Christ?

**PRACTICE THIS** Talk to a pastor or another mature Christian you know and ask that person to share how he or she has grown in the faith.

Then Jesus called a little child to Him, set him in the midst of them, and said, "Assuredly, I say to you, unless you are converted and become as little children, you will by no means enter the kingdom of heaven. Therefore whoever humbles himself as this little child is the greatest in the kingdom of heaven. Whoever receives one little child like this in My name receives Me."

**MATTHEW 18:2-5**

**PONDER THIS** Never lose the wonder of childhood. The Bible says to put away childish things, but the Bible also says to be childlike. A child has wonder and sweetness. Keep that in you—keep the wonder, keep the excitement, keep the joy. Remember when your sins were forgiven. When you get to be a spiritual father or mother, you don't lose the wonder of childhood; you don't cease in the battle of manhood or womanhood, you don't step out of the warfare—you just add to your faith until you become full-grown.

Did you know there ought to be a little boy in every man and a little girl in every woman who's full-grown? It is time to grow, but don't lose your wonder at Christ.

- What are some things you loved about God when you first came to faith?
- What kinds of things often make it difficult to keep childlike wonder in our faith?

**PRACTICE THIS** Sing your favorite hymn or praise song to remember the wonder of your faith.

Little children, it is the last hour; and as you have heard that the
Antichrist is coming, even now many antichrists have come,
by which we know that it is the last hour. They went out from
us, but they were not of us; for if they had been of us, they
would have continued with us; but they went out that they
might be made manifest, that none of them were of us.

**1 JOHN 2:18-19**

**PONDER THIS** When I was a little boy, my dad was in the Coast Guard, and we lived in West Palm Beach. He was stationed in Hobe Sound, Florida. He drove a Ford Model A, and he could come home about forty miles from Hobe Sound. Before he went to duty, he told my brother and me that we had chores to do. And then we knew that when Dad came home, we had to report. I must confess I was not always very diligent in doing everything my father told me to do.

But if you know anything about a Ford Model A, it has a peculiar sound. You can hear it about a block away. I could hear my dad's car coming when he would turn in our neighborhood. We'd be out playing baseball, and if I saw that black Ford Model A coming, I would give a couple of different reactions. If I had done what my dad told me to do, I'd just take off and run to him, reach in the window, hug his neck, and kiss him—it would be such a joy to see him. Other times when I heard that Ford Model A coming, I went the other way. Why? Because I'd not been doing what he told me to do. Now, he was my father either way. I'm going to meet Jesus, but when He comes, I want to meet Him with boldness. I want to meet Him with joy. I want to abide in Him.

- When have you struggled with obeying God's instruction?
- What are some things you can do to prepare for when you meet Jesus?

**PRACTICE THIS** Make a list of ways you want to prepare to meet Jesus. Ask God to equip you in those ways.

For as many as are led by the Spirit of God, these are sons of God. For you did not receive the spirit of bondage again to fear, but you received the Spirit of adoption by whom we cry out, "Abba, Father." The Spirit Himself bears witness with our spirit that we are children of God, and if children, then heirs—heirs of God and joint heirs with Christ, if indeed we suffer with Him, that we may also be glorified together.

**ROMANS 8:14-17**

**PONDER THIS** How much does God love His Son Jesus? Does He love Jesus more than He loves you? That's not what this says. You may say, "No, I can't take that in," but it is true. There is nothing you can do to make God love you any more than He loves you. He loves you as much as He loves His own dear Son.

We are the sons and the daughters of God. Jesus is the firstborn Son, but He's just the firstborn in a family of many brothers and sisters. We are brothers and sisters of Jesus—sons of God, literally. Do you know what "Abba Father" means? Our equivalent would be the name "Daddy." It blesses me when my children call me daddy instead of father because it reminds me of our closeness. Likewise, we can speak to God and call Him "Abba Father." Because I'm a son of God and Jesus Christ is my brother, I have my Father's care, and I'm not a beggar. My Father pledged to take care of me, and He will.

- What would it look like to approach God as your "Abba Father"?
- When have you felt God's closeness in a time of trouble?

**PRACTICE THIS** Approach God as your Abba Father and tell Him about the things that have been weighing you down lately.

Behold what manner of love the Father has bestowed on us,
that we should be called children of God! Therefore the world
does not know us, because it did not know Him. Beloved, now
we are children of God; and it has not yet been revealed what
we shall be, but we know that when He is revealed, we shall
be like Him, for we shall see Him as He is. And everyone who
has this hope in Him purifies himself, just as He is pure.

**1 JOHN 3:1-3**

**PONDER THIS** Did you know God cares for you? His heart is broken when your heart is broken, so it ought to be easy to talk with Him. You don't talk with Him as Judge; He is Judge, but for you, He's more than Judge. You don't talk to Him as Ruler; He is Ruler. You don't talk to Him as King; He is King. But you talk to Him as Father.

We have the Father's companionship. I'm never alone. God is real to me. I don't say that braggingly. It would be strange if I could not say that. I can be shut up alone with Him, and He's never too busy to talk with me.

Sometimes, I get busy, and the phone rings, and I don't want to answer it, but I hate not to answer it. But it doesn't matter how much work I have; if the person on the other end says, "Daddy," I say, "What do you want?" It's all the difference in the world. Why is that? These are my kids. In the same way, there is a relationship with Almighty God that is so wonderful! We are a part of the family of God. You may think He's forgotten you, but He hasn't.

- When was a time you prayed just to talk to God and tell Him what is going on?
- What is your attitude when you talk to God?

**PRACTICE THIS** Talk to God as your Abba Father. Share your joy and burdens.

**19**

Therefore, if anyone is in Christ, he is a new creation; old things
have passed away; behold, all things have become new.

**2 CORINTHIANS 5:17**

**PONDER THIS** A lot of people say they're on the way to Heaven, but there's been no change in their lives. There exists a sort of "easy-believism" where people ask, "Do you believe in Jesus?" We say, "Yes." "Do you believe He died for your sins?" We say, "Yes." Then, they say, "Well, then you're saved." But the devil also believes and trembles. (See James 2:19.) You are saved when you bow the knee to Jesus Christ and make Him the Lord of your life. That's an act of faith, and it is a change.

I want to be very clear here. You're not saved by reforming your life. Our Lord never tells us to clean up before He'll save us. That's backward. We come to Jesus just as we are, but Jesus did not come to save us *in* our sin. He came to save us *from* our sin. If you're not seeking to live a righteous life, then you're not saved. The very word *Christian* means "Christlike," and in Christ, there's no sin. You can't be Christlike and live a life of sin.

- What are some things that have changed in your life since you came to know Christ?

- Why is it important that our lives are changed because of our faith in Jesus?

**PRACTICE THIS** Share with someone how God has transformed your life.

Whoever commits sin also commits lawlessness, and sin is lawlessness. And you know that He was manifested to take away our sins, and in Him there is no sin. Whoever abides in Him does not sin. Whoever sins has neither seen Him nor known Him. Little children, let no one deceive you. He who practices righteousness is righteous, just as He is righteous. He who sins is of the devil, for the devil has sinned from the beginning. For this purpose the Son of God was manifested, that He might destroy the works of the devil. Whoever has been born of God does not sin, for His seed remains in him; and he cannot sin, because he has been born of God.

**1 JOHN 3:4-9**

**PONDER THIS** Once I'm saved, I have a new dynamic: God's life is in me. I have a new desire: I want to be like Him because He's in me, and I'm in Him and abiding in Him. I also have a new deterrent. It says here in this verse, "And he cannot sin, because he has been born of God." This is a present continuous sense. If the God of the Bible lives in you, you cannot habitually live in sin—you just can't do it. If Jesus Christ is in you, you cannot go on carelessly, thoughtlessly, continuously practicing a lifestyle of sin. The Holy Spirit of God in you will tear you up. You will be under conviction, and the Holy Spirit of God will live in you, work in you, and dwell in you. He is delivering you, not only from the penalty of sin and the power of Satan but from the principle of self. You are born again. You have received a new nature, and with that new nature, you have a new dynamic, a new desire, and a new deterrent. You're living for Jesus.

- When have you been convicted by the Holy Spirit?
- What is the difference between conviction and guilt? Why is it important to know this?

**PRACTICE THIS** Pray and confess your sins, acknowledging the areas of conviction in your life.

For I say, through the grace given to me, to everyone who is among
you, not to think of himself more highly than he ought to think, but
to think soberly, as God has dealt to each one a measure of faith.

**ROMANS 12:3**

**PONDER THIS** One way to give a good witness for the Lord Jesus Christ is to tell
what you know, not what you don't. Many of us are afraid to witness because
we're afraid somebody's going to ask us a question we can't answer. Let me give
you the perfect answer. Just say, "I don't know." Isn't that a good answer? You
know, if you tell people that you don't know when you don't know, maybe they'll
believe you when you tell them what you do know. There are a lot of things about
the future that you don't know. Don't worry about it. These things have been
kept from us on purpose. Jesus said, "I still have many things to tell you, but you
cannot bear them now" (John 16:12). And in Daniel's vision, he heard, "...shut up
the words, and seal the book until the time of the end" (Daniel 12:4a).

A 4-year-old can ask questions nobody can answer except God. So don't try to
explain everything. We have hints and clues. The one thing we do know is that
one day, we're going to be like Jesus, and that's good enough for me.

- When have you struggled with the unknowns of the Christian
  faith?

- Why is it difficult to admit we don't know the answer to a
  question? How does admitting this show greater dependence
  on God?

**PRACTICE THIS** Talk to a friend about the faith questions he or she is wrestling
with.

For I know that this will turn out for my deliverance through
your prayer and the supply of the Spirit of Jesus Christ,
according to my earnest expectation and hope that in nothing
I shall be ashamed, but with all boldness, as always, so now
also Christ will be magnified in my body, whether by life or
by death. For to me, to live is Christ, and to die is gain.

**PHILIPPIANS 1:19-21**

**PONDER THIS** Some teenagers were out, and one of them suggested they do something they ought not to do, but a godly girl in that crowd said, "No, I don't want to do that." And one of them began to tease her and said, "Oh, you're afraid of what your dad will do, aren't you?" She said, "No, I'm afraid of what I'd do to my dad." See, that's the difference between law and love! Every person who says, "I am a blood brother of the Lord Jesus Christ," wants to be pure when the Lord Jesus comes. We are to be looking for His coming; we're to be living for His coming, and we ought to be longing for His coming.

You know, when I was a kid, I used to hear preachers preach about the Second Coming of Jesus, and I thought, *Oh, what rotten luck. I won't even get to get married. I won't get to do all those things I want to do. My life's going to be cut short.* The longer I live and the more I see, the more I understand that the best thing that could happen to any of us is for Jesus Christ to come right now. Don't you worry—you're not going to miss out on life if Jesus comes right now. It is all gain.

- How are you living life today with Heaven in mind?
- Where do you feel unprepared for Jesus' return? Why? How might we prepare?

**PRACTICE THIS** Do at least one thing today that has eternal value such as praying for someone, getting to know a non-believer, or investing in your church community.

"A new commandment I give to you, that you love one another; as I have loved you, that you also love one another. By this all will know that you are My disciples, if you have love for one another."

**JOHN 13:34-35**

**PONDER THIS** You don't have to have a lapel pin or bumper sticker to prove you are a Christian—love is the greatest testimony.

A man out in California was one of these guys who was always on time. One morning he woke up, went out, and tried to start his car, and the battery was dead. He asked his wife, "Can I take your car?" She said, "Yes." By this time, he was stuck driving in heavy traffic. He was inching along and then came to a dead stop, and the man behind him honked the horn. He was frustrated but he let it go. After a while, the man behind him blew the horn again. Then the man tapped the horn the third time.

The man threw open the car door, went back to the driver behind him, and tapped on the window. He yelled at the driver, "Listen, you, I don't want you to blow your horn at me one more time. I can't move my car!" The driver behind him said, "Doesn't that bumper sticker mean what it says? Honk if you love Jesus?" He said, "Oh, I do love Jesus. I am so sorry." This is a funny example, but we all need to take the saint off the dashboard and put him behind the steering wheel. We need to stop showboating our Christian title and begin living it out in our love.

- When are you most likely to be guided by your emotions instead of by love?
- When have you seen an example of someone loving others well?

**PRACTICE THIS** Extend an act of love or service to another person today.

And by this we know that we are of the truth, and shall assure our hearts before Him. For if our heart condemns us, God is greater than our heart, and knows all things. Beloved, if our heart does not condemn us, we have confidence toward God. And whatever we ask we receive from Him, because we keep His commandments and do those things that are pleasing in His sight. And this is His commandment: that we should believe on the name of His Son Jesus Christ and love one another, as He gave us commandment.

**1 JOHN 3:19-23**

**PONDER THIS** When you have love in your heart, you're going to find a wonderful thing—your conscience will be clear. Your conscience is not an enemy; it is a friend, something unique put in you that God did not put into animals. Have you ever thought about it? Animals can't blush, and animals can't laugh. A little boy once called the conscience the part of us that feels bad when everything else feels good. But that's not really true. That may be the world's frivolous definition of conscience, but it's that part that God has put in each of us to focus our actions and make moral judgments. The Bible teaches that everyone should have a good conscience. For believers in Jesus, the conscience is driven by the Holy Spirit.

In Acts 24:16, Paul said, "This being so, I myself always strive to have a conscience without offense toward God and men." In Christ, when I learn to love and live by love, I'm going to have a good conscience. And when I have a good conscience, I'm going to have great confidence. And when I have great confidence, I'm going to have a gracious communion. The Holy Spirit will be whispering to my heart that I belong to Jesus and He to me.

- When was a time you remember the Holy Spirit led you by your conscience?
- How is this different than the way people outside of Jesus recognize the conscience?

**PRACTICE THIS** Consider where God might be leading you by His Spirit today. Respond in obedience.

If we receive the witness of men, the witness of God is greater; for this is the witness of God which He has testified of His Son. He who believes in the Son of God has the witness in himself; he who does not believe God has made Him a liar, because he has not believed the testimony that God has given of His Son. And this is the testimony: that God has given us eternal life, and this life is in His Son.

**1 JOHN 5:9-11**

**PONDER THIS** When you get on an airplane to fly, you've likely never seen that pilot, and you've never examined that airplane, but you'll trust them to fly across oceans and land. That's faith. You live by faith every day of your life, and you put your faith in normal people. "If we receive the witness of men, the witness of God is greater." Men can lie. The Holy Spirit is truth. The Holy Spirit witnesses to us. That's the reason I'm never moved when a man says, "Well, I can't believe." He's a liar. If you want to believe, the Holy Spirit will enable you to believe.

Suppose Brother Bob and Brother Jim are arguing with me about apple pie. I have an apple pie, and I've just eaten a big slice of it. And Jim says, "I don't believe there is any apple pie. It doesn't even exist." And Bob says, "Well, I believe it exists, but it's no good." Do you think those two guys are going to disturb me? See, I have the witness in myself. The Bible says, "Taste and see that the LORD is good" (Psalm 34:8a). One way to find out whether apple pie is good or not is to taste and see. That's our job: invite people to taste and see.

- Why do we often find it easier to put faith in people instead of God?
- Where in your life do you want to grow deeper in your faith in God?

**PRACTICE THIS** Share with a confidant the area in which you want to grow deeper in your faith.

Who is he who overcomes the world, but he who believes that
Jesus is the Son of God? This is He who came by water and blood—
Jesus Christ; not only by water, but by water and blood. And it
is the Spirit who bears witness, because the Spirit is truth...

**1 JOHN 5:5-8**

**PONDER THIS** So many times, we're trying to make everybody else have the same emotional experience we have. In some churches, they used to have altars where you came to kneel and get saved. There is nothing wrong with that, but it's not necessary. You can be saved in the back of the room. You can be saved up front. You can be saved in an airplane. You can be saved in a submarine. You can be saved anywhere. But this man came to one of those old-fashioned prayer benches to get saved, and there were some of the brothers and sisters in his country church who came to help him.

One kneeled down alongside him while he was praying and said, "Brother, hold on. You'll never get saved if you don't hold on." Another well-meaning person came up right after that and said, "Brother, let go! I never did get saved until I finally let go." And somebody else came right after that and said, "Oh, man, look for a bright light." He said, "When you see that bright light, you'll know you're saved." Later, the man said, "You know, between trying to hold on and let go and look for that light, I almost didn't make it."

Don't impose your emotions on people. We are different emotionally. The witness of the Spirit is not an emotional experience. It is a certainty. God's Spirit speaks to your spirit, and He tells you, "You are Mine."

- What emotional experiences have you had in your faith?
- How have your experiences affected the way you share with others? How can you be careful not to impose emotional responses on others?

**PRACTICE THIS** Reflect on the significant moments of your faith. Journal about things that were emotional and may have been personal to you. Also, write down truths from Scripture about our unchanging God that the Holy Spirit has assured you of.

In Him also we have obtained an inheritance, being predestined according to the purpose of Him who works all things according to the counsel of His will, that we who first trusted in Christ should be to the praise of His glory. In Him you also trusted, after you heard the word of truth, the gospel of your salvation; in whom also, having believed, you were sealed with the Holy Spirit of promise, who is the guarantee of our inheritance until the redemption of the purchased possession, to the praise of His glory.

**EPHESIANS 1:11-14**

**PONDER THIS** Do you know what the word *guarantee* means in verse 14? It means "a down payment." If you are going to buy a house, you put down some money to begin with, and that means you're coming back for the whole thing. Now, the Holy Spirit that you have in your heart who seals you into Christ is the earnest, the pledge that one day our Lord is coming back for his purchased possession. Why? He's got so much invested in me. He put the down payment in my heart. The Holy Spirit is the guarantee of our inheritance. Thanks be to God for this salvation and guarantee we have in Jesus. When others are wandering like ships at sea on a dark and stormy night without a rudder or a compass, God has pulled back the veil of eternity and shown us what happened before the world was brought into space. He has shown us what we're going to be and what we're going to have. And even more than that, He has put the down payment in our hearts. It is a promise that He is with us until He comes again.

- What excites you about the gifts you have received from Jesus?
- How are you reminded of your inheritance in Christ?

**PRACTICE THIS** Take some time to write about what it would be like if you always remembered your heavenly inheritance. Then, pray over what you've written.

For if our heart condemns us, God is greater than our heart,
and knows all things. Beloved, if our heart does not condemn
us, we have confidence toward God. And whatever we ask
we receive from Him, because we keep His commandments
and do those things that are pleasing in His sight."

**1 JOHN 3:20-22**

**PONDER THIS** Imagine you and your spouse are having one of those arguments that can be heard about three blocks away. Christians can do this. They take their eyes off the Lord, and they're at one another's throats. Whatever else they're doing, they are not dwelling together as heirs of the grace of life. Imagine right after this argument and the storming off, the mother goes in to check on the baby, and she comes out with a frightened look on her face. The baby is very sick, and you're both believers, and you know you need to pray. What happens? Usually, at that moment, you feel like fools praying in that atmosphere, that hostility, that venom, but you know what you do? You say, "I'm so sorry, I was wrong, I was a fool, forgive me." She says, "It was my fault too," and you reconcile. After that, the conscience is clear, the assurance is back, and you can pray. But you cannot pray with a condemning heart. When you still have enmity between one another, you won't be united in prayer. If you don't have a good conscience, you cannot have great confidence, and if you don't have great confidence, you can't get your prayers answered. Love gives a good conscience, and when love gives a good conscience, love gets great confidence.

- When have you lost sight of your identity in Christ in a hard moment?
- Why is reconciliation with others so important in the Christian life?

**PRACTICE THIS** Consider the last angry argument you had. If you have not already, pursue peace with the person with whom you were angry.

Let no corrupt word proceed out of your mouth, but what is good for necessary edification, that it may impart grace to the hearers. And do not grieve the Holy Spirit of God, by whom you were sealed for the day of redemption. Let all bitterness, wrath, anger, clamor, and evil speaking be put away from you, with all malice. And be kind to one another, tenderhearted, forgiving one another, even as God in Christ forgave you.

**EPHESIANS 4:29-32**

**PONDER THIS** If you have anger in your heart, if love is not there, that doesn't mean the Holy Spirit of God forsakes you. If you are in Christ, He cannot, and He will not leave you. You are sealed by the Holy Spirit unto the day of redemption. What grieves the Holy Spirit? It is these things: bitterness, wrath, anger, clamor, and evil. Bitterness is an unresolved hurt. Somebody's hurt you and done you wrong. It may be real, it may be imaginary, but you perceive that somebody has done you wrong. Bitterness turns to wrath. The word *wrath* has the idea of heat, something burning, sort of a slow burn. The best illustration I can give is to think of some oily rags in an attic or a closet, smoldering with the heat building up.

What's the difference between wrath and anger? Wrath is that slow burn, but anger is when somebody opens the door, and the oxygen hits those rags, and they burst into flame. You say, "Well, I lost my temper." You probably found it. You know, when a person says, "I lost my temper," what they're saying is, "It's not really my fault, it's not really me, I lost it." No, what is happening is that you're showing what's in your heart. In those moments, the Holy Spirit has not forsaken you, and you have Him in you to equip you and help in those moments you feel prone to bitterness, wrath, and anger.

- When was the last time you lost your temper?
- What would it look like to seek God when you feel prone to bitterness, wrath, and anger?

**PRACTICE THIS** Write out a verse to memorize and reflect on the next time you feel prone to sinful anger.

Therefore do not be unwise, but understand what the will of the Lord is. And do not be drunk with wine, in which is dissipation; but be filled with the Spirit, speaking to one another in psalms and hymns and spiritual songs, singing and making melody in your heart to the Lord, giving thanks always for all things to God the Father in the name of our Lord Jesus Christ, submitting to one another in the fear of God.

**EPHESIANS 5:17-21**

**PONDER THIS** Be filled with the Spirit. There's no place for the devil when you're filled with the Holy Spirit. The Holy Spirit is not some sort of a liquid with you as the jug; that's not the idea. To be filled with the Spirit of God means there's not one room in your life where God is off-limits. There's not one closet He doesn't have a key to. You are filled with the Spirit in your sex life, in your business life, in your political life, in your church life, in your social life, in the big things and the little things, in your money, in your exercise, in your sleep, in your eating, in your lying down, in your waking up. This is the heart we need to have: "Jesus, I give you the keys to it all; I am filled with Your Spirit." When you're filled with the Holy Spirit, there's no more room for Satan.

If there's room for Satan, the Spirit is grieved, and you are not filled with the Spirit. Don't try to repent until you're honest and face your sin, don't try to resist until you've repented, and don't try to be filled until you resist Satan and yield to God's blessed Holy Spirit.

- What areas of life have you submitted to God's authority?
- In what areas of life have you struggled to give God authority? What needs to change?

**PRACTICE THIS** Pray and surrender to God the areas of life over which you have not given Him full control.

The LORD God planted a garden eastward in Eden, and there
He put the man whom He had formed. And out of the ground
the LORD God made every tree grow that is pleasant to the
sight and good for food. The tree of life was also in the midst of
the garden, and the tree of the knowledge of good and evil.

**GENESIS 2:8-9**

**PONDER THIS** Many think of belonging to the Lord as taking bad medicine to get well. The idea of serving God is painful to them. The idea of being a Christian is negative; it's something you endure. They believe God is a cosmic killjoy. If that is you, you better get that negative idea of God out of your heart and mind. God is not some sort of a cruel, vengeful deity sitting upon a throne somewhere hurling down thunderbolts of wrath.

The truth is, if Satan can get you to think negatively about God, he has you. Can you imagine the glories of the Garden of Eden? Can you imagine how beautiful Eden must have been? Not so long ago, I was at Butchart Gardens in Canada. Those gardens are indescribably beautiful. As you walk through, you wonder what the Garden of Eden must have been like. God, with a smile on His face, said, "Adam and Eve, I made that for you. Help yourself." But there was one tree that God said, "Don't eat of it." That wasn't a threat; it was a warning. Every time God says, "Thou shalt not," He's saying, "Don't hurt yourself." And every time God says, "Thou shalt," He's saying, "Help yourself to abundant life." God loves you. Life with Him is good because you are with Him. The devil doesn't want you to know that.

- When have you had a negative view of God? How did that impact your relationship with Him?
- What helps you see the goodness of God?

**PRACTICE THIS** Write down all the reasons God is good. Remind yourself of His character traits and praise Him for those qualities.

> Now Joseph had a dream, and he told it to his brothers; and they hated him even more. So he said to them, "Please hear this dream which I have dreamed: There we were, binding sheaves in the field. Then behold, my sheaf arose and also stood upright; and indeed your sheaves stood all around and bowed down to my sheaf."
>
> **GENESIS 37:5-7**

**PONDER THIS** Let God put a dream in your heart. I was about Joseph's age when God called me into the ministry. I was in high school, and my pastor told me that God had a plan for everybody's life. And I wanted to know God's plan for my life. So, I said, "Lord, I don't know what You want me to do, but whatever it is, I want You to show me Your will, and whatever it is, I want to do it."

Now, God spoke to Joseph through a dream. He may speak to you some other way. But the point is this: God has a plan for your life. Would you like to know what God's plan for your life is? Remember, Joseph just had a vision. He had a hint, but that's all. God didn't give him a road map. I think Joseph would have been perturbed had God told him about the pit, the prison, the accusations, and everything else. But he had a dream—something he aspired to. Romans 12:1-2 is such a wonderful verse for formulating our God-given dreams. It says to be transformed by the renewing of your mind so you may prove what is the good, acceptable, and perfect will of God. Do you want to know the will of God? There's the formula: presentation plus transformation equals realization.

- What is a dream God has given you?
- When have you desired a road map of God's will for you? How have you learned to trust God with the details of your life?

**PRACTICE THIS** Pray and then write down some of the dreams you have for the future. Consider how these might bring God glory.

I beseech you therefore, brethren, by the mercies of God, that you present your bodies a living sacrifice, holy, acceptable to God, which is your reasonable service. And do not be conformed to this world, but be transformed by the renewing of your mind, that you may prove what is that good and acceptable and perfect will of God.

**ROMANS 12:1-2**

**PONDER THIS** Have you presented yourself to God? Most people have never done that. Most people say, "If I did that, no telling where I'd end up. I'd be a missionary over in a place of poverty." But it's time to present yourself to Him. Sign the contract, hand it to Him, and tell Him to fill it in. Don't be afraid. Because when you present yourself to Him, you're transformed. "Be not conformed to this world, but be transformed." The word *transform* is the word from which we get our English word *metamorphosis*. You will have a divine metamorphosis.

What is a metamorphosis? *Meta* means "change," and *morphose* means "form." It's a change of form. For example, the caterpillar goes into the cocoon and comes out as a butterfly. It has gone through metamorphosis. The inner nature of that caterpillar is a beautiful butterfly. What is the inner nature of a child of God? It's God. It is glory. It is Jesus. Christ lives in you. When you present yourself to Him as a living sacrifice, there will be a metamorphosis, and that which is on the inside will come to the surface.

- How difficult do you find it to present yourself fully to God?
- What has caused you to hold back from presenting yourself to God?

**PRACTICE THIS** Present yourself to God in prayer and bring to Him the things you have been holding back.

Then Joseph's master took him and put him into the prison,
a place where the king's prisoners were confined. And he was
there in the prison. But the LORD was with Joseph and showed
him mercy, and He gave him favor in the sight of the keeper of
the prison. And the keeper of the prison committed to Joseph's
hand all the prisoners who were in the prison; whatever they did
there, it was his doing. The keeper of the prison did not look into
anything that was under Joseph's authority, because the LORD
was with him; and whatever he did, the LORD made it prosper.

**GENESIS 39:20-23**

**PONDER THIS** We need to be careful about bitterness. Bitter people are not nice to be around. Sometimes, pastors get bitter. I know a pastor who served a church for many years. For some reason, the people in that church turned on him; they began to criticize him, and finally, they dismissed him. This pastor asked repeatedly, "How could they do that to me after all I did for them? How could they do that?" And he was very bitter. I thought the shame was he didn't say, "After all I did for God." Not for them, but for God.

If you look to people to supply your needs and recognize your worth, you're going to be disappointed in life. And you're going to get bitter. One of the greatest tests of life is not how you react when you're punished for doing wrong but how you react when you're persecuted for doing right. Joseph had done right. He was persecuted and tested but there was not a shred of bitterness in the life of Joseph. How? Because God was with him.

- When was the last time you were bitter? How did that cause you to act toward others? Toward God?
- Have you ever asked God to be with you when you were tempted with bitterness? How might this change things?

**PRACTICE THIS** Talk to a friend about how bitterness manifests itself in your life. Ask him or her to keep you accountable when you move toward bitterness.

Trust in the LORD with all your heart, and lean not on
your own understanding; in all your ways acknowledge Him,
and He shall direct your paths.

**PROVERBS 3:5-6**

**PONDER THIS** You don't find the will of God; the will of God finds you. You get your heart right with God. You present yourself to Him. You have the mind of Christ; you get in the stream, and you'll find out that God will be guiding you.

God has a dream for you. I'm not telling you God has promised to fulfill your fantasies. I'm talking about a God-given dream. How can I tell whether my dream is a God-given dream? Think about it. Pray over it. When I was a kid, I said, "Lord, what do You want me to do?" And then, after a while, I got a little inclination in my heart. "Lord, I think You want me to preach." And then it was, "Lord, do You want me to preach?" Then, after a while, it was, "Lord, if You don't want me to preach, you better let me know." And then, finally, "Lord, I know this is what You want." Check your dream out. Soak it in prayer. God will guide you.

- When have you felt God guide you to do something?
- Why is it important to be discerning and prayerful when you think you may have a God-given dream?

**PRACTICE THIS** Ask another mature Christian about the ways God led him or her throughout life.

"Peace I leave with you, My peace I give to you; not as the
world gives do I give to you. Let not your heart be troubled,
neither let it be afraid."

**JOHN 14:27**

**PONDER THIS** When Joyce and I lost our son, we left to be with family while we were grieving. When Joyce and I were leaving our church parsonage close by the church we served at, I could see the yellow light as it was streaming out of the open windows of the church, and the congregation was singing, "No, never alone. No, never alone. He hath promised never to leave me, never to leave me alone. I've seen the lightning flashing, I've heard the thunder roll, I've felt sin's breakers dashing, trying to conquer my soul. But I heard the voice of Jesus, telling me still to fight on, for He's promised never to leave me, never to leave me alone."

I would not take anything for the conscious presence of God. And this little phrase that speaks about Joseph's life: "The LORD was with Joseph" (Genesis 39:2a). In prison, God was with him; in the pit, God was with him; in slander, God was with him; in business, God was with him; in pain, God was with him; in prosperity, God was with him. He's dying, God was with him. God is in Christ, and if you want God with you in good times and hard, you need Jesus.

- When have you needed God's presence in a hard time?
- Who do you know that needs to be reminded that God is with them today?

**PRACTICE THIS** Check in on somebody who is going through a hard time. If this person has a relationship with Jesus, remind him or her of God's presence through hard times.

Therefore humble yourselves under the mighty hand
of God, that He may exalt you in due time.

**1 PETER 5:6**

**PONDER THIS** Over and over again in the Bible, we are told to wait upon the Lord. When you don't understand, don't be unwilling to wait. A preacher who was in a hard spot said to me, "I know that God put me here. I just wonder if He remembers where He put me." God knows where you are. The very hairs of your head are numbered. And the God that was with Joseph when he was a lad, the God who was with Joseph when he was serving in Potiphar's house, was the God who was with Joseph when he languished, forgotten in prison.

God has His schedule. When you don't understand, don't demand to understand, don't fail to be faithful, don't bow to bitterness. God is never late, but He's never ahead of time. It's like the sun coming up. One thing about the sun coming up is you can't hurry it, and you can't stop it. That's the way God is. God is always on time. Wait on God. Don't be unwilling to wait. Humble yourselves under the mighty hand of God. In due time, He'll lift you up. When you don't understand, don't get feverish. Wait on Him.

- When have you struggled to trust God's timing?
- What are some reasons we often want to rush God?

**PRACTICE THIS** Make a list of things that you have been impatient about. Pray over that list and ask God to help you trust His timing with those things.

And Jesus said to them, "I am the bread of life. He who comes to Me
shall never hunger, and he who believes in Me shall never thirst."

**JOHN 6:35**

**PONDER THIS** Do you know what the name *Joseph* means? It means "abundance or the one who adds to." It means "a multiplier." That's what Joseph was. What does the name *Jesus* mean? It means "Jehovah Saves." And He is also the one whose life is full of abundance. Jesus said, "The thief does not come except to steal, and to kill, and to destroy" (John 10:10). Who is the thief? Satan. He is the great subtractor. But Jesus said, "I've come that you might have life, and have it abundantly." He is the Joseph who adds to, who multiplies, and who gives abundance.

A little girl once saw a communion table at the front of the sanctuary. The little girl had been learning math—the plus signs and the minus signs. She looked and saw the cross on the communion table, and she asked her mother, "Why is the plus sign there?" It is a funny question but carries a serious reminder, Jesus Christ died upon that cross to add to us life and to give it abundantly.

- How has Jesus added to your life?
- Why is it important to remember Jesus is the only one who gives in spiritual abundance?

**PRACTICE THIS** Thank God for the opportunity to receive abundant life through Jesus.

Husbands, love your wives, just as Christ also loved the church
and gave Himself for her, that He might sanctify and cleanse her
with the washing of water by the word, that He might present her
to Himself a glorious church, not having spot or wrinkle or any
such thing, but that she should be holy and without blemish.

**EPHESIANS 5:25-27**

**PONDER THIS** Who is the bride of Jesus? It is the Church. The Church is not the building but the people. Don't abuse the bride of Christ. Jesus loves His bride. He loves us. He's working on us that He might present us to Himself a spotless bride, without blemish or any such thing.

God wants you saved; He wants you to be a part of the Church, His bride. He wants you to know Jesus. And He's saying to you, "If you've never come, then come now." It is beautiful to be a part of the Church, the bride of Christ. If you have come, hear Jesus calling, "Go tell the others. Tell them that I'm not dead, but I'm alive. I am now at the right hand of the Majesty on high. I have made provision for you. And I want you to come and live with Me forever." This is the hope and calling we have. Jesus is the only hope of a dying world!

- How have you cared for the bride of Christ, the Church? How can you do so in the future?
- Why do we often struggle with loving the bride of Christ?

**PRACTICE THIS** Pray for your pastors, ministers, members, and volunteers at your church.

> Then Joseph said to his brothers, "I am Joseph; does my father still live?" But his brothers could not answer him, for they were dismayed in his presence. And Joseph said to his brothers, "Please come near to me." So they came near. Then he said: "I am Joseph your brother, whom you sold into Egypt. But now, do not therefore be grieved or angry with yourselves because you sold me here; for God sent me before you to preserve life."

**GENESIS 45:3-5**

**PONDER THIS** Consider what it was that brought Joseph's brothers to Egypt to begin with. They had a hunger. There was a famine in the land of Canaan. If we never had any needs, we wouldn't come to our Lord. God allows us to have heartaches and pains that point us to Him. Joseph was speaking roughly to his brothers and so overcome with emotion that he had to leave the room and literally weep.

Are you having troubles? Are you having heartaches? Are you having difficulties? Are you having disappointments? Is there pain in your life? There is! That is the silken cord that God is using to draw you to Himself. He loves you. No matter what the appearances may seem, I'm telling you that God loves you, and God's love is greater than all of our sins. What a moment when Joseph said, "Look, I am Joseph!" His brothers didn't know this gospel song, but I believe they could have sung, "Once I was blind, but now I see." Joseph wept tears of joy because he was able to make himself known to his brothers. And there's joy in Heaven when one sinner comes home, is there not?

- When have you grown in your relationship with God during a hard time?
- How do you react when you have sinned: do you run away from God or do you run toward Him? Why?

**PRACTICE THIS** Pray and lay before God all the hurts and difficulties you are facing as you come to Him.

"Hurry and go up to my father, and say to him, 'Thus says your son Joseph: God has made me lord of all Egypt; come down to me, do not tarry. You shall dwell in the land of Goshen, and you shall be near to me, you and your children, your children's children, your flocks and your herds, and all that you have. There I will provide for you, lest you and your household, and all that you have, come to poverty; for there are still five years of famine...'

**GENESIS 45:9-13**

**PONDER THIS** All of the Gospel can be summed up in these two phrases, "Come unto me; Go ye into all the world." That's it. Jesus says, "Come to Me." They came. He said, "All right. Now, go and tell others." What right do we have to call ourselves children of God if we fail to obey Him? Our Lord has given us a Great Commission. We're to go into all the world and share the Lord Jesus Christ.

A little boy had a toy car he got at Christmas. It wouldn't work. His dad said, "What's wrong with it?" He said, "I think the 'go' is broke." I think that's what's wrong with the Church. We are to go. To say that all Christians are missionaries is just another way of saying all Christians are Christians.

What are we to share? Number one, we once rejected Jesus. Number two, God has raised Him up on high. Number three, He has a name that is above every name. Number four, the world is now at His feet. Number five, He is the fairest of ten thousand. Number six, He has forgiven all of our sins. Number seven, He wants us to be with Him and to share His glory. That's what they were to tell about Joseph, and that's what we're to tell about Jesus.

- Do you know how to share the Gospel? When was the last opportunity that you had to share it?
- Who are some people in your life that need the hope of the Gospel?

**PRACTICE THIS** Practice sharing the Gospel with a fellow Christian and then share that hope with someone else you know.

*"Come to Me, all you who labor and are heavy
laden, and I will give you rest."*

**MATTHEW 11:28**

**PONDER THIS** In Genesis 45, Joseph's brothers would never have known who he was had he not revealed himself to them. He was older, dressed like an Egyptian, and spoke the Egyptian language. The only way they could know him was for him to say, "Look, I'm Joseph."

Likewise, the only way you'll know Jesus is for Jesus to reveal Himself to you. You'll never figure Him out. But you've been brought by divine providence to receive this message that God the Holy Spirit might speak to you, and Jesus is saying unto you, "I am Jesus. I'm the Son of God. I want to save you." So, you lay your intellectual pride in the dust and let Him reveal Himself.

Now, like Jesus, Joseph revealed himself to his brothers. Like Jesus, Joseph forgave and restored his brothers. Genesis 45:4-5 says, "And Joseph said to his brothers, 'Please come near to me.' So, they came near. Then he said: 'I am Joseph, your brother, whom you sold into Egypt. But now, do not therefore be grieved or angry with yourselves because you sold me here, for God sent me before you to preserve life.'" Tragedy became triumph. Notice in these verses that Joseph gave an invitation. He said, "Come to me," and they came. They responded by coming to him. It is time for you to come too.

- Why is it important to remember it is Jesus who initiates the relationship with you and not the other way around?
- What are some obstacles you face when coming to Jesus?

**PRACTICE THIS** Come to Jesus in prayer. Bring before Him your sin, struggles, shame, and burdens.

And they told him, saying, "Joseph is still alive, and he is governor over all the land of Egypt." And Jacob's heart stood still, because he did not believe them. But when they told him all the words which Joseph had said to them, and when he saw the carts which Joseph had sent to carry him, the spirit of Jacob their father revived.

**GENESIS 45:26-27**

**PONDER THIS** In Genesis 45:24, Joseph told his brothers not to be troubled. He was not trying to minimize their sin. What he was doing was maximizing the grace of God. Calvary, from man's viewpoint, was Earth's greatest tragedy. From God's viewpoint, it was Earth's greatest triumph. "You meant evil against me; but God meant it for good" (Genesis 50:20). When Hell was doing its worst, God was doing His best when Jesus died upon that cross. Do you see the picture here?

Not only did Joseph convict his brothers and reveal himself to them, not only did he forgive them and restore them, but here, finally, he commissioned his brothers. Our faith is summed up in this; "Come to Me and go to all the world." Joseph said to his brothers, "Come to me, come here. I will forgive you. I will restore you. Now I want you to go, and I want you to tell the message." They are going now as evangelists. His brothers, the ones who put him to death, have been forgiven, restored, and sent out.

This is the message: We once rejected Jesus. Now He has been raised on high, He's been given a name above every name, and the world is at His feet. He is the fairest of ten thousand. He has forgiven our sins. He wants us to be with Him and share His glory. And that's the message that they preached. They preached Joseph was risen, rich, and reigning.

- What message do you share about Jesus?
- What are some things that are discouraging from the world's perspective but are triumphs from God's perspective?

**PRACTICE THIS** Share the triumph of Jesus with someone today.

By faith Joseph, when he was dying, made mention of the departure
of the children of Israel, and gave instructions concerning his bones.

**HEBREWS 11:22**

**PONDER THIS** Do you want to smile at death? Do you want to practice the presence of God in the time of death? There's no way you can do it without faith. And what is faith? Faith is not positive thinking. Faith is not following a hunch. Faith is not hoping for the best. I love optimists, but that's not faith. Faith is not self-confidence. Self-confidence is all right if your confidence is first in the Lord. Faith is not wishing upon a star. What is faith? Faith is getting a word from God and believing it.

Hebrews 11:1 tells us what faith is. It says, "Now faith is the substance of things hoped for, the evidence of things not seen." That word *hope* does not mean maybe so, perhaps so. *Hope* in the Bible means rock-ribbed assurance based on the Word of God. God had made a promise to Abram. God cannot lie. Joseph, therefore, in the time of death, could smile at death because he had the unbreakable promises of God. Faith is not naming it and claiming it. You can't claim it until God names it. Faith is standing on the promises of God.

- What has God said that you need to put faith in this week?
- What would it look like to have faith when you think about death? What would change?

**PRACTICE THIS** Spend some time reading the Bible to learn about the promises of God from the Word of God. Consider Hebrews 11.

And Joseph said to his brethren, "I am dying; but God will
surely visit you, and bring you out of this land to the land of
which He swore to Abraham, to Isaac, and to Jacob." Then
Joseph took an oath from the children of Israel, saying, "God
will surely visit you, and you shall carry up my bones from here."
So Joseph died, being one hundred and ten years old; and
they embalmed him, and he was put in a coffin in Egypt.

**GENESIS 50:24-26**

**PONDER THIS** Faith is not shaken by appearances. When Joseph quoted this promise that God had made, from all appearances, there was no reason for them to think of ever leaving Egypt. Joseph was the prime minister there. They had it good there. They were living a life of ease. They had come from the land of Canaan to Egypt because of a famine. There was no famine in Egypt. They were in a place of privileged position.

Emotions don't really matter when it comes to God's Word. In this passage, nothing is said about Joseph's emotions one way or the other. I don't know what they were, but they really did not matter much. Feelings come and go, and feelings are deceiving. The Bible is the Word of God, and nothing else is worth believing.

Don't take counsel with your emotions as to whether or not a promise of God is true. Your emotions are the shallowest part of your nature. Salvation is the deepest work of God. God doesn't do the deepest work in the shallowest part. Put your confidence in the unshakeable power of God, not in your reasoning and not in your emotions.

- When have your emotions influenced you negatively?
- Why is it important to trust the Word of God even when your emotions tell you otherwise?

**PRACTICE THIS** Think about an area where your emotions are dictating your decisions instead of God's Word. Bring these to God in prayer.

Then the LORD said to Moses, "Depart and go up from here, you
and the people whom you have brought out of the land of Egypt,
to the land of which I swore to Abraham, Isaac, and Jacob, saying,
To your descendants I will give it. And I will send My Angel before
you, and I will drive out the Canaanite and the Amorite and the
Hittite and the Perizzite and the Hivite and the Jebusite. Go up to a
land flowing with milk and honey; for I will not go up in your midst,
lest I consume you on the way, for you are a stiff-necked people."

**EXODUS 33:1-3**

**PONDER THIS** Do not settle for protection, provision, or a promised land without God's presence. When you have God's presence, you need nothing more, but you should settle for nothing less.

There are many today who are saying, "I have salvation. I have eternal security. I'm not walking in joy. I'm not walking in victory. God is not real to me. But I honestly expect to go to Heaven." And when the pastor asks how many of you know if you were to die today, you'd go to Heaven, you lift your hand. But if you would be honest with me, you would say, "Pastor, God is not real in my life. I do not have the manifest presence of God in my life. I have His protection, I have His provision, I have His promise, but I do not have that presence of God in my life."

That is faulty logic. Don't think just because you have provision and protection you're right with God. I remind you that even a nonbeliever has certain provisions: food and air and clothes and houses. And you know, we can be so preoccupied with getting that provision and that protection and claiming that promise that we fail to have His presence.

- Is God real in your life right now? Why or why not?
- When has God's presence been real to you?

**PRACTICE THIS** Ask another Christian to share with you how to press into God's presence every day.

"I am the LORD, and there is no other; there is no God besides Me. I will gird you, though you have not known Me, that they may know from the rising of the sun to its setting that there is none besides Me. I am the LORD, and there is no other."

**ISAIAH 45:5-6**

**PONDER THIS** What is an idol? Anything you love more than God is an idol. What is an idol? Anything you fear more than God is an idol. What is an idol? Anything you serve more than God is an idol. Anything you trust more than God is an idol. Is there something that you love more, fear more, serve more, or trust more than almighty God? If there is, no wonder God's presence is not real in your heart and in your life. You have divided devotion.

If the glory of God is gone in your life if God is not real to you, ask this question: *Is there anyone or anything that takes precedence over God in my life?* You say, "Well, I give God a place in my life." God doesn't want a place in your life. You say, "Well, I give God prominence in my life." But God demands preeminence in your life. He will take nothing less. God's throne is not a duplex. Is there anything that is a greater controlling factor of your behavior? Is there a relationship that means more to you? Is there treasure that means more to you? Is there anything that gets more of your attention than almighty God? Then it should not come as a surprise to you that because of that golden calf in your life, God says, "I'm not going with you. I'll not be in the midst of you. I just won't do it." God will not accept divided devotion.

- If you are honest, what is God's place in your life?
- How can you give God preeminence in your life? Why is that important?

**PRACTICE THIS** Pray and surrender authority of your life before God. Confess where you have been holding onto control.

Therefore be imitators of God as dear children. And walk in love, as
Christ also has loved us and given Himself for us, an offering and a
sacrifice to God for a sweet-smelling aroma. But fornication and all
uncleanness or covetousness, let it not even be named among you,
as is fitting for saints; neither filthiness, nor foolish talking, nor coarse
jesting, which are not fitting, but rather giving of thanks. For this you
know, that no fornicator, unclean person, nor covetous man, who is
an idolater, has any inheritance in the kingdom of Christ and God.

**EPHESIANS 5:1-5**

**PONDER THIS** When a person has fellowship with God, it follows that he or she
has the ability to love. There is nothing more debilitating, nothing more dulling,
nothing more harmful to the ability to love than pornography. God wants you to
love. But there are many things that are disguised in the world as love that are
not. Pornography is not based on love. It destroys love. It is based on lust.

What's the difference between love and lust? Lust wants to get. Love wants to
give. Pornography is based on lust. It looks at people as objects to gratify one's
selfishness. The Bible says we're to love others as we love ourselves. You should
have some love for yourself. And when you have love for yourself, then you're
going to have love for others. Because you're going to want others to be treated
as you want to be treated, according to your own self-respect.

What treasures should we not trade for anything? Number one is a clean heart.
How wonderful it is to have a clean heart, to walk in the light, and to have fellowship
with God. Is any filth, dirt, or pornography worth losing a clean heart? Number
two is the ability to love. Don't you want to be able to love people? Consider the
treasure before you give into the trap.

- How has God grown your ability to love others?
- What are some things in your life that are holding back your
  ability to love others (such as pride, pornography, or self-
  seeking)?

**PRACTICE THIS** Confess to another Christian the struggles that are inhibiting
your ability to love God and others.

Then the LORD answered me and said: "Write the vision
and make it plain on tablets, that he may run who reads
it. For the vision is yet for an appointed time; but at the
end it will speak, and it will not lie. Though it tarries, wait
for it; because it will surely come, it will not tarry."

**HABAKKUK 2:2-3**

**PONDER THIS** I read a story about a young man who went to a revival. The preacher preached from John 5:24, "Most assuredly, I say to you, he who hears My word and believes in Him who sent Me has everlasting life, and shall not come into judgment, but has passed from death into life." The boy believed that message, gave his heart to Christ, and was saved. When he gave testimony of that account, he said, "That night, when I walked home, it seemed as if Satan were perched on my shoulder, whispering in my ear, saying 'You're not saved; you're not good enough; you're not strong enough. You didn't do this; you didn't do that; you'll never make it." He went home, and Satan kept taunting him. He sat on the couch in his living room, and the doubt continued. He said, "I got to thinking, well, maybe I'm not saved. I'd better look at that verse again."

And he picked it up, "Most assuredly, I say to you." He said, "Well, Jesus is speaking." He read, "he who hears My Word." He said, "I've heard it." He read, "and believes in Him who sent Me." He said, "I believed." He read, "has everlasting life." He said, "I have everlasting life. There, devil, read it for yourself!" From that moment on, he had assurance. You see, it is the Word of God, not your feelings, that gives assurance.

Faith is not shaken by reason; it is not shaken by emotion; it is not shaken by delay.

- When have you experienced doubts in your faith? Why is important to turn to the Bible in these moments?
- How do you keep yourself anchored in the truth of the Bible daily?

**PRACTICE THIS** Encourage a friend who is experiencing a time of doubt or trial in his or her faith.

And Moses took the bones of Joseph with him, for he had placed
the children of Israel under solemn oath, saying, "God will surely
visit you, and you shall carry up my bones from here with you."

**EXODUS 13:19**

**PONDER THIS** Why did Joseph say, "Take my bones with you?" Why was that so important to him? I mean, after all, he was dead. Joseph wanted to be a part of what God was doing.

Have you ever seen the tombs in Egypt? They are incredible! There are so many valuables there that belonged to King Tut. If you go to the British Museum, you can see many different ancient mummies. It's something to see, but I'm glad you can't find one of Joseph in there. Joseph was not a materialist. He had all of this wealth. He could have built a colossal monument. But, instead of building a physical monument, he built a monument of faith.

So many people today are living for this world only. Joseph wanted to be a part of what God was doing. All of the success of Egypt meant nothing to him. He wanted to leave a monument of faith.

If you know the Lord, the unbreakable promises of God, and the unshakeable power of God, then you will experience that undeniable peace of God when it comes time to die. Every time they saw that coffin with Joseph's bones, they were reminded of the brevity of life and the length of eternity. If they were living in prosperity, those bones reminded them that one of these days, they had to leave it all. And if they were living in adversity, those bones reminded them that there was a better day coming.

- Who in your life has left a monument of faith?
- What would it look like for you to build a monument of faith in your life? What would change? What would stay the same?

**PRACTICE THIS** Acknowledge and thank a person who is building a monument of faith with his or her life.

By faith Moses, when he was born, was hidden three months by his parents, because they saw he was a beautiful child; and they were not afraid of the king's command. By faith Moses, when he became of age, refused to be called the son of Pharaoh's daughter, choosing rather to suffer affliction with the people of God than to enjoy the passing pleasures of sin, esteeming the reproach of Christ greater riches than the treasures in Egypt; for he looked to the reward.

**HEBREWS 11:23-26**

**PONDER THIS** Moses was faced with position, possessions, pleasures, and all these things. If he went the devil's way, every sensual desire would be satisfied.

Every person has to come to the place where he or she makes a clear decision. The Bible speaks of the pleasures of sin. Don't be so foolish as to say to young people, "There's no pleasure in sin. You're going against the Bible." There are pleasures of sin. The devil is too smart to go fishing without any bait on his hook. There are pleasures, and there are treasures, and you are going to have to choose between the two.

It was not easy for Moses, and it will not be easy for you. That's the reason you have to make a radical, dramatic, clear choice. If you don't choose, you're going down. The Bible says Moses esteemed the reproach of Christ greater than the treasures in Egypt.

- Why is temporary pleasure so appealing to us?
- Do you treasure the things of Christ? What are some ways your life displays valuing His treasure over the pleasures of the world?

**PRACTICE THIS** Share with someone the treasure Christ is to you.

If we confess our sins, He is faithful and just to forgive us
our sins and to cleanse us from all unrighteousness.

**1 JOHN 1:9**

**PONDER THIS** I used to pastor a church in Fellsmere, Florida. There's a sugar mill there, and I would go witness to the men at the sugar mill. They had a big garage there where they fixed the tractors and other equipment. One of the members of my church ran that big garage machine shop. His shop was not what you would expect. The floors were clean and slick. There was no trash, nothing just lying around. There was no grease. Everything was clean. The tools were all put up in a certain place.

I looked at that place, and I stood in awe of how clean it was because it was a machine shop. Then I noticed something unusual. That man had painted every corner of that machine shop snow white. I asked him about it. I said, "Why are the corners white?" He said, "I found out that if you keep the corners white, you can keep the rest of the shop clean." He wouldn't allow anybody to put anything in a corner. Keep the corners of your mind clean. Don't just try to clean up the main part. Keep it all perfectly clean. Let God make you perfectly clean.

The question is, do you long to be perfectly clean? Would you like to say there is nothing between your soul and the Savior? That is the starting point.

- Have you allowed Christ to "clean the corners" of your heart? Why or why not?

- What is a corner in your life God wants to clean?

**PRACTICE THIS** Have a time of reflection, confession, and repentance, considering what areas of your heart need to be cleaned by Christ.

How can a young man cleanse his way? By taking heed
according to Your word. With my whole heart I have sought You;
oh, let me not wander from Your commandments! Your word
I have hidden in my heart, that I might not sin against You.

**PSALM 119:9-11**

**PONDER THIS** When you have Scripture in your heart and mind, your heart and mind are tied up in who God is. Casual thoughts and casual reading of the Bible are like a bee just flitting over the surface of a flower. Memorization is like the bee going down into the heart of the flower and gathering the nectar. Meditation is like taking it back to the hive and making honey out of it. We need to gather the Word of God so we can meditate on the Word of God.

You see, God gave you a memory. So many people remember what they should not remember and forget what they should remember. What Scripture memory does is this: it helps you to remember what you should and to forget what you should. The mind is a marvelous thing. A mind can think about itself thinking. It's an incredible thing. And you can hide God's Word in your heart. This is why the Psalmist says, "Your word I have hidden in my heart, that I might not sin against You."

- What verses do you have memorized? How did you learn these?
- What are some negative thoughts that play over and over in your mind? What are some verses that could anchor you in the truth of God's Word when those thoughts come to mind?

**PRACTICE THIS** Work to memorize a new verse by writing it down and putting it in a place you will see every day.

"But the hour is coming, and now is, when the true worshipers
will worship the Father in spirit and truth; for the Father
is seeking such to worship Him. God is Spirit, and those
who worship Him must worship in spirit and truth."

**JOHN 4:23-24**

**PONDER THIS** When I was a little kid, my daddy sold Buick automobiles for East Coast Motors down in West Palm Beach, Florida. He would leave the house with his briefcase in hand and kiss my mother goodbye before he left for a day of work. I had no earthly idea where he went, what he did, or what he said. But when he would come back home, I would welcome him home. I didn't have to know what he did or how he did it to know and love him. He was my daddy; I loved him because of who he was to me.

I don't understand today where God goes when He goes to work—how He flings out the stars and scoops out the oceans and heaps up the mountains and runs this mighty Universe. There are a lot of things about God I don't know, but that doesn't bother me. You don't know either, but the truth is, you don't have to know all that your Father does for Him to be your Father. Little children can look to Him and say, "Father," and the Bible teaches that when we are saved, God has sent forth the Spirit of His Son into our hearts crying, "Abba, Father." (See Romans 8:15.) When you worship, you must worship the right person. Don't hold back your worship because you don't understand all the details.

- What are some questions you have asked God that have held you back from worshiping Him?
- When is it easy for you to forget God's role as your unchanging Father?

**PRACTICE THIS** Encourage a friend who feels far from God in his or her faith. Remind him or her of the truth that God is his or her heavenly Father even through the unknowns.

Or do you not know that your body is the temple of the Holy
Spirit who is in you, whom you have from God, and you are not
your own? For you were bought at a price; therefore glorify
God in your body and in your spirit, which are God's.

**1 CORINTHIANS 6:19-20**

**PONDER THIS** When I was a little boy, I was part of a wonderful church. As you walked in the door of that very small auditorium, there was a sign over the door that said, "The LORD is in His holy temple. Let all the earth keep silence before Him" (Habakkuk 2:20). When I walked in there, I knew I'd come to the holy place. Now, don't get me wrong, I'm not putting down that place, but there is a flaw with attaching that quote to a building. Because do you know where the sanctuary is now? Right here, in me. Paul said, when you're in Christ, your body is a temple of the Holy Spirit. (See 1 Corinthians 3:16; 6:19.)

You know, there are people who wouldn't think of defiling this place. Some of you would not smoke in here, but as soon as you get out, you light up. You say, "Well, I wouldn't smoke in there—that's the church." But the truth is, you're the sanctuary. Some of you would not use language in the church that you would use outside of church. Why is that? You're the temple of God. God lives in you! That is the sanctuary to keep clean through His Spirit, in church and out of church, when everyone sees you and when no one is around.

- What are some things that you do outside of the church that do not honor God?

- How should the understanding that you are the temple of the Holy Spirit change the way you live?

**PRACTICE THIS** Pray and ask God to show you where you are not reflecting the Holy Spirit in your life.

Beware, brethren, lest there be in any of you an evil heart of unbelief
in departing from the living God; but exhort one another daily,
while it is called "Today," lest any of you be hardened through the
deceitfulness of sin. For we have become partakers of Christ if
we hold the beginning of our confidence steadfast to the end.

**HEBREWS 3:12-14**

**PONDER THIS** Where's the place of worship? Worship can be any time and any place, but there is something significant about our coming together to worship. However, the significance of coming together is not primarily that we come to worship at church but that we bring our worship to church. Ideally, we have been with the Lord all week long. And so, when we come together, we don't come to church to get filled up; we're already full of God. We gather to celebrate together. We bring our worship.

Do you know what you're saying when you go to church? Number one, you're saying, "God is important to me," and you're saying, "You people are important to me." My brothers and sisters in Christ are important to me. That's why we "[do] not [forsake] the assembling of ourselves together" (See Hebrews 10:25.), but we exhort one another. So many in my church bless me when I see them—the choir, the Sunday school teachers, the musicians, the members. As we worship, as I look out there and look at all the people in my church, those who are smiling and nodding and saying, "Amen," that is a blessing to me.

- Who are the people you are encouraged by at your church? How can you let them know?
- What kind of attitude do you typically bring to church? Is it an attitude of celebration? Why or why not?

**PRACTICE THIS** Share a word or note of encouragement with someone in your church today.

For God is my witness, whom I serve with my spirit
in the gospel of His Son, that without ceasing I
make mention of you always in my prayers.

**ROMANS 1:9**

**PONDER THIS** We worship the Lord in spirit and in truth. What does it mean to worship in spirit? You don't just worship God with your hands and your knees and your eyes and your mouth—that's involved, but worship needs to come from within. You have to serve God with your spirit. If you don't enjoy worshiping, the problem is in your heart. If worship seems boring to you, you are not worshiping God in spirit and in truth. You may think a church service is just listening to a sermon or singing songs, but it is more than that!

You have to worship God in spirit! And to worship God in spirit, the Holy Spirit has to be in your spirit! "You received the Spirit of adoption by whom we cry out, 'Abba, Father'" (Romans 8:15). If you don't enjoy coming to church, if it's tedious, tasteless, a bore, and a drag to you, remember the joy of your salvation, go to a gathering, and see God work in a powerful way to remind yourself of His Spirit at work!

- Do you enjoy worship services? What do you like about them? What is more difficult for you about them?
- Have you ever found yourself stuck in the motions, going to church as a routine but taking no joy in it? How can we turn to the Lord in these moments?

**PRACTICE THIS** Spend some time in prayer asking God to restore the joy of your salvation and lead you to worship Him in spirit and truth as He desires.

Who is wise and understanding among you? Let him show by good conduct that his works are done in the meekness of wisdom. But if you have bitter envy and self-seeking in your hearts, do not boast and lie against the truth. This wisdom does not descend from above, but is earthly, sensual, demonic. For where envy and self-seeking exist, confusion and every evil thing are there. But the wisdom that is from above is first pure, then peaceable, gentle, willing to yield, full of mercy and good fruits, without partiality and without hypocrisy. Now the fruit of righteousness is sown in peace by those who make peace.

**JAMES 3:13-18**

**PONDER THIS** If a dog has a nasty bone in his mouth and you try to take it away from him, you might get bitten. But if you put a steak on the ground and the dog sees the steak, he'll drop the bone to get the steak. That dog discerns. He looks: Here's the bone, there's the steak. There's a discernment. He thinks, "That is better than this." Then there's a choice. He says, "I want the steak. I choose the steak." Then he refuses the bone.

You're going to have to spend some time with your children to help them understand what the values of life are. I would not trade anything for fellowship with God. The ability to have a godly family is valuable and precious. Don't let them sacrifice these things. Lead them to Christ. Help them to see through Satan's lies. All of their sin struggles are based on a lie. The lie is that this is somehow good, tantalizing, titillating, that it will somehow satisfy. It is all a lie. Satan is a liar. Show your children the One who is the way, the truth, and the life. (See John 14:6.)

- Who has taught you the most about discernment? How has that impacted you?

- How do you seek to communicate the value of Christ to those around you?

**PRACTICE THIS** Share with another person how precious and valuable Jesus is to you.

Unless the LORD builds the house, they labor in vain who build it; unless the LORD guards the city, the watchman stays awake in vain. It is vain for you to rise up early, to sit up late, to eat the bread of sorrows; for so He gives His beloved sleep.

**PSALM 127:1-2**

**PONDER THIS** Imagine you are at the pool, and there is a beach ball in the water. You could keep it under the water as long as you sit on it. But suddenly, it pops up to the surface again. Even if you have two or three people trying to keep it under, you can only hold it down so long before it comes back up. That's the way people often fight sin. They say, "I'm not going to do this anymore. I don't like this. I'm against it." And they put it down in their minds, but then it just comes to the surface again. And they are fighting a hopeless battle.

Let me tell you one way to keep that ball sunk. Let the air out of it. You need to let the air out of Satan's lies, too. One way is to remove temptations. This is also a way to help others avoid sin. Ultimately, there is absolutely nothing you can do to keep your kids from sin because God gave them a will. But I'll tell you one thing I don't want to do: I don't want to build a home that is dangerous for children. If they want to climb over the wall and jump off, that will break my heart. But I don't want to have the kind of home where they fall accidentally because I have not removed the temptations from that home. Do you understand what I am saying? You need to at least build the wall.

- What are some boundaries against temptation you have in your home? How are they beneficial to you and your family?
- What are some sin struggles that keep popping back up in your life? What are some lies from Satan you need to "let the air out of"?

**PRACTICE THIS** Pray and consider what sin struggles repeatedly arise in your life. Repent and surrender them to God.

Therefore be imitators of God as dear children.

**EPHESIANS 5:1**

**PONDER THIS** Do you have any unconfessed, unrepented sin? I want to give you a testimony. You may think I'm bragging, but I am not. I don't have any unconfessed sin in my life—none. You say, "Oh, you think you're a super Christian?" No, I'm a normal Christian. That is the normal Christian life. I would be a fool to stand up here and try and preach without the breastplate of righteousness.

Now, you're not going to win the war with pornography if all you fight is pornography. What about honesty? What about pride? What about selfishness? You say, "Pastor Rogers, you mean to tell me you don't have any problem fighting the devil?" I fight him all the time. "You mean to tell me you don't fail?" I fail. I'm not saying I'm perfect. God knows I'm not. But I'm telling you, there's no reason that any man, woman, boy, or girl cannot be as pure and clean as the driven snow. "If we confess our sins, He is faithful and just to forgive us our sins and to cleanse us from all unrighteousness" (1 John 1:9). Why would I want to drag sin around? Why would I want to start the day with the baggage of sin when I can be clean? It's so simple. If we confess our sins, He is faithful and just to forgive us our sins and to cleanse us from all unrighteousness. Not some, all. Thank God for that.

- When was the last time you confessed sin to God?
- Why is it important to deal with our sin as it comes up instead of keeping it around?

**PRACTICE THIS** Pray and talk to God about your sin. Consider all your sins, not only the ones that are most public or obvious.

But when He saw the multitudes, He was moved with compassion
for them, because they were weary and scattered, like sheep
having no shepherd. Then He said to His disciples, "The harvest
truly is plentiful, but the laborers are few. Therefore pray the
Lord of the harvest to send out laborers into His harvest."

**MATTHEW 9:36-38**

**PONDER THIS** We don't fight alone. I need you to pray for me. People tell me from time to time, "Pastor, I'm praying for you." Many times, tears will come to my eyes when someone says that. There are six billion people on Earth. Some people have never been prayed for one time. If you have anybody praying for you, you're blessed. We need to pray for one another. Husbands need to pray for their wives. Wives need to pray for their husbands. Parents need to pray for their children. The pastor needs to pray for his congregation. The congregation needs to pray for the people. We're in the battle together, and it's a real battle, isn't it? Let's hold one another up in prayer. Let's encourage one another. I don't want us to lose this war.

We may be on the verge of one of the greatest spiritual revivals the world has ever seen. Things are happening—there's a quickening. I speak to pastor friends, and I ask how it's going. They say, "I don't understand it, but God is moving in our church. Things are happening. Souls are getting saved." How encouraging! The power of prayer is incredible.

- What are the things you pray for most often?
- How active is your prayer life? What are some things that cause you to pray more? What are things that prevent you from praying?

**PRACTICE THIS** Reach out and let someone know you are praying for him or her today.

For I delivered to you first of all that which I also received: that Christ
died for our sins according to the Scriptures, and that He was buried,
and that He rose again the third day according to the Scriptures.

**1 CORINTHIANS 15:3-4**

**PONDER THIS** The word *gospel* comes from a combination of words—telling good things. The Greek word itself literally means "good news." The Gospel is "the good news of the death, burial, and resurrection of Jesus Christ." The best news the world ever heard came from a graveyard outside Jerusalem, and it is this: "He is not here; for He is risen" (Matthew 28:6a).

But good news is not good news unless there's the possibility of bad news. Suppose I said to you tonight, "I've got good news for you. Your house is not on fire." Well, that kind of falls flat unless you feel that your house may have been on fire. But imagine you're in the hospital; perhaps a person you love is in the operating room, and you're waiting in the waiting room. Then the doors swing open, and the surgeon comes out, takes that mask from his face, and says, "I've got good news." That's good news because you were unsure of what you might hear. The good news is the death, burial, and resurrection of Jesus Christ. The bad news that makes the good news good is found in 1 Corinthians 15:3: "Christ died for our sins." This is the major thing. No matter what else you do, if you don't get this, you have missed it. As somebody said a long time ago, "The main thing is to keep the main thing the main thing, and the main thing is the Gospel."

- What is the danger of emphasizing one part of the Gospel over another?
- How do you seek to keep the Gospel as the main thing in your life?

**PRACTICE THIS** Pray and ask God to give you the opportunity to share the Gospel with someone else this week.

"Fear not, for I am with you; be not dismayed, for I am
your God. I will strengthen you, yes, I will help you, I
will uphold you with My righteous right hand."

**ISAIAH 41:10**

**PONDER THIS** As a teen, I prayed and asked the Lord Jesus Christ to come into my heart and my life. I know I would never have made it had it not been for the Gospel of Jesus Christ, which not only saved me but also strengthened me. And I am being saved day by day. Salvation is a crisis when you trust Christ, but it is a crisis followed by a process as He pours His life into you day by day. Those of you who are saying, "Well, I'd like to be saved, but I'm afraid I can't live it"—you can't. I can't live it. Nobody has ever lived the Christian life but Jesus Christ. But He will live it in you and through you. I promise you on the authority of the Word of God, if you trust Jesus Christ, He will come into your heart. He will give you a new nature. Believe it and be saved. Believe it and be strengthened.

Isn't it great that we can be saved? Isn't it better that we can be saved and know it? It is thrice wonderful that we can be saved, know that we're saved, and know that we can never, ever lose it. I am secured by the Gospel of the Lord Jesus Christ. I stand amazed. I stand assured. I stand secured and strengthened by the Gospel of our Lord and Savior, Jesus Christ.

- How has God strengthened your faith?
- Have you ever been overwhelmed trying to live the Christian life on your own power? Why won't that work?

**PRACTICE THIS** Write down a list of ways you'd like to grow in your faith. Ask God to help you grow.

For by grace you have been saved through faith, and that not of yourselves; it is the gift of God, not of works, lest anyone should boast.

**EPHESIANS 2:8-9**

**PONDER THIS** I was on an airplane with a man who was a member of a denomination that believes you have to be baptized to be saved. I said, "What if I were a businessman on this plane with you, and we heard we were minutes away from a deadly crash? What would you do if I asked, 'Sir, would you tell me how to be saved?'" He said, "I wouldn't have a message for you." Is that not sad? In that logic, you have to take the "whosoever" out of the Bible and say, "Whosoever would believe in the Lord Jesus Christ and be fortunate enough to be near water and have a preacher there to baptize him—and some would say, 'and be of my denomination'—will be saved." Do you see what that does? It emasculates the Gospel. It takes the good news out of the Gospel. I am so everlastingly glad that I can say to anybody, anyplace, "Believe on the Lord Jesus Christ, and you will be saved." (See Acts 16:31.) It is totally, completely by grace. It extends to every person. It extends to every place, and it extends to every problem. There's only one thing that ultimately matters, and that's your relationship with God. There's no other message that has an answer to sin, sorrow, and death but the Gospel of our Lord and Savior, Jesus Christ.

- What are some conditions you feel tempted to add to the Gospel?
- What's a recent example of God's grace in your life?

**PRACTICE THIS** Practice sharing the Gospel with someone. Are you prone to make much of grace or works in sharing with others? Evaluate how you can grow in sharing the Gospel.

Come now, you rich, weep and howl for your miseries that are
coming upon you! Your riches are corrupted, and your garments are
moth-eaten. Your gold and silver are corroded, and their corrosion
will be a witness against you and will eat your flesh like fire. You
have heaped up treasure in the last days. Indeed the wages of the
laborers who mowed your fields, which you kept back by fraud,
cry out; and the cries of the reapers have reached the ears of the
Lord of Sabaoth. You have lived on the earth in pleasure and luxury;
you have fattened your hearts as in a day of slaughter. You have
condemned, you have murdered the just; he does not resist you.

**JAMES 5:1-6**

**PONDER THIS** I know some people who are making money, but they don't need
any more money. They are really just kind of keeping score, and they don't
want that money in circulation. God wants money in circulation; God wants
everything in circulation. There is enough to go around. There is enough to take
care of everything, and when God created the world, He made everything with
a propensity and the ability to give. The sun gives, and we have light. The earth
gives, and we have life. The trees give, and we have air, food, and wood. There
is a reciprocal service that God has put into humanity, but some people can't
trust the Lord. They say, "I've just got to keep hoarding it up. I've just got to keep
stashing it away."

A bell, somebody said, is not a bell until you ring it; a song is not a song until you
sing it; love is not love until you give it away; joy is not joy until you share it; and
wealth is not really wealth until you spend it. What good is paper sitting around
somewhere? Use it for God's glory!

- When have you given generously? How did you receive a
  blessing as a giver?
- Why do we wrestle with the temptation to keep money and
  things to ourselves? Does this reflect God's heart? Why or why
  not?

**PRACTICE THIS** Pray and ask God who you can give generously to, and act on
His answer.

Do not overwork to be rich; because of
your own understanding, cease!

**PROVERBS 23:4**

**PONDER THIS** You are in financial bondage if you have a desire to get rich quickly. We tell a young person, "Make all the money you can, so long as you make it honestly." That's bad advice. A man who's making all the money he can is going to be making money when he should be praying, soul-winning, witnessing, or going fishing. He's in bondage. Feel sorry for the man whose goal is to be rich. Your goal should be to live for the Lord. The Bible says in Matthew 6:33, "But seek first the kingdom of God and His righteousness, and all these things shall be added to you." If wealth is what motivates you, you're in financial bondage. You're in financial bondage if you don't have treasure in Heaven.

You may call it your house or your car, but fifty or one hundred years from now, somebody else will hold possession of it. Isn't that true? We only have earthly possessions for a little while and we're stewards. All areas of your life, including your finances, should be used for God's glory.

- What are some ways you might be in bondage to money?
- How does Jesus offer freedom from this?

**PRACTICE THIS** Consider what place money has in your life. Discuss with another friend ideas on how you can use money for God's glory.

"Will a man rob God? Yet you have robbed Me!" But you say," "In what way have we robbed You?" "In tithes and offerings. You are cursed with a curse, for you have robbed Me, even this whole nation. Bring all the tithes into the storehouse, that there may be food in My house, and try Me now in this," says the LORD of hosts, "If I will not open for you the windows of heaven and pour out for you such blessing that there will not be room enough to receive it."

**MALACHI 3:8-10**

**PONDER THIS** A man was seen driving down the highway in a red Ferrari. On the back of that Ferrari was a bumper sticker that said, "He who has the most toys when he dies wins." That's wrong. If you want to know how wealthy you are, add up everything you have that money can't buy, and death can't take away, then you'll know. Or, to put it another way, are the things you're living for worth Christ dying for? Think about it. It's not wrong to have possessions. As a matter of fact, God wants you to have possessions. God gives you possessions to make you a steward over them. But you can be financially in bondage as a poor person, and you can be financially in bondage as a wealthy person.

It's about time we stopped buying things we don't need with money we don't have to impress people we don't like. It's about time we learn what God had to say about how to make money, how to use money, how to spend money, how to save money, and how to give money. God wants to open the windows of Heaven and pour out a blessing on you.

- How do you use your possessions for God's glory?
- How does your faith affect how you make, use, and spend your money?

**PRACTICE THIS** Look up different passages about money and ask God where you could grow in stewardship for His glory.

Now godliness with contentment is great gain. For we brought
nothing into this world, and it is certain we can carry nothing out.
And having food and clothing, with these we shall be content.
But those who desire to be rich fall into temptation and a snare,
and into many foolish and harmful lusts which drown men in
destruction and perdition. For the love of money is a root of all
kinds of evil, for which some have strayed from the faith in their
greediness, and pierced themselves through with many sorrows.

**1 TIMOTHY 6:6-10**

**PONDER THIS** Many of us just think if we simply hold our financial position, we are being biblical, but we are not. We are stewards; we are to invest and see our investments grow. When you invest, you need to examine your motive for investment. If your motive is greed, or if your motive is pride, that is not from God. If you have Jesus, you are rich. And to whom little is not enough, nothing is enough. Godliness with contentment is great gain because we brought nothing into this world, and it is certain that we will carry nothing out.

In 1 Timothy 6:17, Paul told Timothy, here's what you tell your church members: "Command those who are rich in this present age not to be haughty, nor to trust in uncertain riches but in the living God, who gives us richly all things to enjoy." Isn't that good advice? We are stewards who are managing what God has given to us. As good stewards, we need to take what God has put in our hands and prayerfully ask, "How much of this shall I use? How much of this shall I give? And how much of this shall I invest for the glory of God?"

- Where do you struggle with contentment? How is that reflected in your finances?
- How do you seek to discern between a want, a need, or a prompting from God?

**PRACTICE THIS** Ask a fellow Christian how he or she uses resources for God's glory.

As you do not know what is the way of the wind, or how
the bones grow in the womb of her who is with child, so
you do not know the works of God who makes everything.
In the morning sow your seed, and in the evening do not
withhold your hand; for you do not know which will prosper,
either this or that, or whether both alike will be good.

**ECCLESIASTES 11:5-6**

**PONDER THIS** There are some things we don't know. How do we know the mind of the Spirit? Who knows the ways of God any more than we understand how a baby is formed in its mother's womb? There are some mysteries in life that are under the sovereign control of Almighty God, and therefore, you must trust Him. You have to say, "Lord, I just look to You. I realize I've got to make investments. I realize that I must prepare. I realize that I must be willing to venture, but after I've done all that, who knows what's going to happen? So, Lord, I trust You."

Proverbs 3:5-6 says, "Trust in the LORD with all your heart, and lean not on your own understanding; in all your ways acknowledge Him, and He shall direct your paths." People are so uptight because they're worried about their finances. You don't have to live in that bondage. You can come to Him and say, "Lord, it's in Your hands. I don't know what the future holds, but I know you, Lord, and I know that You love me." You don't have to know the exact way that He will provide, but you can trust that He will provide when you follow Him.

- What are some things you have entrusted to God? What are some things you have not entrusted to God?

- Have you seen an example of trusting God with the unknown? What was that like? What did you learn from that experience?

**PRACTICE THIS** Talk to God about the areas in which you struggle to trust Him. Surrender your life, possessions, and finances to Him.

Give, and it will be given to you: good measure, pressed down, shaken
together, and running over will be put into your bosom. For with
the same measure that you use, it will be measured back to you."

**LUKE 6:38**

**PONDER THIS** I heard about a corn farmer who had two boys. While the other boys were off fishing and hunting and running around, this farmer's sons were working in the cornfields. Somebody asked that farmer, "Why do you work those boys so diligently? You don't need all that corn." He said, "I'm not raising corn—I'm raising boys." Likewise, God is not simply raising money. What God is doing is growing Christians.

One sign that you're getting right with God is that you trust God with your finances. You can sing all you want about how you love Jesus and all of that. You can have crocodile tears in your eyes, but the consecration that doesn't reach every part of your life, even your wallet, has not reached your heart. It's just idle talk.

I saw a bumper sticker that said, "Tithe if you love Jesus. Anybody can blow their horn." God wants your heart. That's the reason He asks us to give because "where your treasure is, there your heart will be also" (Matthew 6:21). The Lord knows what He's up to. He just wants you to put Him first. That's the reason he says in Matthew 6:33, "But seek first the kingdom of God and His righteousness, and all these things shall be added to you."

- What would it look like to trust God with your finances?
- What makes it hard to prioritize God in our finances?

**PRACTICE THIS** Look at your budget and pray about where you could grow in trusting God with your finances.

"Therefore do not worry, saying, 'What shall we eat?' or 'What shall we drink?' or 'What shall we wear?' For after all these things the Gentiles seek. For your heavenly Father knows that you need all these things. But seek first the kingdom of God and His righteousness, and all these things shall be added to you."

**MATTHEW 6:31-33**

**PONDER THIS** After our wedding, Joyce and I had about fifty or sixty dollars to begin our marriage. We took our honeymoon on that. We didn't have anything. But we had each other, and we had Jesus. I worked my way through school in all manner of jobs—packing fruit, selling automobiles, doing construction, working as a butcher, and working in a department store. Even in that difficult time, when our finances were stretched thin, we gave beyond the tithe.

And I can tell you that through these years we've tithed, we've seen this verse to be true. God enabled us to give away amounts of money that I thought we'd never be able to give. He has proven to us that His Word is true. "Try me," God says in Malachi 3:10. Put me to the test. See if it's true. Would you trust God with your finances that way? Would you give generously to sit back and watch His provision?

- When have you given generously for God's glory, even if it didn't make sense on paper? What happened?
- What are some fears that arise when you consider tithing generously?

**PRACTICE THIS** Pray about where you could give generously for God's glory.

Blessed be the God and Father of our Lord Jesus Christ, who has blessed us with every spiritual blessing in the heavenly places in Christ, just as He chose us in Him before the foundation of the world, that we should be holy and without blame before Him in love, having predestined us to adoption as sons by Jesus Christ to Himself, according to the good pleasure of His will, to the praise of the glory of His grace, by which He made us accepted in the Beloved.

**EPHESIANS 1:3-6**

**PONDER THIS** Do you have all the love you need? Or all the patience you need? Or all the courage you need? Or all the faith you need? Or all the wisdom you need? In general, do you have all you need? Few would say yes unless you understand where I'm coming from. Ephesians 1:3 says, "God has blessed us with every spiritual blessing in the heavenly places in Christ." So why don't we have them? We haven't taken hold of what we've received. We need to put the foot of faith on the promises of God and say, "That is mine."

When you are living in victory, it's not according to your ability; it's your response to His ability. In Romans 8:37, Paul said, "Yet in all these things we are more than conquerors through Him who loved us." It is time to claim the spiritual blessings you have in Him. Live in the victory of Jesus.

- When do you feel needy in your faith? How do you respond in those moments?

- What is the difference between believing victory is our responsibility and seeing victory as our response to God's ability?

**PRACTICE THIS** Talk to God about the areas in which you struggle to trust His victory.

Because Your lovingkindness is better than life, my lips shall praise
You. Thus I will bless You while I live; I will lift up my hands in Your
name. My soul shall be satisfied as with marrow and fatness, and
my mouth shall praise You with joyful lips. When I remember
You on my bed, I meditate on You in the night watches.

**PSALM 63:3-6**

**PONDER THIS** This passage illustrates the path to God's victory. Young David is
fleeing from wicked and jealous King Saul, who is chasing him for his life. David
wonders whether he will be killed. How could David live victoriously like that?
He'd been meditating.

Do you know what a constant habit of mine is? I like to get a verse of Scripture
and go to sleep with it. I'll run it through my mind, chew on it, and soak on it. It's
a wonderful thing to do. Let the last word be His Word, and go to sleep thinking
about the Word of God. That's what David did. It was in his mouth because it was
in his mind, and because it was in his mouth and in his mind, it was in his manner
of life. The Word of God is not given to satisfy your curiosity and to scratch your
intellectual itch. It's given to lead you to obedience that leads to a knowledge
of God that leads to victory. The real proof that we believe in the Bible is that
we obey it. And when we obey it, God reveals Himself to us in such wonderful
ways. You're saying to God, "I trust You so much that I'm going to obey You in
everything You tell me." And God says, "I'm going to manifest Myself to you."

- What are some habits that remind you of God's truth?
- Why is it hard for us to obey God's Word?

**PRACTICE THIS** Choose a verse to read before bed and meditate on that verse
as you go to sleep.

Trust in the LORD with all your heart and lean not on your own understanding; in all your ways acknowledge Him, and He shall direct your paths. Do not be wise in your own eyes; fear the LORD and depart from evil. It will be health to your flesh, and strength to your bones.

**PSALM 63:3-6**

**PONDER THIS** Why is it difficult for us to trust the Lord with all our hearts? It's hard to trust someone you don't know. I mean, if a perfect stranger were to walk up to you today and say, "Will you do something for me?" What's your first question? "What is it?" If Joyce were to say to me, "Adrian, will you do something for me?" I might say, "What is it?" And then she might say to me, "Just trust me." I'd say, "Yes." Do you know why? I know her that well. I can trust her because I know her.

You can't trust someone you don't know. If you're having difficulty trusting the Lord, you have not learned to know Him and love Him. To know Him is to love Him. And then, to love Him is to trust Him. And then, to trust Him is to obey Him. And to obey Him is to be blessed. So, it begins with knowing the Lord, and if you're having difficulty trusting the Lord, may I suggest that you spend some time getting to know the Lord. We're not to trust our own understanding. So many times, we want to say, "Well, this is the way I think." Very frankly, we make a terrible mistake when we trust our own understanding.

- Where do you struggle to trust God?
- When was a time when you were close to God? Why was it easier to trust Him in that time?

**PRACTICE THIS** Spend some time in God's Word getting to know Him better.

Love has been perfected among us in this: that we may have boldness in the day of judgment; because as He is, so are we in this world. There is no fear in love; but perfect love casts out fear, because fear involves torment. But he who fears has not been made perfect in love. We love Him because He first loved us.

**1 JOHN 4:17-19**

**PONDER THIS** I read a young man's poem about his commitment to Christ. He was devoted and steadfast in His words, ready to follow the Great Commission. He wrote about how God would equip him through His Spirit for the task to which He was called. He said he was a part of the fellowship of the unashamed. That is powerful.

We need church members like that. We need a pastor like that. We need a choir like that. The reason many of us do not know the will of God for our lives is we have not come to the recipe, "Trust in the LORD with all your heart, and lean not on your own understanding; in all your ways acknowledge Him, and He shall direct your paths" (Proverbs 3:5-6). Until you've done that, don't complain about not knowing the will of God. You say, "Well, Pastor, if I were to do that, no telling what He'd have me to do. He might send me as some missionary in Africa. He might make me marry some boring person."

Don't be afraid of the will of God. I love that Scripture says, "Perfect love casts out fear" (1 John 4:18a). That doesn't mean you love God perfectly. None of us has ever done anything perfectly except sin. It's not my perfect love for Him that casts out fear. It's His perfect love for us!

- Why is it difficult for you to know God's will?
- When was a time you sought God's will? How did that approach change your perspective on daily life?

**PRACTICE THIS** Ask a pastor or Bible study leader how he or she seeks the will of God. Consider any principles he or she shares that you might follow.

These things we also speak, not in words which man's wisdom teaches but which the Holy Spirit teaches, comparing spiritual things with spiritual. But the natural man does not receive the things of the Spirit of God, for they are foolishness to him; nor can he know them, because they are spiritually discerned.

**1 CORINTHIANS 2:13-14**

**PONDER THIS** A natural man is one who's only had one birth. He is born into the natural world, and he is bound by the material world. He can never know the things of the Spirit of God until he has a second birth. Look at verse 14, "The natural man does not receive the things of the Spirit of God."

If you were to come into a room where music is playing and I say to you, "Smell that music," you'd say, "That's impossible." Now, that wouldn't mean that there was anything wrong with your nose; it just would mean that the nose is the wrong organ for perceiving music. You don't smell music; you hear music. There may be nothing wrong with your mind, but that is the wrong organ for knowing God.

The soul is missing. You know God primarily with your soul, which is the organ of spiritual knowledge. Human wisdom is superficial, transitory, limited, and dangerous. You can't know God through human wisdom. You know God in your soul, according to His Spirit, who speaks to your soul.

- What is the difference between knowing God with your mind and with your soul?
- When have you felt God's presence through the Holy Spirit? What did you learn about God in that time?

**PRACTICE THIS** Ask God to help you know Him in your soul through the presence of His Spirit.

"Ask, and it will be given to you; seek, and you will find; knock,
and it will be opened to you. For everyone who asks receives, and
he who seeks finds, and to him who knocks it will be opened."

**MATTHEW 7:7-8**

**PONDER THIS** One night when I was down in Orlando, Florida, I tried to sleep, but I had a rock for a pillow. That is saying a lot because I am a sound sleeper. All night long, God just said, "Adrian, you're going in the wrong direction—you're trying to pour water uphill. You're in the wrong place. You need to move out somewhere on the Interstate 40 corridor and see if there's property out there." So, I talked to some of the leadership of my church. I said, "Don't think I'm crazy, but let me tell you something that God has put in my heart." It had been so discouraging to see where the doors were shut. But God was giving us a different direction. In this new opportunity, God said, "Come on in." God just opened the door.

That's the way God leads. He'll do it through His Word. He'll do it when you pray, and the Spirit of God speaks to your heart. He will do it through sanctified wisdom. God will renew your mind and use it and give you wisdom, and then God will open doors and God will shut doors. God doesn't leave you wandering around like a ship without a rudder, a mast, a compass, or a sail on a dark and stormy night. God will guide His people.

- Have you ever gotten frustrated when God closed a door? What did you do?

- How can you tell when God is opening a door?

**PRACTICE THIS** Consider what doors God may be opening or closing in your life right now. Pray for wisdom and discernment to follow His direction.

He who is faithful in what is least is faithful also in much; and
he who is unjust in what is least is unjust also in much.

**LUKE 16:10**

**PONDER THIS** When I played football, I was always grateful if I had the ball and a man was down the field in front of me, throwing blocks and moving those obstacles. Do you know God does some downfield blocking for you? You may not even know He's been doing it. It's not merely enough to know the will of God, not enough to only have direction. We've got to have power, where God makes our paths straight for us through the wilderness. God's done that for me so many times. God has given me a job and a message, and then He just picks me up and carries me. He'll do that for you, too. Proverbs 3:5 says, "Trust in the LORD with *all* your heart." Look in verse 6, "In *all* your ways acknowledge Him." Look in verse 9, "*all* your increase." When your worship, your walk, and your wealth are given over to Him, you'll know the will of God. Put those "alls" in there! Don't play games with God! Are you serious about knowing and doing the will of God? You say, "Oh, I wish I knew the will of God." Just do it in the small things. Do it in the things nearest to you. "He who is faithful in what is least is faithful also in much."

- What is a small thing you need to entrust to God today?
- Which "all" do you struggle with the most from today's devotion?

**PRACTICE THIS** Surrender to God your all. Journal about this surrender so you can recall this moment you entrusted your life to Him.

But he who is spiritual judges all things, yet he himself is rightly
judged by no one. For "who has known the mind of the Lord
that he may instruct Him?" But we have the mind of Christ.

**1 CORINTHIANS 2:15-16**

**PONDER THIS** Do you know a good prayer for when you begin to study the Word of God? It is Psalm 119:18, "Open my eyes, that I may see wondrous things from Your law." When you pray that prayer and are filled with the Holy Spirit, a part of you will know that "never knew before," and a part of you will see that "never saw before."

People who live by divine illumination are going to be a mystery to those around them. Today's verse says, "But he who is spiritual judges all things." That is, he or she has a penetrating insight into the way things work. These people have supernatural wisdom. "Yet he himself is rightly judged by no one." The world is not going to understand us. I'll tell you; we're going to know some things that they won't know, and they're really going to think we're the crazy ones. They're going to say, "There's something wrong with that person." You see, we're tuned in where others are not. We are marching to the beat of a different drum. They can't understand us because we have the mind of Christ, and they don't understand Christ.

- How do you seek to have the mind of Christ on an ongoing basis?
- What is something you understood in a new way after coming to faith?

**PRACTICE THIS** Talk to a friend about how your mindset has changed since you began following Jesus.

Then Mary said to the angel, "How can this be, since I do not know a man?" And the angel answered and said to her, "The Holy Spirit will come upon you, and the power of the Highest will overshadow you; therefore, also, that Holy One who is to be born will be called the Son of God. Now indeed, Elizabeth your relative has also conceived a son in her old age; and this is now the sixth month for her who was called barren. For with God nothing will be impossible."

**LUKE 1:34-37**

**PONDER THIS** The Virgin Birth does not depend on your understanding for its validation. There are a lot of things we don't understand. We don't understand how a brown cow can eat green grass and give white milk that we churn and turn to yellow butter. We don't understand that. Most of us don't even understand how a windshield wiper works. We know it works. It takes the water off the windshield. But if I asked you to draw a diagram and describe to me what makes the windshield wiper go back and forth, many could not do it. If you are an engineer, you could do that, but there would be other things you couldn't explain. There are a lot of things we don't understand, but we experience.

Now, Mary asked a good question: "How can this be, since I do not know a man?" Many people ask, "Isn't the Virgin Birth a biological impossibility?" The angel, in effect, answered for us: "Is there anything too hard for God? With God all things are possible."

- What is something in life you don't understand but experience and believe?
- What parts of Jesus' birth are hard for you to comprehend? How can you pursue faith when you don't understand?

**PRACTICE THIS** Spend some time thanking God that we don't need full understanding to possess belief in Him.

Then the angel said to them, "Do not be afraid, for behold, I bring you good tidings of great joy which will be to all people. For there is born to you this day in the city of David a Savior, who is Christ the Lord."

**LUKE 2:10-11**

**PONDER THIS** Some time ago, when we still used landlines and operators to find phone numbers for people, a lady received a message that told her she had inherited a fortune of more than a million dollars. She was flabbergasted. She didn't even know she had a relative with that kind of money. She was so excited she didn't know what to do. She was home by herself. She went to the telephone, picked it up, and said, "Operator! Get me somebody on the line! Anybody! I want to tell them what has happened." Shouldn't we feel that way about Jesus?

The angel said, "I bring you good tidings of great joy which will be to all people." Jesus Christ is not only the Savior of one group or region; He is the Savior of the world! This is Good News to all people.

The world needs Jesus. Jews and Gentiles need Jesus. Young and old need Jesus. Rich and poor need Jesus. Intellectual and illiterate need Jesus. People here, there, and everywhere need Jesus. This is the Good News we have to share!

- Who in your life needs to know Jesus?
- Does sharing the Good News of Jesus excite you? Why or why not?

**PRACTICE THIS** Pray together with a friend regarding who you could share the Good News with, than practice sharing the Gospel with your friend.

But if the Spirit of Him who raised Jesus from the dead dwells in
you, He who raised Christ from the dead will also give life to your
mortal bodies through His Spirit who dwells in you. Therefore,
brethren, we are debtors—not to the flesh, to live according to the
flesh. For if you live according to the flesh you will die; but if by
the Spirit you put to death the deeds of the body, you will live. For
as many as are led by the Spirit of God, these are sons of God.

**ROMANS 8:11-14**

**PONDER THIS** Do you remember anticipating Christmas as a child? Perhaps the Christmas tree was decorated in the family room. Maybe your family hung stockings by the chimney. There were presents under the tree, and you could hardly wait until Christmas morning. In Scripture, there was a man who was waiting for Christmas like this. His name was Simeon. He was looking, waiting, longing, and anticipating the coming of Jesus Christ into this world. Then, one day, God led him to the temple to meet the Messiah, baby Jesus.

Did you know that the same Spirit that led Simeon to the temple so long ago to meet the Lord Jesus and hold Jesus in his arms is the same Holy Spirit who wants to guide you? Are you sensitive? Can God speak to you? How about your prayer life? So often in our prayer lives, we're telling God things. We think God's some sort of heavenly Santa Claus. We come with a shopping list of the things we want, and we say, "Now, listen, Lord, your servant speaks," when we ought to say, "Speak, Lord; Your servant is listening."

- What does your prayer life look like? What are things you most often pray about?
- Do you crave to see God work the way Simeon did? Why or why not?

**PRACTICE THIS** Take some time in prayer to listen to God rather than only speaking to Him.

Then Simeon blessed them, and said to Mary His mother,
"Behold, this Child is destined for the fall and rising of
many in Israel, and for a sign which will be spoken against
(yes, a sword will pierce through your own soul also), that
the thoughts of many hearts may be revealed."

**ROMANS 8:11-14**

**PONDER THIS** What makes the difference in individuals? It's not education. It's not social status. It's not environment. People can be raised in the same family and end up different. One child loves God, and the other child does not love God. Cain and Abel had basically the same environment. There were two thieves on the cross, one crucified on Jesus's right hand and one on the other. One of those thieves cursed and spit blasphemies in the face of Jesus; the other said, "'Lord, remember me when You come into Your kingdom'" (Luke 23:42b). The same sun that melts ice hardens clay. The same sermon that brings people to Jesus can harden people and turn them away from Jesus. But it's not the sermon that really does it. The sermon only reveals the heart. What is really in you is determined by how your heart resonates with the preaching of Jesus. What you do with Jesus determines what Jesus does with you. You can accept Him, or you can reject Him. You can crown Him, or you can crucify Him. But you cannot ignore Him. You must do something.

- How did you reject Jesus before coming to know and trust Him?

- How are you responding to Jesus now? Where can you grow to know Him?

**PRACTICE THIS** Pray for those who have hearts that are hard toward Jesus and the Gospel.

"He who believes in the Son has everlasting life; and he who does not believe the Son shall not see life, but the wrath of God abides on him."

**JOHN 3:36**

**PONDER THIS** Christ is the solid rock. Christ is the foundation stone. Christ is the cornerstone. And He's before you today. You can build on Him or stumble over Him, but you cannot go around the Lord Jesus Christ. He is the One who determines your destiny. Either Jesus Christ will be your Savior, or He will be your judge. He will be a stepping stone or a stumbling stone, but you have an appointment with Jesus Christ. He is inescapable. He is inevitable. He is unavoidable. The baby that Simeon held in Luke 2 is the Christ of your destiny, one way or the other. Simeon said, in effect, "Mary, this baby is going to be like a sword in your heart. He's going to divide between your natural emotions as a mother and your desire for the will of God. And you're going to find this conflict between natural emotions and the spiritual life, between your soul and the Spirit." All who have received the Lord Jesus Christ as our personal Savior and Lord feel that sword on the inside, do we not? It's the pull of the old life and the desire of the new life.

Do you feel that conflict? When you give your heart to Jesus Christ, you become twice-born, you let the Spirit of God come into you, and there's going to be a division in your life between the old and new natures.

- When have you felt the pull of the old life? How do you respond in these moments?
- How does Christmas remind you of your new life in Christ?

**PRACTICE THIS** As you prepare for Christmas, consider how the Christmas story has impacted your faith.

Then Simeon blessed them, and said to Mary His mother,
"Behold, this Child is destined for the fall and rising of
many in Israel, and for a sign which will be spoken against
(yes, a sword will pierce through your own soul also), that
the thoughts of many hearts may be revealed.

**LUKE 2:34-35**

**PONDER THIS** A man went down to the train station and people were getting off the train and meeting loved ones. And there was embracing and kissing and great joy. But he saw some men walk up; they had a man in handcuffs, and they were leading him away on the train. Evidently, he was going to jail. His wife and children were weeping and wailing as the man was being led away. That's a picture of the coming of Jesus. What joy it will be to those of us who know Him. What joy it will be when we have that grand reunion, when we meet our loved ones when Jesus comes. But how sad it will be for some, who'll be bound and cast into outer darkness.

Jesus is dividing, and He will divide for all eternity. At the judgment, He will divide between the sheep and the goats, the saved and the lost. His decision will not be based on finances or the opinion of society but on the Lamb's Book of Life. We divide people by social status. We say upper class, middle class, and lower class. But God divides right and left, saved or lost. He is the Christ with the sword in His hand. The baby in Bethlehem changed the playing field. Will you share in the joy when He comes?

- On what basis do you most often judge people? What does God judge by?
- Why is it important at Christmas to remember the coming return of Jesus?

**PRACTICE THIS** Share the hope of Jesus with others as you tell the story of the first Christmas.

But while he thought about these things, behold, an angel of the
Lord appeared to him in a dream, saying, "Joseph, son of David,
do not be afraid to take to you Mary your wife, for that which is
conceived in her is of the Holy Spirit. And she will bring forth a
Son, and you shall call His name Jesus, for He will save His people
from their sins." So all this was done that it might be fulfilled which
was spoken by the Lord through the prophet, saying: "Behold,
the virgin shall be with child, and bear a Son, and they shall call
His name Immanuel," which is translated, "God with us."

**MATTHEW 1:20-23**

**PONDER THIS** People race their theological motors to try to illustrate the Trinity. They say, "It's like this; it's like that." We try to compare God to something. But there's only one God, so there's nothing to compare with Him. You can compare one thing to another, but you can't compare God with anything because there is no other God. There are reflections of His Trinity in everything—reflections, but not proofs. Time and space make our Universe. Time is past, present, and future. Space is height, width, and depth. All belong together. Each is distinguishable, but all are inseparable. You can't have a past without a present, you can't have a present without a future, and you can't have a future without a past. Each is distinguishable; all are part of one. In each example, three things are distinguishable, and yet they are inseparable, not proof of the Trinity, only a reflection.

A wise man said, "Don't try to explain the Trinity; you'll lose your mind. Don't deny it; you'll lose your soul." We know of the Trinity by divine revelation as we open the Word of God. The only knowledge we have of the Most High is as He discloses Himself to us.

- How have you seen the Trinity at work?
- How does growing in your understanding the Trinity change the way you view Christmas?

**PRACTICE THIS** Praise God this Christmas for all of who He is and thank Him for the reality of His Triune being.

"I am the door. If anyone enters by Me, he will be saved, and
will go in and out and find pasture. The thief does not come
except to steal, and to kill, and to destroy. I have come that they
may have life, and that they may have it more abundantly."

**JOHN 10:9-10**

**PONDER THIS** During the Second World War, a very wealthy man with a rare art collection had a son in the Royal Air Force. Unfortunately, the son was shot down in flames and died, leaving this man with no other descendants. When the man died, he instructed that there be an auction for his collection. The art collectors came from all over, ready to bid. And the auctioneer said, "First of all, we're going to auction one painting." It was a painting of a man. It was the wealthy man's son, the one who died. To the art collectors, it was valueless, and nobody bid. But an old friend of the family, who knew the boy and had seen him grow up, thought it would be nice to have a painting of that lad. And he bid on it.

There was no other bid. The auctioneer said, "Do I hear any other bids? Very well, it is sold to this individual." And then he said, "The auction is over." They said, "No, there are other paintings." He said, "No. The will states that whoever buys this picture gets the entire collection. Whoever gets the son gets all the rest." Friend, I want to tell you that God has a Son, and when you get Jesus, you get it all.

- How do you remind yourself daily of the value of Jesus?
- What are some of the blessings you have experienced because of Jesus?

**PRACTICE THIS** Talk to a friend and share how you have seen the value of Jesus.

In that hour Jesus rejoiced in the Spirit and said, "I thank You, Father, Lord of heaven and earth, that You have hidden these things from the wise and prudent and revealed them to babes. Even so, Father, for so it seemed good in Your sight. All things have been delivered to Me by My Father, and no one knows who the Son is except the Father, and who the Father is except the Son, and the one to whom the Son wills to reveal Him."

**LUKE 10:21-22**

**PONDER THIS** What is the great need in the world today? Is it information? We're drowning in a sea of information. If it is information that we need, God would have sent us an educator. Is it technology? If technology had been the need, God would have sent a scientist or a developer. Is it money? Do you think that your problems would be solved if you had more money? If money had been the need, God would've sent an economist. Do you think the need is more leisure? Maybe God should have sent an entertainer. No, our greatest need is salvation. So, God sent a Savior.

I'm amazed, in wonder, and blessed that He sent the message to humble shepherds. And Herod, the king, never quite got it. He never quite understood. But humble shepherds understood the message. Why? Because God has "hidden these things from the wise and the prudent and has revealed them unto babes." Do you want to understand Jesus Christ? Then lay your intellectual pride in the dust and come to Him and say, "Lord, reveal the truth to me."

- What are some of the world's problems you are worried about?
- How does Jesus as Savior give you hope as you look to the New Year?

**PRACTICE THIS** Pray and submit the worries you have to God. Remind yourself of the hope you have in the Savior.

Therefore we make it our aim, whether present or absent, to be well pleasing to Him. For we must all appear before the judgment seat of Christ, that each one may receive the things done in the body, according to what he has done, whether good or bad.

**2 CORINTHIANS 5:9-10**

**PONDER THIS** Some years ago, I heard about a young pastor who was hired by a church, and one of the ladies in that church said to him, "You're going to have a difficult time trying to please all 300 of us." He said, "Madam, there's only One I'm going to try to please; His name is Jesus. If I please Him, that should be good enough for the rest of you." Jesus is the One we serve. We don't primarily serve other people.

Now, there's only one question that you ask after you bow the knee to Jesus Christ and receive Him as Lord, Master, and Savior of your life. It's the question that the Apostle Paul asked on the road to Damascus, "Lord, what do You want me to do?" (See Acts 9:6.) The best advice anybody ever gave to another person was the advice Mary gave that day Jesus turned water into wine. Mary said to the servants, "Whatever He says to you, do it" (John 2:5b). You'll never get better advice than that. Ask Him today, "Lord, what do You want me to do?"

- Have you ever asked, "Lord, what do You want me to do?" What makes us hesitant to ask this question?
- How can you discern what the Lord would have you do?

**PRACTICE THIS** Ask "Lord, what do You want me to do?" See what He brings to mind and consider it in light of His Word and the wisdom of other Spirit-filled believers.

"Now therefore, fear the LORD, serve Him in sincerity and in truth, and put away the gods which your fathers served on the other side of the River and in Egypt. Serve the LORD! And if it seems evil to you to serve the LORD, choose for yourselves this day whom you will serve, whether the gods which your fathers served that were on the other side of the River, or the gods of the Amorites, in whose land you dwell. But as for me and my house, we will serve the LORD."

**JOSHUA 24:14-15**

**PONDER THIS** We need to fear the Lord. Now, I'm not talking about a negative fear. Do you know the difference between a slave and a son? A slave fears his master's lash, but a son fears his father's displeasure. I don't want to break God's heart. The best illustration I can give you of the kind of fear I'm talking about comes from Mark 4:35-41 when Jesus stilled the waves. The disciples came to Him distressed, saying, "Teacher, do You not care that we are perishing?" (Mark 35:38b). "But He said to them, 'Why are you so fearful? How *is it* that you have no faith'" (Mark 35:40)? And Jesus rebuked that kind of fear. But listen to the very next verse: "And they feared exceedingly, and said to one another, 'Who can this be, that even the wind and the sea obey Him'" (Mark 35:41)! He rebuked them for fearing wrongly and in the very next verse they feared Him in a wonderful way. One kind of fear was condemned because it was faithless. The other was exonerated and commended because it was reverential awe. Never get careless about your Christian life. Never lose the reverence. Have a careful reverence for God.

- What does it mean to fear the Lord in reverence?
- How does fearing the Lord change your faith? How does not fearing the Lord inhibit your faith?

**PRACTICE THIS** Resolve to pursue proper fear of the Lord in the year to come. Consider how that may change different aspects of your life.

"Now therefore, fear the LORD, serve Him in sincerity and in truth, and put away the gods which your fathers served on the other side of the River and in Egypt. Serve the LORD! And if it seems evil to you to serve the LORD, choose for yourselves this day whom you will serve, whether the gods which your fathers served that were on the other side of the River, or the gods of the Amorites, in whose land you dwell. But as for me and my house, we will serve the LORD."

**JOSHUA 24:14-15**

**PONDER THIS** It is important to have steadfast worship. Joshua said, "We will serve the LORD." He said, "I don't know what choice you're going to make. I can't force you to make that choice. You can serve other gods if you want to, 'But as for me and my house, we will serve the LORD.'" He was dedicated to sincere, scriptural, and steadfast service to our Lord.

Joshua said, "If I have to, I'll stand alone." The closer we get to the end of the age, the more you're going to have to stand alone. Noah stood alone and was, no doubt, called a bigot and a fool. Elijah stood alone before the 450 prophets of Baal. Amos stood alone before the king's court. You may have to stand alone.

We should never divide over incidentals, but we ought to divide over idolatry. Joshua said, if you want to serve those gods, you can go ahead. But I'm going to serve the Lord. Divide over issues leading to idolatry. Divide over issues leading people to worship something other than God. Whatever we face, we need to resolve that we will serve the Lord.

- What are some less important issues you feel tempted to divide over? What issues are worth dividing over?
- What does steadfast service to the Lord look like? Is that reflected in your life? Why or why not?

**PRACTICE THIS** Commit to steadfast service to the Lord. Write a list of things that need to change to make that happen.

For the Scripture says, "Whoever believes on Him will not be put
to shame." For there is no distinction between Jew and Greek,
for the same Lord over all is rich to all who call upon Him. For
"whoever calls on the name of the LORD shall be saved."

**ROMANS 10:11-13**

**PONDER THIS** When Jesus spoke of some forsaking him, Simon Peter said, "Lord,
I'll go with you to prison and to death" (Matthew 26:35, author's paraphrase). And
then Peter cursed and swore and denied that he even knew the Lord Jesus. Why?
Because it was a boast of the flesh. Do you want to maintain your victory? You'd
better realize that as you have reverence and resolve, you also need a reliance
that says, "God, I can't do it. But God, you can do it in me, and I'm going to let
you." In the truest sense of the word, victory is not your responsibility; it is your
response to His ability.

I have wonderful news for you. The Bible says it clearly and plainly, "Believe on
the Lord Jesus Christ, and you will be saved." (See Acts 16:31.) To be saved means
every sin is forgiven. To be saved means Jesus Christ lives in your heart to give you
peace, power, and purpose. And to be saved means you go to Heaven when you
die or when Jesus comes. The word *believes* means more than intellectual belief.
It means "trust, reliance, and commitment." Trust Him. Rely on Him. Commit
your life to Him, and you will be saved.

- What are some things you feel like God is leading you toward in
  the year to come?
- Have you ever prayed with a resolve to serve God and a reliance
  on Him? What impact did this have on you?

**PRACTICE THIS** Pray with a resolve to rely on God and serve Him in the year to
come.

notes

**A**drian **Rogers**, one of America's most respected Bible teachers, faithfully preached the Word of God for 53 years—32 of those years as senior pastor of the historic Bellevue Baptist Church near Memphis, Tennessee.

He wrote 18 books and over 80 booklets giving strength and encouragement on subjects such as marriage, prophecy, evangelism, and the Christian walk.

In 1987 he founded Love Worth Finding Ministries to communicate the glorious Gospel of Jesus Christ with millions around the world. The message of God's love continues today, and as he so aptly put it, "Truly, the sun never sets on the ministry of Love Worth Finding."

## WILL YOU SUPPORT
## LOVE WORTH FINDING?

This ministry is funded primarily by gifts from
Christians committed to sharing God's Word with
lost and hurting people from all walks of life.

———————

If this resource has been a help to you,
please consider joining with us to bless
others with the Gospel of Jesus Christ.

**lwf.org**/give

FIND ANSWERS AND ENCOURAGEMENT AT **lwf.org**

**LOVEWORTHFINDING**®
WITH ADRIAN ROGERS

2941 Kate Bond Road  Memphis TN 38133  (901) 382-7900